Palgrave Macmillan Series in International Political Communication

Series Editor: Philip Seib, University of Southern California (USA)

From democratization to terrorism, economic development to conflict resolution, global political dynamics are affected by the increasing pervasiveness and influence of communication media. This series examines the participants and their tools, their strategies and their impact. It offers a mix of comparative and tightly focused analyses that bridge the various elements of communication and political science included in the field of international studies. Particular emphasis is placed on topics related to the rapidly changing communication environment that is being shaped by new technologies and new political realities. This is the evolving world of international political communication.

Books Appearing in This Series

*Media and the Politics of Failure: Great Powers,
Communication Strategies, and Military Defeats*
By Laura Roselle

*The CNN Effect in Action: How the News Media Pushed the
West toward War in Kosovo*
By Babak Bahador

Media Pressure on Foreign Policy: The Evolving Theoretical Framework
By Derek B. Miller

New Media and the New Middle East
Edited by Philip Seib

The African Press, Civic Cynicism, and Democracy
By Minabere Ibelema

Global Communication and Transnational Public Spheres
By Angela M. Crack

Latin America, Media, and Revolt ...tion *in Modern
Mesoamerica*
By Juanita Darling

Japanese Public Opinion and the I
Edited by Robert D. Eldridge a

African Media and the Digital Pι
Edited by Okoth Fred Mudhai, Wisdom J. Tettey, and ι α... a

D1367464

Islam Dot Com: Contemporary Islamic Discourses in Cyberspace
  By Mohammed el-Nawawy and SaharKhamis

Explaining News: National Politics and Journalistic Cultures in Global Context
  By Cristina Archetti

News Media and EU-China Relations
  By Li Zhang

Kurdish Identity, Discourse, and New Media
  By Jaffer Sheyholislami

Al Jazeera English: Global News in a Changing World
  Edited by Philip Seib

AL JAZEERA ENGLISH

Global News in a Changing World

Edited by

Philip Seib

First published in 2012 by
PALGRAVE MACMILLAN®
in the United States—a division of St. Martin's Press LLC,
175 Fifth Avenue, New York, NY 10010.

Where this book is distributed in the UK, Europe and the rest of the world,
this is by Palgrave Macmillan, a division of Macmillan Publishers Limited,
registered in England, company number 785998, of Houndmills,
Basingstoke, Hampshire RG21 6XS.

Palgrave Macmillan is the global academic imprint of the above companies
and has companies and representatives throughout the world.

Palgrave® and Macmillan® are registered trademarks in the United States,
the United Kingdom, Europe and other countries.

ISBN: 978–0–230–34020–6 (hc)
ISBN: 978–0–230–34021–3 (pbk)

Library of Congress Cataloging-in-Publication Data

Al Jazeera English : global news in a changing world / edited by
Philip Seib.
        p. cm.—(Palgrave Macmillan series in international political
communication)
Includes bilbiographical references.
ISBN 978–0–230–34020–6 (hardcover : alk. paper)—
ISBN 978–0–230–34021–3 (trade pbk. : alk. paper)
    1. Al Jazeera English (Television network) 2. Television broadcasting of
news—Qatar. 3. Broadcast journalism—Qatar. 4. Television broadcasting of
news—Objectivity—Qatar. I. Seib, Philip M., 1949–
PN1992.92.A393A43 2012
070.4'332—dc23   2011030903

A catalogue record of the book is available from the British Library.

Design by Newgen Imaging Systems (P) Ltd., Chennai, India.

First edition: February 2012

10 9 8 7 6 5 4 3 2 1

Printed in the United States of America.

Contents

Figure and Tables

Figure

Tables

Acknowledgments

My thanks to all the chapter authors, who did a fine job of analyzing complex topics during a time of rapid change. It was a pleasure to work with them.

Thanks also to Al Anstey, managing director of Al Jazeera English, and his colleagues at the channel who were unfailingly helpful to me and the book's other authors.

At Palgrave Macmillan, Farideh Koohi-Kamali and Sarah Nathan are a formidable team—always supportive and always thorough. Working with them is a pleasure.

At the University of Southern California, Ernest Wilson, dean of the Annenberg School for Communication and Journalism, and Geneva Overholser, director of the School of Journalism, were, as always, fully supportive of my work. My colleagues at USC's Center on Public Diplomacy are so efficient and thoughtful that I was able to carve out some time away from the office to work on this project. My research assistant, Arezou Rezvani, with diligence and good cheer, found whatever material I needed.

The most notable single accomplishment to date of Al Jazeera English is its coverage of the Arab revolutions of 2011. But it is the women and men who went into the streets of Tunis, Cairo, and elsewhere to claim freedom and build democracy, and whose courage could be seen during the newscasts of Al Jazeera English and other channels, who deserve a special salute.

PHILIP SEIB
Los Angeles
June 2011

Introduction

Philip Seib

For Al Jazeera English (AJE), the Arab revolutions of 2011 offered an opportunity that news executives dream about. It was the biggest story of the century, it was happening on home territory, and the channel had the expertise and the reportorial staff on the ground at levels its competitors could not match. For English speakers around the world, AJE was the indispensable, go-to source of information about what was happening in the streets of Tunis, Cairo, Sanaa, and elsewhere in the suddenly rebellious region.

Only five years old in 2011, AJE had, since its inception, proclaimed itself to be offering a new kind of journalism—with emphasis on covering the global South and providing a "voice for the voiceless." It had one of the best-known brand names in the world and an inexhaustible source of funding, the royal family of Qatar. However, it was burdened—at least in some quarters—by the political baggage that came with the Al Jazeera label. After a half-century of Western hegemony in the television news business, Al Jazeera Arabic, which began broadcasting in 1996, had redefined journalism in the Arab world. It addressed social issues long considered taboo, challenged entrenched Arab leaders, pointing out the corruption they sanctioned, and it criticized the West, particularly the United States, for invading Muslim countries and killing tens, or more likely hundreds, of thousands of civilians.

A channel such as AJE is, by its technological nature, supranational. Conventional borders are irrelevant, and that fosters a broad perspective on events. By satellite (and, for those without access to it, through streaming Internet content), AJE has given the world a chance to look at events through a prism that differs significantly from the Western-created lens that for so long defined the world's definition of "news." As the only English-language broadcaster in Gaza during the 2008–2009 war there, and with its intensive coverage of the 2011 Arab uprisings, AJE has attracted an audience tired of staid, traditional journalism that is too eager to embrace conventional wisdom and fails to capture the passions imbuing those events that shape people's lives. The Arab world, with all its political complexity and turmoil, is a magnet for the rest of the world's attention, and AJE takes full advantage of this region being its home.

AJE's coverage, like that of any news organization, is far from perfect. It sometimes slips into cheerleading and self-congratulation, and it sometimes makes mistakes. Journalism is an imperfect craft, and AJE's work is evidence of that. Nevertheless, the world of news is richer for having AJE as part of it.

*　*　*

This is, as best as I can tell, the first book to be devoted to the work of AJE. It was completed during "Arab spring"—the first months of 2011—when AJE was providing intensive, and sometimes exultant, coverage of democratic surges in the Arab world. As we wrote our chapters, we had a sense that the events we were watching might be prologue to even broader change. How would the coverage of events in the Arab world by AJE and others affect those with democratic yearnings in Tanzania, Venezuela, Kazakhstan, and even China? Would the images from Cairo's Tahrir Square inspire and galvanize forces for change elsewhere? I think the answer to that is, Yes; the questions being: when, to what extent, and with what level of success?

AJE is very much still a work in progress, five years old when this book was written and with its influence on the rise. The people who work for the channel are serious, committed journalists, and they will certainly study their own coverage carefully, looking for ways to build upon the journalistic foundation they have constructed. They are also sophisticated about the ways of global politics, and they appreciate the influence they wield. As their parent company continues to expand—with Al Jazeera Turkish, Al Jazeera Swahili, and Al Jazeera Balkans being readied—the presence of Al Jazeera (and Qatar) throughout the world is becoming more pronounced and its brand of journalism more pervasive.

Characterizing "Al Jazeera journalism" is difficult. It is a mix of good, fundamental reporting and audience-grabbing technique, with a presumed political agenda in the background that some claim tilts the Arabic channel toward the interests of the Muslim Brotherhood and Hamas. The Al Jazeera channels certainly reflect the interests of the emir of Qatar, who, by some accounts, sees his oil- and gas-rich country as "the next Saudi Arabia" in terms of wielding global, wealth-based influence. You will not find stories about allegations of corruption in Qatar on Al Jazeera channels, nor will you find its leaders portrayed in unflattering ways. Some critics of Al Jazeera point to that as evidence of lack of objectivity and independence, which might be true, but in that regard this media empire is like those elsewhere in the world that are loathe to carry stories that might offend their proprietors or commercial sponsors.

The authors have varied perspectives; they come from Egypt, Israel, Norway, Palestine, and the United States. They are all well-versed in journalism and politics, which—despite journalists' claims of apolitical purity—are inextricably linked. We look at more than the Middle East, because AJE is a *global* news channel, similar in some ways to CNN and the BBC, but with emphasis on areas that often remain outside mainstream news coverage. The chapters by Michael Kugelman and Amelia Arsenault that evaluate AJE's reporting and audience-building in South Asia and sub-Saharan Africa underscore the significance of extending coverage priorities beyond the traditional power centers of North America and Europe.

Shawn Powers addresses the origins and early development of the channel, and Will Youmans analyzes the political controversy, especially in the United States, that has kept AJE unavailable, except via the Internet, in more than a hundred million American households. In their chapters, Hussein Amin and Tine Ustad Figenschou look at the foundations of AJE's audience makeup and news content. Rima Najjar Merriman, a Palestinian, and Eytan Gilboa, an Israeli, have written two very different analyses of AJE's coverage of Israel's Operation Cast Lead in Gaza during 2008 and 2009. Mohammed el-Nawawy (who, it should be noted, was coauthor of *Al Jazeera,* the first book about the network) examines the content of AJE's website during the controversy about the so-called Ground Zero Mosque and the role that a news organization might play in calming tensions that are often fueled by biases and incorrect information. In the book's final chapter, which I wrote, I consider AJE's brief history to date and its prospects for the future within the context of technology-driven changes in global geopolitics.

All that is a lot for one book, and we do not pretend that we have come close to exhausting the topic of AJE's significance. Our main hope is to spur discussion and further studies about AJE and the ways that international news providers are changing journalism and the global public sphere.

* * *

To return to the Arab spring, the confluence of journalism and politics, particularly during the heady days when democracy was visibly taking root and spreading its first tendrils, has altered the way the world works. As much of the Arab world showed in 2011, courage is most likely to spread when it is visible. AJE was a crucial player in bringing about that visibility, and in doing so marked its own coming of age and pointed the way for the development of global journalism in the years to come.

CHAPTER 1

The Origins of Al Jazeera English

Shawn Powers

INTRODUCTION

What precipitates the launch of a global news network is an important question for international communication and globalization research and for anyone seeking to understand how news organizations work in the new global media environment. The early motivations often determine the reach, mission, journalistic culture, and longevity of any global media endeavor. And global news—the Al Jazeera Network, the BBC World Service, CNN International, Voice of America (VOA), to name just a few—represent the bedrock and most publicly recognized means of international communications.

Yet, despite their importance, global news networks are often written about simply in episodic contexts (e.g., the rise of Al Jazeera Arabic, or the emergence of a CNN Effect) rather than within an empirical and analytical analysis. Using analysis grounded in political economy theory, this chapter addresses such oversights by situating the genesis of Al Jazeera English (AJE) within the evolving nature of geopolitics, cross-cultural communication, and neoliberalism in contemporary society.

First, I outline the genesis of AJE in the context of one important question: what motivates the launch of a global news network, and how does that inform and shape the network's mission, trajectory and, eventually, success and/or failure? Second, in order to provide context for the motivations and mission of the new channel, I outline the history of the Al Jazeera Network, focusing on both the Arabic-language news broadcaster and Qatari government out of which AJE was born. Third, I provide a chronology of Al Jazeera's drive to reach English-speaking audiences, including the geopolitical context that shaped the channel's initial outlook and leadership. Finally, I map the transition from the early iterations of AJE—conceived of as entirely independent of its Arabic sister, Al Jazeera—to its launch in 2006, where the channel was more fully integrated into the Al Jazeera Network and was operating under the authority of, rather than independent from, its Arabic-language partner, Al Jazeera.

Understanding AJE in a Historical Context

What motivates the creation of a global news network? On one level, the answer is simple: power. For private and publicly supported news networks alike, the first goal is to reach and inform a target audience deemed important by the network's managerial team, be it a board of directors or a Ministry of Foreign Affairs. While the goals of reaching a target audience can be political (e.g., shaping foreign opinion abroad) or financial (e.g., attracting an audience that appeals to advertisers), in both cases the ability to reach one's target audience will, ostensibly, provide the broadcaster power either in leveraging foreign opinions or in negotiations with advertisers keen on reaching members of their loyal audience.

For example, the BBC's Empire Service, as it was officially christened in 1932, was an effort by the British government to use radio to communicate and assert particular power relations with the citizenry of its empire. It was seen as a tool of governance, by highlighting the achievements of British society and policies while civilizing the "uncivilized" with programing featuring the exquisite lifestyles and politics of the British upper class.[1] Today's BBC World Service, a direct descendent of the Empire Service, still operates with a familiar mandate, albeit less about maintaining an empire and more focused on development and modernization in less developed societies.[2]

In 1942, the U.S. government launched the Voice of America (VOA) in order to counter Axis propaganda with accurate news and occasional editorials explaining the rationales for U.S. foreign policies. In the case of the VOA, the goal was to reach the democratically inclined elite, to connect them to American foreign policy objectives, and in so doing, influence the trajectory of domestic politics in foreign countries. While the VOA and its offshoots Radio Free Europe and Radio Liberty were important elements in shaping foreign public opinion during the Cold War, their original mandate as an advocate for American interests continues to burden contemporary American broadcasters who struggle to establish credibility with audiences skeptical about their impartiality. Thus, for both the BBC and the VOA, two of the world's oldest and best known international broadcasters, their early origins have had important consequences for their long-term success, both in perception and in practice.

For profit-driven news networks as well, the initial goal centers on the question of power. In the case of CNN, launched in 1980 by Ted Turner, the goal was to fill a gap in the market for news consumption that catered to a growing number of influential business and political elites. According to Turner, CNN's model for 24-hour news programing was inspired by the success of talk radio: "There was an unmet demand for busy people to access televised news anytime of the day. Radio news demonstrated a niche, and the television business was way behind. So I created the Cable News Network."[3] Of course, in the case of CNN, the "power" generated by the news network stems from its ability to sell a specific, global, upper class, and business-oriented audience to advertisers. But it was that power that led to CNN's substantial profits in the 1990s and created a model for successful 24-hour news channels, such as EuroNews, Bloomberg TV, Sky News, MSNBC, and Fox News.

AJE was launched in the context of vast market opportunities and geopolitical necessities. In the aftermath of the attacks on 9/11, and the U.S.-led invasion of Afghanistan, there was a growing demand for high-quality, timely reporting from the greater Middle East and other parts of the non-Western world historically underreported by Western news networks. In the eyes of Al Jazeera's management, there was a "market failure" in terms of there being a demand for reporting from Afghanistan and the Middle East in English, based on Western journalistic sensibilities, that, according to then-editor-in-chief, Ibrahim Helal, their channel was well situated and "morally obligated" to meet, given its unique vantage point and expertise.[4]

AJE's launch was driven by geopolitical motivations as well. While there was certainly a market failure in terms of high quality and timely journalism from the region accessible to English-speaking audiences, filling such a gap required substantial resources, as launching a global news network able to report from underdeveloped parts of the world would be expensive. And given that it was unlikely that such an investment would provide substantial financial return in the short term, the launch of an English-language global news network had to be in the best interest of its chief financier— Emir Hamad bin Khalifa Al Thani—and his oil-and-natural-gas-rich microstate, Qatar. To more fully understand the geopolitical motivations and context within which AJE was launched, one must first understand how AJE's sister channel, Al Jazeera Arabic, came to be.

In the Beginning, There Was Al Jazeera

AJE, of course, grew out of an existing news organization: Al Jazeera, and it is important to note that AJE's identity and mission are tethered to its older, Arabic-speaking sister, Al Jazeera. The original Arabic-language network was launched in 1996 after the current emir of Qatar, Sheikh Hamad bin Khalifa Al Thani (1952–), seized power from his father in a coup d'état and placed Qatar on path toward greater market liberalization, cultural openness, and international prestige. In one of his first emiri decrees, Sheikh Hamad abolished the Qatari Ministry of Information, the bureaucratic arm historically responsible for controlling the press, and established Al Jazeera. The news channel began broadcasting on November 1, 1996, at first terrestrially from Qatar, and for only a few hours per day. At the outset, there were three factors that helped it become the most watched and the most powerful news network in the region, each of which also helps explain the origins and challenges facing AJE: (1) its mission and financial support; (2) its commitment to hiring professional journalists with in-depth local knowledge; (3) access to international communications infrastructure.

First, Al Jazeera's mission was to produce programing that was journalistically sound and free from government interference. In the Middle East, no such mandate had ever been given to a news network that would broadcast from within the region, and thus Al Jazeera appealed to both reporters interested in practicing uncensored journalism and audiences keen on watching news that wasn't merely government propaganda. Sheik Hamad pledged to let Al Jazeera "report the news as they see it," adding, "I believe criticism can be a good thing and some discomfort for government officials is a small price to pay for this new freedom."[5] In order to help ensure the news channel achieved its mission, Sheikh Hamad pledged a grant of US$137 million to Al Jazeera, enabling it to initially operate without concern for generating significant advertising revenue. Since then, the emir has supported the Network with an annual grant of approximately $100 million, in addition to an estimated $1 billion investment to launch AJE.[6]

Building on its initial mission to provide uncensored and critical reporting on the region's political elite, Al Jazeera's mission is often summed up as "the opinion and the other opinion," a reference to its goal of exposing audiences to all sides of an issue. The channel quickly established credibility with audiences as it consistently challenged official accounts of news offered by the region's ministries of information, a first in the Arab world. And in its sensationalized coverage championing the Palestinian Intifada, and its opposition to international sanctions on Iraq and coalition attacks on Iraqi civilians, the network became known as the voice of the Arab Street, reflecting and even fighting for the collective Arab citizenry. Marc Lynch describes the period from 1996 to 2004 as the "Al Jazeera Era" due to its huge significance in Middle East politics and unmatched popularity among audiences from around the region.[7] Put another way, Al Jazeera identified a market failure—an unmet demand for accurate 24-hour news broadcast from within the region—and offered a journalistic product that provided an unmatched news service from within the region while standing up to established centers of power, both Arab and Western, using highly sophisticated presentation technologies and striking, dramatic aesthetics.

Second, Al Jazeera consistently sought out journalists with experience reporting throughout the region and with training in investigative reporting typically associated with "Western journalism." This effort was substantially helped early on when, just months before Al Jazeera was launched, the British-Saudi joint venture BBC Arabic collapsed after a series of disagreements between the Saudi financiers and BBC editors over editorial freedom. As a result of the falling out, the Middle East was flooded with hundreds of BBC trained, politically active journalists, 150 of whom were hired to build the journalistic core of Al Jazeera's news team. As a result, in addition to its attractive and persuasive on-screen presenters, the channel's content was far superior in quality and depth when compared to other sources of news in the region.

Third, and perhaps most importantly, in November 1997 Al Jazeera secured access to the coveted C-band transponder (the most powerful transponder) on the Saudi-owned communications satellite Arabsat, thus making its programing available to anyone in the Middle East who had a small, cheap satellite dish. Al Jazeera's ability to secure space on Arabsat was due to a technical mix-up months earlier, when a French company, Canal France International (CFI), broadcast an explicit adult program to approximately 30 million Arab viewers who had tuned in expecting children's educational programing. This led to CFI being dropped from Arabsat, thus creating an opening for Al Jazeera on the only communications satellite then broadcasting to the Middle East. As a result, the network quickly ramped up its news output, moving from 6 hours of programing a day to 18, and by 2008, to 24 hours a day.[8] Since then, Al Jazeera has moved to Egyptian-owned Nilesat and is accessible without charge to anyone in the region with a simple, standard satellite dish.

Once Al Jazeera was accessible to the broader Arab public the network grew into the role of the political provocateur. Its programs covered taboo topics previously considered to be off limits for discussion, such as women's rights, homosexuality, political corruption, and many others. It also dispatched journalists throughout the region to get a better sense of the mood of the different Arab Streets, creating an extended network of journalists with local knowledge of every country in the region. Al Jazeera often aired the "dirty laundry" of Middle Eastern autocrats and dictators, except Qatar's, generating attention from Arab publics and their governments.[9]

Marc Lynch (2006) argues that the network can be credited for the creation of an "Arab public sphere…or spheres," where open, deliberative discourse on matters of public interest became more and more notable and sophisticated.[10] While every government in the region at one point or another tried to combat the influence of Al Jazeera by banning its journalists from operating in their countries, or closing down their local bureaus, eventually it became clear that the network had opened a Pandora's Box of free expression that would forever change the expectations of Arab citizens. Though scientifically correlating changes in political opinions to changes in news consumption is difficult, studies have found a direct relationship between Arab viewing of Al Jazeera and opinions in favor of democratic governance.[11]

This, however, is only one side of the story. Al Jazeera's launch in 1996 was not merely part of an effort toward political liberalization, but was also motivated by geopolitical calculations. In 1995, the new emir was confronted with attacks in the Saudi and Egyptian press questioning his legitimacy as the rightful ruler of Qatar. Al Jazeera was launched, in part, to give the Qatari emir a megaphone to challenge the Egyptian and Saudi governments by broadcasting programing featuring popular Egyptian and Saudi political dissidents. The fact that its journalistic core consisted of journalists who had previously been fired due to their criticisms of human rights conditions in Saudi Arabia made Al Jazeera a thorn in Saudis' side. In addition, several notable Egyptian political dissidents were invited to join the network and given space to create program content that was, at times, highly critical of Egypt's President Mubarak.[12]

More broadly, by employing journalists from throughout the region's 22 countries, Al Jazeera became a powerful tool to combat media attacks on Qatar, not through refutation, but rather by redirecting the news agenda. The simple fact that the Qatari population was among the smallest in the region meant that there was always more demand for news about corruption and political scandals in almost any other country in the region, where there were more interested citizens and more well-known, controversial leaders than those located in Qatar.

Over the course of its relatively short tenure, Al Jazeera has put Qatar on the map and continues to provide the Qatari government with a powerful tool in shaping Arab politics. As a clear demonstration of the network's geopolitical significance, nearly every country in the region had pressured Sheikh Hamad, via diplomatic channels, to shut down Al Jazeera, at times closing embassies, recalling ambassadors, and even shunning corporate interests that conduct business with the network.

By 2005, Qatar had received over 450 official complaints from governments both within and outside the region.[13] Moreover, continued opposition to the network's reporting in Syria and Yemen, for example, and its credited role in helping protest movements oust Tunisia's Ben Ali and Egypt's Mubarak, demonstrate just how geopolitically important the broadcaster is for Qatar.[14]

Helal, former editor-in-chief of the channel, explained: "Al Jazeera is like the nuclear option. Its track record of causing trouble for Arab governments, and its record of mobilizing the Arab masses gives Qatar a weapon in its foreign relations. The implicit threat the channel represents gives Qatar an upper hand in political negotiations."[15] Egyptian political analyst Amr Choubaki agrees that Al Jazeera has built Qatar's international prestige, but argues the relationship between the channel and its Qatari financiers is not as simple as Helal suggests: "Qatar created Al Jazeera, but now Al Jazeera is creating Qatar. It's like when you build a robot and eventually lose control of it and it controls you."[16] Al Jazeera's transition into English-language content production, and eventually the launch of AJE, helps provide an answer as to which of the two perspectives is more accurate.

MAKING AL JAZEERA ACCESSIBLE IN ENGLISH: FROM TRANSLATION TO AL JAZEERA NET

In the immediate aftermath of the 2001 American-led invasion of Afghanistan Al Jazeera was the only international news network with a bureau operating in Kabul, Afghanistan. According to Al Jazeera producer Imad Musa, the initial impetus for an English language Al Jazeera was in response to a market failure in the arena of international newsgathering: "The idea of English-language programing came to us after 9/11, when we were fielding an average of 60 calls a day from American viewers wanting to know what Al Jazeera was saying!"[17] With 9/11 fresh on the minds of many in the West, and in America in particular, Western news networks rushed correspondents to the region in an effort to get their own vantage points of the war on the Taliban, Al Qaeda, and Osama bin Laden. But coverage was difficult, and expertise on the war-torn country was sparse. Al Jazeera emerged as the world's leading news outlet broadcasting from Afghanistan, with a team of correspondents having been stationed there for some time, well-connected, and able to navigate the unique contours of the severely underdeveloped country. As a result, news organizations around the world were interested in purchasing and rebroadcasting Al Jazeera's Afghanistan footage, including networks in Indonesia, Japan, India, the UK, Germany, and the United States. All of a sudden, the young network that had become infamous for its role in regional politics was a globally recognized international news network. Footage was repackaged and sold to networks around the world.

In late 2002, Al Jazeera began to talk about directly appealing to a broader, English-speaking audience. Ali Mohammed Kamal, Al Jazeera's director of marketing, started promoting a "repositioning" of the organization, "accompanied by the introduction of English subtitles and dubbing of broadcasts into English." His rationale was straightforward: "We are trying to create a dialogue between East and West, and Muslim and Christianity. If we provide more information and education there will be more understanding and more peace."[18]

Yet, as Al Jazeera's footage from Afghanistan began to reach American viewers, it became clear that the channel's reporters were telling a different story than that which was being sold by the coalition forces to Western reporters. Able to record and broadcast from unique vantage points inside the country, often without the guidance or approval of coalition forces, Al Jazeera captured a story of a civilian sector that was increasingly devastated by coalition attacks and far from supportive of the international intervention. As the narrative of benign humanitarianism began to fall apart, Western policymakers in particular challenged Al Jazeera's focus on civilian casualties as anti-American, even deeming the channel's coverage a threat to the efficacy of the entire military operation. While demand for Al Jazeera's coverage continued to grow around the world, in America the channel was increasingly portrayed as taking the side of Al Qaeda, the Taliban, and Osama bin Laden. American networks stopped rebroadcasting Al Jazeera's footage, in part due to pressure from the Bush administration to shun the network, and even refused to air several new bin Laden tapes that Al Jazeera had uncovered in 2001 and 2002.[19]

Thus, while consumers continued to demand a fresh perspective on news from the broader Middle East, cultural sensibilities superseded Al Jazeera's ability to fill the market. As a result, Al Jazeera's management decided that merely repackaging their Arabic news broadcasts for English audiences wouldn't do given the different expectations and cultural mores for Western audiences, particularly in the American market. Rather than merely translating their footage, what was needed was a separate outlet that drew from the Arabic channel's brand and ethos but catered to global English-speaking audiences desiring more comprehensive and accurate footage from the Middle East and Afghanistan.

Steve Clark, former director of News for ITN, Sky News, and the Middle East Broadcasting Corporation (MBC), was a key architect of Al Jazeera's English-language channel. Clark traced the current iteration of the AJE back to 2003, in what he describes as "a formative year for Qatari-U.S. relations, Al Jazeera's first real attempt to penetrate the American market, and as a result, for the Al Jazeera Network."[20] Clark argued that in 2003, the Bush administration's pressure on Qatar's Sheikh Hamad to tone down Al Jazeera's sensational and critical reporting had "profound implications for how the English-language initiatives were formed."[21] Given the network's continued dependence on funding from the emir, and Qatar's close relations with the Bush administration and growing desire to be recognized as a modern, forward-thinking developed country, AJE came into being during a time of careful balancing between Qatar's foreign relations and the integrity and brand of the established and popular Al Jazeera Channel.

Al Jazeera's first effort at specifically reaching English-speaking audiences was an English-language website launched on March 24, 2003, just five days after the U.S.-led coalition had invaded Iraq. Officially called Al Jazeera Net, the web initiative was designed in close consultation with the BBC World Service in an effort to ensure its sophistication and ability to connect with Western audiences.[22] A team of younger journalists launched the site, operating within the broad editorial scope of the network, but independently from the Arabic-language channel and website. According to Joanne Tucker, a BBC-trained Cambridge University graduate tapped as the site's first managing editor, "we want it to be a global citizen's home page."[23]

Twelve hours after its launch, a series of denial of service attacks targeted the website, leaving it offline for over twenty-four hours. When it was finally back online, a group called Freedom Cyber Force Militia hacked the news sites servers to redirect web browsers to a picture of the U.S. flag accompanied by the slogan: "Let Freedom Ring." A follow-up attack redirected readers to another web page with a similar message: "God bless our troops."[24] Soon thereafter, Al Jazeera's web providers, Horizons Media and Information Services and Akamai Technologies, cancelled their contracts with Arabic satellite news channel, leaving the network without a secure place to host its English-language website.[25] Importantly, the decisions to sever ties with the network were not made for commercial reasons, as Al Jazeera Net was willing to compensate the web hosts for their additional services and site security. As Tucker recalls, "There was nonstop political pressure on these companies not to deal with us."[26] In the same month, Yahoo and AOL terminated their advertising contracts with Al Jazeera, and the New York Stock Exchange (NYSE) and NASDAQ revoked press credentials from Al Jazeera's reporters.[27] Al Jazeera's hope of reaching American audiences had proven much harder than had originally been expected. As a result, the original web effort was postponed for a relaunch later in 2003.[28]

Around the same time, Qatar continued to move toward greater reform and to demonstrate to the world that it was indeed on a path of rapid Western modernization. For example, in March 2003, Sheikha bint Ahmed Al Mahmoud was appointed as minister of education, Qatar's first woman minister. A month later, on April 7, the elections to the Central Municipal Council elected 29 representatives for Qatar's only elected body, including Sheikha Yusuf Al Jeffairi, Qatar's first woman civic councilor. Later that month, 96.6 percent of Qataris (68,987 voters) approved a draft constitution via referendum, paving the way for the formal election of a legislative advisory council.[29] (It should be noted that although the population of Qatar was about 1.7 million in 2011, only a small number are actual citizens, and the rest are mostly workers from South Asia and elsewhere.)

The same day the Qataris went to the polls embracing the most expansive constitutional reform in the young country's history, commander of U.S. Central Command Army Gen. Tommy Franks, and Secretary of Defense Donald H. Rumsfeld met with American troops at Central Command Forward headquarters outside of Doha, Qatar. As Qatar embraced Western democratic reforms, its military ties with the United States and coalition forces grew as well.

It was on the back of these reforms, as well as its growing military alliance between the United States and Qatar, that the Qatari emir came to visit President Bush and his administration in Washington, DC, in May 2003. The Qatari emir was given the treatment of a close ally of the United States, including meetings with President Bush and his cabinet, as well as public opinion leaders and high-level journalists. As the most prominent Arab ally supporting the U.S.-led invasion of Iraq, President Bush thanked the Sheikh Hamad, adding, "We are proud to say you are a friend. We appreciate your silent support. The emir presents a strong example to be followed in that area of the world. He is a reformist."[30] During the visit, Sheikh Hamad also had an "excellent meeting" with Secretary of Defense Donald Rumsfled, where both promised to have long-term military cooperation between the United States and Qatar.[31] Up until this point, while the Bush administration had been highly critical of Al Jazeera's coverage of the U.S.-led war in Iraq, its anger over the news network had not spilled over into the diplomatic ties with the Qatari government. In fact, the Bush administration had found Sheikh Hamad as a helpful ally, not only in hosting CENTCOM just outside of Doha, but also in helping rein in anti-American journalists and programing. According to a Qatari senior government official, "pressure from the emirate had contributed to lessened hostility toward the U.S.-led coalition in the later stages of its Iraq war coverage."[32]

While in Washington, Sheikh Hamad was interviewed by the *Washington Times'* David R. Sands regarding Qatar as a model for democratic reform in the region. In response to a question about Al Jazeera's reception in the West, Sheikh Hamad noted, "We do recognize that Al Jazeera has its faults. That's normal." In the first public announcement from a Qatari official regarding the possible launch of Al Jazeera in English, the emir added that he "hoped a planned new English-language version of the network could provide a bridge between the Arab world and the West."[33]

The proposed mission of providing a bridge between the Arab world and the West is, importantly, in line with Qatar's stated foreign policy doctrine, which is based on moving past narrow national interests toward cross-cultural mutual understanding and shared interests. For example, according to Qatar's Deputy Prime Minister and Minister of Foreign Affairs Sheikh Hamad Bin Jassim Bin Jabr Al-Thani (Sheikh HBJ), "We think that the international community has finally reached an understanding of the basics of peaceful coexistence, a condition that gives answers to the problems facing the nations and societies of the world. Such understanding is based on dialogue and cooperation in service of the common best interests of all parties."[34] Al Jazeera in English, as a portal for the "global citizen," working toward bridging the divide between East and West, can be seen both as an important addition to the marketplace of ideas and, similar to the original Al Jazeera channel, as a helpful asset in pursuing Qatar's foreign interests.

Sheikh Hamad's Washington trip represented a high point in Qatar-U.S. relations. One day after the emir's interview with the *Washington Post*, on May 11, 2003, the UK's *Sunday Times* reported that the CIA obtained government papers tying Iraqi intelligence (the Mukhabarat) directly to Al Jazeera's managing director Mohammed Jassem al-Ali. The documents described how, through three Iraqi intelligence agents working at the network, Saddam Hussein's regime was able to shape coverage favorable toward his government, including suppressing stories of the notorious 1988 gas attacks on the Kurdish town of Halabjah, the largest chemical weapons attack against civilians in history.[35] Later that month, Jassem al-Ali stepped down from his post at Al Jazeera and returned to his management position with Qatar TV.

Then, on May 21, days after a deadly Al Qaeda attack in Morocco, Al Jazeera broadcast a three-minute clip from a tape it had received from Al Qaeda, featuring Egyptian physician and the intellectual force behind Al Qaeda, Ayman al-Zawahiri. In it, Zawahiri noted the attacks of 9/11 and called for further terrorism against the West: "The Crusaders and Jews understand only the language of killing and blood. They can only be persuaded through returning coffins, devastated interests, burning towers and collapsed economies."[36] The tape sent Western governments scrambling, heightening security to maximum levels, prompting the United States, UK, and Germany to close embassies in Saudi Arabia. The Pentagon also deployed antiaircraft batteries around Washington, DC.[37] Washington was quick to condemn the airing of the video, noting its focus on calling for further attacks alone meant that the recording itself wasn't newsworthy, but simply an incitement to violence. Richard Boucher, spokesman for the U.S. State Department, bluntly asked, "Why would a television channel air this kind of repeated threats and statements calling on people to commit horrible crimes against innocent people?" adding, "Airing this tape is an irresponsible act. We clearly expressed this to the Qatari government and said it publicly."[38]

While tensions grew, diplomatic relations remained stable. In June 2003, President Bush went on a seven-day "victory tour" of the Middle East and Europe, including a final stop in Doha to meet Sheikh Hamad, U.S. ambassador Paul Bremmer, and General Tommy Franks.[39] The visit was the first time a sitting American president had ever been to in Qatar.[40] President Bush also allotted time to speak to approximately 2,500 coalition troops at Camp As Sayliyah, 20 miles outside of Doha, where he once again expressed gratitude toward Qatar for its help in the invasion of Iraq: "I want to thank the members of the armed forces of Qatar and I want to thank the Emir of Qatar, with whom I just met, for his hospitality and for his friendship to the United States of America."[41]

Yet, over the coming months, Western governments—and the Bush administration in particular—grew tired of what they perceived as Al Jazeera's support for and connections to extremist groups and Iraqi insurgents. In September 2003, Tayssir Allouni, the Al Jazeera journalist who managed to interview Osama bin Laden just weeks after the attacks of September 11, was arrested by Spanish authorities and accused of having close links with Al Qaeda. Allouni was charged and eventually found guilty and sentenced to seven years of house arrest in Spain.[42]

In October, John R. Bradley, managing editor of the Saudi newspaper *Arab News*, reported that the Bush administration had finally delivered an ultimatum to the Qatari government: "If Al Jazeera failed to reconsider its news content…the US would in turn have to reconsider its relations with Qatar." The story quoted an e-mail obtained from a former senior member of the Al Jazeera channel that described a meeting that had been held in late August where members of the U.S. House, Senate, FBI, CIA, Pentagon, and State Department had reached a unanimous proposal "to advise Bush to warn the Qatari government to close Al Jazeera or, as a first step, replace its current journalists with others who are moderate and neutral." The memo that resulted from the meeting threatened to cancel the 50-year-old defense treaty between the United States and Qatar, including the transfer of American military assets out of Qatar and withdrawing all U.S. support for the tiny Gulf state.[43]

In the aftermath of Bradley's story, hostility toward Al Jazeera only increased. Later that month, the Iraqi National Congress imposed a two-week ban on Al Jazeera's Baghdad reporters following accusations of collusion with Iraqi insurgents while U.S. forces detained two additional Al Jazeera employees suspected of having prior knowledge of a suicide bomber attack at a police station in Baghdad. Al Jazeera also reacted to the controversies, as management worked to tone down perceived anti-American or coalition bias. According to one Al Jazeera reporter, "there has been unprecedented tension in the Al Jazeera newsroom that is home to both the Arabic and English language web sites' staff as a result of senior editors being increasingly reluctant to give the go-ahead to controversial story ideas."[44] As an indication of how seriously the network was reacting to the recent controversies, Al Jazeera's management intervened and removed two political cartoons from its Arabic and English websites "without hesitation" after the U.S. State Department complained about their "inflammatory" and "offensive" content.[45]

At the same time, the English-language website was also experiencing a new set of difficulties, this time related to management and staffing. Joanne Tucker, the managing editor of the initial effort, left in August 2003. Tucker was replaced by Al Jazeera Net senior editor, Yvonne Ridley, who was terminated in November 2003.[46] In addition to Tucker and Ridley, Ahmed Shaykh and Alison Balharry had also been brought on to steer the Network's English-language initiatives, both leaving in less than a few months over "clear disagreements over how news coverage will proceed."[47] As a result, feelings of discontent and fear among the Al Jazeera Net journalists grew. According to one staff member, "All that talk about bridging cultural gaps has turned out false and the managers here are interested in having docile Filipino and Indian workers."[48] In an effort to assess the level of dismay, upper management sent out contracts owed to journalists. "The management said that they will shut the site down and are now waiting to see how many people will sign on to their contracts before deciding."[49] Given its difficulties in engaging English-speaking audiences, as well as its devitalized staff, by the end of 2003, Al Jazeera Net's future was unclear.

Around the same time, in December 2003, Qatar's Minister of Foreign Affairs Sheikh HBJ had scheduled a series of meetings with senior Bush administration officials in Washington, DC, Sheikha Moza, the wife of the Sheikh Hamad, had also planned the trip and was scheduled to meet with senior figures in the Department of Education and to have lunch with First Lady Laura Bush. The trip was scheduled as a follow-up to Sheikh Hamad's previous trip, an effort to further strengthen cooperation over foreign policy, defense, and education. But, amidst the growing anger over Qatar's inability to rein in Al Jazeera, the Bush administration, at the behest of the National Security Council, downgraded the trip, cancelling Sheikha Moza's lunch with the first lady and a number of Hamad Bin Jasim Thani's meetings at the Department of Defense and State Department. Insulted, the Qataris reacted to the changed itinerary by cancelling the trip altogether.[50]

According to AJE architect Steve Clark, it was this cancelled trip that solidified Sheikh Hamad's decision to invest substantially to create a news network that would once and for all clear Al Jazeera's name in the West. Tired of an overwhelming focus on Al Jazeera in the day-to-day operations of Qatari foreign affairs, Sheikh Hamad, Sheikh HBJ, and others decided that reining in Al Jazeera's Arabic channel would never be seen as enough for Western policymakers. Moreover, Al Jazeera Net had failed to generate sufficient interest among enough talented, credible journalists, and as a result had failed to penetrate Western markets. Due to ongoing controversies over its staff, the initiative was starting to damage the Network's reputation, and thus its long-term ability to operate successfully in the West. As a result, the Qatari leadership, in consultation with Al Jazeera's management, decided it was better to launch a fresh, ambitious global news channel that would represent Al Jazeera's brand and reputation to the world, while utilizing the most advanced technologies and recruiting prestigious, well-known international talent.[51] According to Marwan Bishara, a senior-level journalist for the network and familiar with the decision-making process, "as the first global news channel based in the Middle East looking outward, the new global network offered a completely different perspective from the BBC and CNN, challenging dominant news narratives and agendas and reversing the global flow of information." He added that "the Al Jazeera in English initiative was grounded in the idea of building greater understanding between different peoples and different cultures through cross-cultural news media storytelling."[52] Given the ongoing difficulties Al Jazeera's Arabic channel continued to face in the West, the Qatari leaders sought to establish its global, English-language channel independent from Al Jazeera's existing operations.

From Al Jazeera International to Al Jazeera English

In order to avoid many of the challenges that Al Jazeera Net faced, Al Jazeera's management brought in a number of highly respected outsiders to lead the planning and launching of Al Jazeera's English-language global news network, initially named Al Jazeera International. Nigel Parsons—former head of APTN, the television arm of Associated Press news agency, and journalist at the BBC World Service—was hired as managing director. In addition, Steve Clark, a BBC-trained journalist who had previously worked as the news director of Middle East Broadcasting Corporation (MBC) and as a senior executive at ITN and Sky News joined Al Jazeera International as director of news. Paul Gibbs, a former BBC news and current affairs executive was hired as director of programing. The three became the core network architects, tasked with hiring hundreds of journalists to staff the global operation and securing distribution agreements around the world, all from Doha.[53] Between the three, only Clark had substantial experience working in the Middle East, some of which took place from MBC's broadcasting headquarters in London. From the perspective of many working on the Arabic side of the Network, Al Jazeera International quickly became known as the "British Boys Network," not only because of their British citizenship, but also due to their reliance on UK business practices and journalism models.[54]

Al Jazeera didn't officially announce its intention to launch Al Jazeera International until October 27, 2004, at the Cable and Satellite Broadcasters Association in Asia convention in Hong Kong. It was there that Nigel Parsons outlined the network's initial vision: "Our target audience is everyone who speaks English. We will have a slightly different agenda than the Arabic speaking channel. There will be four major news centres including Doha, London, and Washington, in addition to Kuala Lumpur."[55] Later, Parsons provided a bit more detail about the Network's global expansion:

> Our mission is emphatically not to do an English translation of the Arabic channel. This won't be an anti-Western or anti-U.S. station. We will target an international audience and fill a gap in international news in order to meet growing demands for news from around the world that is not filtered through the lens of the West.[56]

Combined with resentment toward the importation of a British management team that had little knowledge of or interest in Al Jazeera's institutional history and mission, Parson's comments were taken by many on the Arabic side of the Network as an implicit suggestion that they were, in fact, broadcasting anti-Western programing. "Why go through the trouble of constantly explaining that you are not like Al Jazeera unless you think that what Al Jazeera is doing is someone bad," a veteran presenter at the Arabic satellite channel asked.[57] From early on there was clear tension between the English-language and Arabic-language channels, with almost no interaction between the two.

In July 2005, amidst growing difficulties in securing cable and/or satellite distribution deals in North America and Europe, Al Jazeera hired the international public relations firm Brown Lloyd James (BLJ) to soften its image. According to a press release announcing BLJ's goals, "A brand-building drive will target the US media to soften entry to global markets. The second and more ambitious phase will see BLJ promote the channel's complete editorial independence from its sister Arabic channel."[58] Once again, the English-language channel's efforts to distance itself from the Al Jazeera brand were seen by veteran journalists at the the Arabic-language channel as a clear sign of disrespect toward an organization that they had worked to build from scratch and were tremendously proud of.

In September 2005, Sir David Frost announced his departure from Sky News for Al Jazeera International. Frost was recruited by his former colleague, Steve Clark, and was seen as a huge boon for the network's credibility with Western audiences. In addition to Frost, the channel also brought on a number of familiar faces from established international broadcasters, including Riz Khan (former presenter for CNN International and the BBC World Service); Trish Carter (former head of Current Affairs and News for Television New Zealand); Sue Phillips (former managing director of News World International at the Canadian Broadcasting Corporation) and Jane Dutton (former presenter and reporter for CNBC Europe and BBC World). Moreover, to help boost its credibility with American audiences, the Network hired Josh Rushing, a former U.S. marine captain who served in the United States Central Command media office during the invasion of Iraq, and David Marash, a Jewish American and Emmy-award-winning ABC News and Nightline journalist. From the perspective of its British architects, the channel had assembled an all-star cast of journalists and presenters well suited for news consumers in the North American and European markets. Yet, notably absent from the channel's premier journalists, or its management, were Arabs.

In its original conception, the channel was supposed to launch by the end of 2004. Then, once its mission expanded to taking on the global news establishment, the channel was given an extra year to build the global network of journalists and bureaus required for such an ambitious effort. But, as 2005 came to an end with no hint of a launch date for Al Jazeera International, many started to wonder what was taking the channel so long to get its act together. Bureau Chiefs had been hired in Washington, DC, London, and Kuala Lumpur, in addition to hundreds of journalists who were already receiving salaries, none of whom was actually reporting the news.

By early 2006, the tensions between the English-language and the Arabic-language networks had come to a head. Growing animosity on the Arabic side of the network had become explosive, as Al Jazeera International was receiving tremendously positive coverage in the international press, and its journalists were receiving wages significantly higher than their Arabic counterparts, as well as substantial perks such as tuition remission for their children to go to private schools in Doha and complimentary travel from Doha to their home countries several times a year. Moreover, the newly christened Al Jazeera International headquarters towered over the Arabic network's headquarters in Doha, featuring more space, better technology, and modern design. On top of these tangible differences, the constant chatter from Al Jazeera International management and journalists differentiating themselves from their Arabic sister had left a widespread feeling of resentment among the journalists who had worked tremendously hard to build Al Jazeera's brand and reputation, at times risking their lives in covering conflicts in Iraq, Afghanistan, and Palestine. According to an Al Jazeera presenter speaking off the record due to a network decree, "we felt used, unappreciated, and even 'colonized' a bit. Over the short period of two years, we had gone from Kings and Queens of the Arab world to peons when compared to a 'British Boys Network' that is trading on our names, our blood, and our reputations. Many of us are heart broken."[59]

As anger and animosity grew, with no clear resolution in sight, Al Jazeera's board of directors stepped in and outlined a restructuring of all of Al Jazeera's channels (Al Jazeera Arabic, Al Jazeera Net, Al Jazeera Sports, Al Jazeera International, and Al Jazeera Documentary) into the Al Jazeera Network. On March 23, 2006, Sheikh Hamad Bin-Thamir Al Thani, chairman of the board of directors of Al Jazeera satellite network and cousin of Sheikh Hamad, appointed Waddah Khanfar, then director of Al Jazeera Arabic, as director general of the entire Al Jazeera Network. According to the chairman of the board, "The decision to create this post is in line with efforts to reinforce the institutional structure of the network and to facilitate integration among its channels." While the move to create an institutional structure organizing all of the Network's different channels and initiatives was long overdue, the timing of the restructuring, right before the planned launch of Al Jazeera International, was seen as a clear intervention on behalf of the board of directors to place Al Jazeera International under the authority of Waddah Khanfar, a well-established Al Jazeera journalist-turned-manager who represented the core of the organization's original principles and outlook.

According to Americas Bureau Chief Will Stebbins, "from that moment on, we went from operating independently from the Arabic channel to working under its Director. The entire relationship between the two channels had to be renegotiated, and we weren't even sure if we had a seat at the negotiating table." Stebbins goes on, "Waddah inherited an organization that he had little hand in shaping, and as a result, we all knew big changes lay ahead. For starters, we needed to be much better integrated with the Arabic language channel in order to ensure we didn't dilute the brand or deviate from their journalistic style."[60] Parsons' public statements quickly took on a new tone compared to his previous rhetoric. "We are here to build on the heritage of Al Jazeera and bring their brand of fearless journalism to a much wider audience. We are not completely divorced from one another."[61]

In an effort to further integrate Al Jazeera International's operations and mission into the broader Network, on May 31, Ibrahim Helal was appointed deputy managing director for News and Programmes, to work directly below Nigel Parsons, and above Clark and Gibbs. Helal was previously the editor-in-chief of Al Jazeera Arabic Channel and had worked at BBC Arabic and at the BBC World Service Trust. Importantly, Helal had been with the Network since its launch in 1996 (he was one of the 150 BBC Arabic journalists who joined Al Jazeera after the Saudi-funded Orbit TV backed out of its agreement with the BBC) and was well respected throughout the organization. He had worked closely with Waddah Khanfar. According to Nigel Parsons, "Having Ibrahim join us at the English-language channel not only further professional-izes our staff with a top-flight newsman, it also solidifies us as a family built around the core spirit of Al Jazeera," adding, "Ibrahim will have a quality-control responsibility to assure that news content across the channels is consistent."[62] Ten weeks later, on August 13, 2006, Paul Gibbs resigned over differences of opinion with management, saying competing "visions for the channel" could not be resolved.[63]

Helal returned to Doha from a two-year post in London (with the BBC World Service Trust) by the invitation of the Chairman of the Board of Directors. According to Helal,

> When I returned amidst an impending and rushed launch of Al Jazeera International, I was surrounded by a team of British management who had built an international news network from their own network of friends, from their own backyard. There was no diversity, no Arabs, just a lot of Brits, and most of them didn't understand the difference between ITN or Sky News and Al Jazeera.[64]

Helal's first demand was that the channel delay its launch from later that month until the end of the year, a move that would give him enough time to ensure that the channel's first broadcast would build on Al Jazeera's brand and reputation. He immediately went to work to instilling a "public service" model among the network's journalists, many of whom had worked for profit-driven news organizations previously. He also diversified the recruiting process, steering the network away from the British model, and eventually hiring journalists from 65 different nationalities prior to the channel's formal launch in November 2006.

In October 2006, just one month before Al Jazeera International would launch, Helal intervened once again, this time on behalf of his colleagues working at the Arabic-language channel. Rather than name the English language network "Al Jazeera International," Helal demanded that the network's name be changed to "Al Jazeera English." His rationale was clear and persuasive: "to name this new channel 'International' makes it seem both more important than the Network's other channels and also implies that the Arabic Al Jazeera isn't international. The name itself makes Al Jazeera seem parochial."[65] Less than three weeks before its first broadcast, the Al Jazeera Network issued a public statement announcing the official launching of AJE on November 15, 2006, a day that would coincide with Al Jazeera Arabic's 10-year anniversary.

While Nigel Parsons and Steve Clark stayed with AJE to oversee its global debut, both would leave the organization within 18 months of its first broadcast. As it turns out, each of the three architects of the channel—Parsons, Gibbs, and Clark—would end up having spent more time planning the launch of AJE than they did working for the channel after its first broadcast. The day of AJE's long-awaited launch, Waddah Khanfar celebrated the launch by emphasizing its role in his broader global media network:

> We are extremely proud of what Al Jazeera has achieved over the past 10 years. Al Jazeera today is an international media organization. AlJazeera English will build on the pioneering spirit of Al Jazeera and will carry our media model to the entire world. This new channel will provide the same ground-breaking news and impartial and balanced journalism to the English-speaking world.[66]

In just six months prior to its launch, AJE had been streamlined, rebuilt, reorganized, and restaffed under far different auspices than its architects had originally conceived. The initial Qatari design to launch a news network independent from the Arabic channel's origins had failed due to opposition from the network's journalists and managerial core. As a result, at the time of its launch in 2006, AJE's operations and mission were very much tied to the overall management and reputation of the Al Jazeera Network. To revisit a quote cited earlier from Amr Choubaki, "Qatar created Al Jazeera, but now Al Jazeera is creating Qatar. It's like when you build a robot and eventually lose control of it and it controls you." Clearly, the relationship between the Qatari government and its Al Jazeera Network is not one of absolute deference, and in the case of AJE, one could argue that Al Jazeera came out with the upper hand.

CONCLUSION

This chapter started with a brief discussion of the importance of understanding what motivates the launch of a global news network and how that informs the network's mission, trajectory, and eventual success or failure. In the case of AJE, its initial mandate was motivated by two primary goals: (1) to meet a growing demand for accurate, timely news about the Middle East and other underrepresented parts of the world that could be delivered to English-speaking audiences; (2) to launch a global news network on par with the world's most prestigious news organizations that would, as a result of its association to and generous support from Qatar, help generate goodwill toward the small Gulf state, particularly in the West. While these two goals could, at times, be in tension with one another, due to Qatar's unique economic and political positions—resource rich with national interests closely aligned with neoliberal globalization, international law, and greater cultural hybridity—it was able to both finance and recruit a team of talented journalists interested in such an endeavor.

Compared to other global media organizations, such as the BBC and CNN, AJE stands out not only in its mission but also in its origins. Whereas the BBC World Service is firmly grounded in a history of government-supported, public service broadcasting with the aim of improving international civil societies, CNN's origins and current operations focus on meeting a demand for timely information among audiences attractive to potential advertisers (corporations and governments alike). AJE's origins embody a combination of CNN's market-based and the BBC's public service-based models. It is due to this combination of origins, driven in part by a demand for Al Jazeera's style of journalism to be more accessible in the West and a young emir's desire for his small Gulf state to shape the trajectory of international discourse that explains both AJE's early struggles and its potential strengths moving forward.

In terms of AJE's struggles (which go back to the launch of Al Jazeera Net), the tension between Qatar's geopolitical aspirations and AJE's desire to give a true "voice to the voiceless" explains the network's ongoing challenge to establish credibility with audiences around the world while simultaneously accessing communications systems, such as those in the United States, that are regulated by governments. The channel's ongoing staffing drama—some of which is outlined here—should be read as an example of how such tensions within a news organization can impede the work of its journalists and management.

In terms of strengths, AJE's ability to generate support, both from its host government and from its journalists and audiences around the world, allows the channel to never be beholden to any single constituent, like the BBC is to the British Parliament and CNN is to its stockholders. Indeed, the early iterations of Al Jazeera in English—first merely translated into English from Arabic, and later reenvisioned as independent from Al Jazeera Arabic—each failed because they were too beholden to a particular model of broadcasting. It is its current form, a hybrid model of public and private, quasi-governmental international broadcaster, and quasi-voice of the voiceless that enables AJE to operate successfully in today's complex environment. Its ability to draw interest and support from a range of constituents, from educated American elite to Arab autocrats, provides the channel with the capacity to operate between, rather than dependent on, market forces and geopolitical interests.

Notes

1. Beresford Clark, "The B.B.C.'S External Services," *International Affairs* 35 (1959): 170–180; S. Nicholas, "Brushing Up Your Empire: Dominion and Colonial Propaganda on the BBC's Home Services, 1939–45," *Journal of Imperial and Commonwealth History* 31 (2003): 207–230.
2. For example, see the BBC World Service Trust's "African Media Development Initiative," http://www.bbc.co.uk/worldservice/trust/specials/1552_trust_amdi/index.shtml
3. Author interview, Atlanta Press Club, February 2011, Atlanta, GA.
4. Author interview (telephone), March 25, 2011.
5. Susan Taylor Martin, "Scrappy Al-Jazeera Stands Up," *St. Petersburg Times*, September 22, 2002.
6. John Arlidge, "Al Jazeera: A Fresh Voice or Something a Lot Scarier?," *Real Clear Politics*, April 2 2011, http://www.realclearpolitics.com/articles/2011/04/02/al_jazeera_a_fresh_voice_or_something_a_lot_scarier_109438.html
7. Marc Lynch, *Voices of the New Arab Public: Iraq, Al-Jazeera, and Middle East Politics Today* (New York: Columbia University Press, 2006).
8. Hugh Miles, *Al-Jazeera: The Inside Story of the Arab News Channel That Is Challenging the West* (New York: Grove Press, 2005).
9. Ibid.

10. Lynch, *Voices of the New Arab Public*.

11. Erik C. Nisbet, M. C. Nisbet, D. A. Scheufeke, and J. E. Shanahan, "Public Diplomacy, Television News, and Muslim Opinion," *Harvard International Journal of Press/Politics* 9 (2004): 11–37; S. Abdullah Schleifer, "The Impact of Arab Satellite Television on the Prospects for Democracy in the Arab World," in *The Real (Arab) World: Is Reality TV Democratizing the Middle East?*, ed. Walter Armbrust (Adham Center for Television Journalism, the American University in Cairo and the Middle East Centre, St. Antony's College, University of Oxford, 2005); Larry Pintak, "Satellite TV News and Arab Democracy," *Journalism Practice* 2 (2008): 15–26.

12. Mamoun Fandy, *(Un)Civil War of Words: Media and Politics in the Arab World* (London: Praeger Security International, 2007).

13. Adel Iskander, "Al Jazeera Going Once," *National Public Radio's On the Media*, February 4, 2005, http://www.onthemedia.org/transcripts /2005/02/04/03

14. Shawn Powers, "The Democratic Republic of Al Jazeera," *GSU Magazine* (Summer 2011), http://www.gsu.edu/magazine/2011summer/462.html

15. Deborah Campbell interview with Ibrahim Helal, February, 2009, Doha, Qatar. Notes and transcript retrieved from Campbell in March 2011.

16. Jeffrey Fleishman and Noha El-Hennawy, "Qatar's Ambitions Roil Middle East," *Los Angeles Times*, April 21, 2009.

17. Douglas Quenqua, "Al Jazeera Set to Be a Force in US Media," *PR Week*, January 17, 2003.

18. Quoted in an interview with Poppy Brech, "The Island Goes Global," *Marketing*, October 31, 2002; See also Raymond Snoddy, "The Arab CNN?" *Times* (London), November 1, 2002.

19. Sarah Sullivan, "The Courting of Al-Jazeera," *Transnational Broadcasting Studies* 7 (2001 Fall/Winter), http://www.tbsjournal .com/Archives/Fall01/Jazeera_sjs2.html

20. Author interview, January 22, 2010, London, UK.

21. Ibid.

22. Louise Jury, "BBC Signed Deal with Al Jazeera," *Independent*, January 17, 2003.

23. Quoted in Warren St. John, "Q.& A.; Package from bin Laden: All in a Day's Work," *New York Times*, April 6, 2003, http://www.nytimes .com/2003/04/06/style/q-a-package-from-bin-laden-all-in-a-day-s -work.html?pagewanted=all&src=pm

24. Simon Tsang, "Hacking Al-Jazeera," *Sydney Morning Herald*, April 12, 2003.

25. *EuropeMedia*, "Al-Jazeera's Web Support Cancelled," April 7, 2003.

26. Kevin R. Lang, "Al Jazeera Denied Akamai Services," *Tech*, April 8, 2003, http://tech.mit.edu/V123/N17/17aljazeera.17n.html

27. *Economist*, "Coming of Age," March 29, 2003.

28. Sean Dodson, "Online: Brutal Reality Hits Home," *Guardian*, August 21, 2003.

29. *Freedom House*, "Women's Rights in the Middle East and North Africa Country Reports: Qatar," 2004, http://www.freedomhouse.org /template.cfm?page=181

30. Al-Jazeera TV, "US President Praises Qatar's Silent Support during Emir's Visit to US," *BBC Summary of World Broadcasts*, May 9, 2003.

31. Al-Jazeera TV, "Qatari Emir, US Defence Secretary Discuss Military Ties," *BBC Summary of World Broadcasts*, May 8, 2003.

32. Paul Martin, "Papers Show Saddam's Influence of Arab TV. Al Jazeera Caught in Propaganda War," *Washington Times*, May 12, 2003.

33. David Sands, "Qatar Says Iraq Will Be Democracy Test Case," *Washington Times*, May 10, 2003.

34. H. E. Sheikh Hamad Bin Jassim Bin Jabr Al-Thani, "How to Avoid the Conflict between Civilizations," Opening Session of the *US-Islamic World Forum*, Doha, Qatar, February 17, 2007, http://english.mofa.gov .qa/minister.cfm?m_cat=1&id=29

35. Marie Colvin, "Saddam's Spies 'Infiltrated' Leading TV Network," *Sunday Times*, May 11, 2003; Kim Sengupta, "Al Jazeera TV Sacks Chief Linked to Saddam's Spies," *Independent*, May 28, 2003; John Pike. "Chemical Weapons Programs: History," *Federation of American Scientists*, November 8, 1998.

36. *Al Jazeera*, "Excerpt from al-Zawahiri Audiotape," May 21, 2003; Neil MacFarquhar and Don Van Natta Jr., "New Tape, Linked to bin Laden Aide, Urges More Attacks," *New York Times*, May 22, 2003.

37. Edward Alden and Roula Khalaf, "Security Tightened as Tape Urges al-Qaeda Attacks," *Financial Times*, May 22, 2003.

38. Al Jazeera TV, "USA Raps Qatar, Al-Jazeera TV for Airing Al-Zawahiri Tape," *BBC Summary of World Broadcasts*, May 21, 2003.

39. *Independent*, "Bush-Blair Itinerary," May 30, 2003.

40. Mike Allen, "President: 'Truth' on Arms Will Be Found; New Caution Expressed in Claims about Iraq," *Washington Post*, June 6, 2003.

41. George W. Bush, "Speech at Camp as Sayliyah," Qatar, June 5, 2003.

42. John R. Bradley, "Crunch-Time for Al-Jazeera," *Straits Times*, December 1, 2003.

43. John R. Bradley, "US Threatened to Downgrade Qatari Ties over Al-Jazeera," *Arab News*, October 4, 2003. For a critical reading of the story, see Miles, *Al-Jazeera: The Inside Story*.

44. Arab News, "Saudi Daily Reports US Resolve to Close Down or Tone Down Al-Jazeera," *BBC Summary of World Broadcasts*, October 4, 2003.

45. John R. Bradley, "Fit to Print?" *Al Ahram Weekly*, November 27– December 3, 2003.

46. Iason Athanasiadi, "Al-Jazeera Fires Ridley," *Guardian*, November 17, 2003.

47. Iason Athanasiadis, "Aljazeera's English Experiment in Trouble," *Asia Times*, November 19, 2003.

48. Ibid.

49. Ibid.

50. Al Kamen, "Tough Love by U.S. Angers Key Ally," *Washington Post*, December 17, 2003.
51. Author interview, January 22, 2010, London, UK.
52. Author interview, March 25, 2008, London, UK.
53. Lisa O'Carroll, "Sky Man Poached for Al Jazeera Launch," *Guardian*, September 10, 2004, http://www.guardian.co.uk/media/2004/sep/10/iraqandthemedia.tvnews
54. Author interview (telephone), Mach 25, 2011.
55. Vijaya Cherian, "Inside Al Jazeera," *Arabian Business.com*, March 4, 2005, http://www.arabianbusiness.com/inside-al-jazeera-205552.html
56. Author interview, March 2008, Doha, Qatar.
57. Author interview, March 2008, Doha, Qatar.
58. Alex Black, "Al Jazeera Picks BLJ to Soften English Launch," *PR Week*, July 22, 2005.
59. Author interview, March 2008, Doha, Qatar; for other examples of growing disagreement, see Hannah Allam, "New Al-Jazeera International Channel Sparks Conflict," *Knight Ridder*, March 2, 2006.
60. Author interview (telephone), March 25, 2011.
61. Hannah Allam, "New Al-Jazeera International Channel Sparks Conflict," *Knight Ridder*, March 2, 2006, http://www.commondreams.org/headlines06/0302-08.htm
62. *BBC Monitoring World Media*, "Veteran Journalist Ibrahim Helal Joins Al-Jazeera International," May 31, 2006.
63. Joy Lo Dico, "Resignation Hits al-Jazeera Plans," *Independent*, August 13, 2006.
64. Author interview (telephone), March 25, 2011.
65. Ibid.
66. Aljazeera.net (translated by BBC World Service), November 1, 2006.

CHAPTER 2

The Nature of the Channel's Global Audience

Hussein Amin

Al Jazeera launched its international English-language news channel, Al Jazeera English (AJE), on November 15, 2006. Originally called Aljazeera International and broadcast to more than 80 million households worldwide, the channel became the world's first English-language international news network to originate in the Middle East. The network modeled itself on news organizations like BBC World and CNN International and worked to develop a global identity, rather than positioning itself as the English translation of its Arab sister network.

The channel is broadcast from four centers in Doha, Kuala Lumpur, London, and Washington, DC, and the network's mission is to "provide independent, impartial news for an international audience and to offer a voice to a diversity of perspectives from under-reported regions" and to "balance the information flow between the South and the North."[1] With 65 bureaus strategically placed around the world at a time when other news networks are shuttering expensive foreign operations, AJE has the opportunity to fill a gap in the market for global news shot on location with an immediacy and access that is increasingly unavailable to other networks. Researchers Mohamed el-Nawawy and Shawn Powers note that

> Al Jazeera English stands out from its competitors in that it presents a challenge to the existing paradigms guiding international news broadcasters. It is dominated by neither geopolitical nor commercial interests, and is the first of its kind to have the resources, mandate and journalistic capacity to reach out to typically isolated and ignored audiences throughout the world. It both represents a challenge to "the myth of the mediated centre," while also providing a test case for examining the conciliatory potential of a global satellite channel.[2]

Since its inception, AJE has received nominations and awards for news and programing including the International Emmys, the Royal Television Society, the Monte Carlo Film Festival, YouTube, the Foreign Press Association, the Association of International Broadcasters, Amnesty International,[3] and Columbia University. Despite this success, however, the network still struggles to reach audiences in the West.

At the time of its launch in 2006, the "war on terror" was still in its early days, with hot wars being fought in Iraq and Afghanistan, and Al Jazeera was widely viewed in the West as biased in its reporting and sympathetic to extremist groups in the region as well as the preferred outlet for videos from Osama bin Laden and Al Qaeda. This reputation made the network too "hot to handle for some cable operators," according to the New York Times (2008). Although the network has a footprint that spans the globe, AJE is fully available only through cable systems to U.S. audiences in Washington, DC, Toledo, OH, and Burlington, VT, representing 1.7 percent of American households.[4]

Despite the barriers that have been erected against the penetration of AJE in markets like the United States, the network has continued to grow. As of early 2011, the network's reach had grown from 80 million households to more than 250 million households in more than 100 countries, and these numbers should continue to expand with the network's recent acquisition of a down-linking license for carriage in India, the largest English-language television market in the world[5] as well as with the West's increasing awareness of and demand for the network following its coverage of the uprisings in the Arab World.

TELEVISION

AJE broadcasts reach nearly all countries in the world. Because of the breadth of its coverage, particularly in areas where rating agencies do not operate, it is difficult to estimate the audience size for AJE broadcasts. According to Al Anstey, AJE's new managing director, the network is currently conducting a large-scale research project in 21 countries to provide greater information about the size and profile of the network's audience.[6]

In Europe, AJE is available to the vast majority of households. In addition to extensive satellite coverage, the network is available on standard terrestrial service (Freeview) in the UK and with a DVB-S receiver in Europe through broadcasts on the Astra 1M, Hot Bird 6, Eutelsat W2A, Badr 4, Turksat 2A, Thor 6, Nilesat 102, Hispasat 1C, and Eurobird 1 satellites.[7] These same satellites provide extensive coverage for Africa and the Middle East as well. In Australia, the channel is provided free through the Optus C1 satellite.

AJE was recently granted a license to broadcast over both cable and satellite in India for the first time, potentially increasing the size of their global audience by an additional 115 million households. AJE already has a bureau in New Delhi, which contributed to important international stories such as the Mumbai bombing and the Commonwealth Games.[8]

In North America, access to coverage is more divided, with Canada relatively open to AJE and the United States all but banning the network. AJE began broadcasting in Canada on May 4, 2010. After receiving approval from Canada's federal regulator in November 2009, three of Canada's largest cable providers, Bell TV, Rogers, and Videotron, now carry the digital channel.[9] In June 2010, AJE announced that all digital subscribers of Shaw Cable on channel 175 would be able to access AJE free of charge for a trial period ending in August 2010.[10] The approval process took four years to successfully pass all the hurdles set by the regulator, despite the fact that AJE employs a number of Canadians in leadership positions, including the then AJE managing director, Tony Burman, former editor-in-chief of Canadian Broadcasting Corporation (CBC) News. Other prominent Canadian AJE staff members include Canadian-born journalist Imtiaz Tyab, formerly of the BBC in London and CBC News in Vancouver, and Jet Belgraver, a Canadian documentary and news producer, both based in AJE's recently opened Toronto news bureau. As part of its strategy to fill gaps in coverage of areas and stories that other international news organizations have abandoned, AJE plans to broadcast news affairs and documentary programs relevant to Canadian audiences, including features on Canada's oil sands and the country's controversial climate change policy.[11]

In the United States, a market of 300 million people and hundreds of cable television channels, the network is largely unavailable on television. AJE is available free to air on the Galaxy 19 and Galaxy 23 C-band satellites. Individual newscasts are shown through Link TV on the Direc TV and DISH Network satellite systems.[12] Most Americans, however, don't use satellite dishes to watch television. According to a 2006 study by Arbitron, more than 60% of Americans subscribe to cable television,[13] yet AJE is available to cable subscribers in only three locations in the United States: Toledo, OH; Burlington, VT; and Washington, DC.[14] The number of subscribers reached by these cable providers is relatively small. Burlington Telecom reaches about 3,000 subscribers; Washington, DC-based MHz Networks, reaches nearly 5 million households, and Buckeye CableSystem reaches 150,000 subscribers in northwest Ohio.[15] Viewers can, however, watch it on the Web through AJE's website, YouTube, and online broadcasters.

Link TV, an award-winning satellite network provider based in San Francisco, airs the network 12 hours a day. A recent internal study by Link TV shows that 6.7 million people watch it at least once a week and keep watching for 45 minutes, either through the satellite broadcast or online. The network is available in 33 million U.S. homes, and 60 percent of Link's viewers are 18–34 years old—approximately half the age of the typical network evening news provider and a demographic highly coveted by both politicians and advertisers.[16]

In February 2011, listener-supported network Pacifica Radio KPFK 90.7 fm announced that it would carry a 30-minute news broadcast from AJE each day during the 6:00–6:30 pm time slot. KPFK was originally supposed to launch the broadcast in March but decided to move the launch date up given the events occurring in the Middle East to "provide an additional voice and perspective from the region to the communities of Southern California." The network broadcasts one hour of AJE news in three markets: KPFA in Berkeley, CA; WBAI in New York; and KPFT in Houston, TX, in addition to the Los Angeles, CA, broadcast of KPFK. The broadcasts will also be made available to Pacifica affiliates and streamed live on the Internet.[17]

In March 2011, Free Speech TV, an independent, publicly supported, nonprofit television network that broadcasts and webcasts independently produced programing like *Democracy Now!* preempted its regular programing to air Al Jazeera's coverage of the unrest in the Middle East. AJE live news feeds are available on Free Speech TV on DIRECTV channel 348, DISH network channel 9415, and on www.freespeech.org.[18]

INTERNET AND SOCIAL MEDIA

Cable and satellite transmission of AJE is only part of the network's strategy. Viewers unable or unwilling to watch AJE broadcasts on television can access the network's programing through the Internet and have done so in the millions.

In March 2003, in response to Al Jazeera's coverage of the war in Afghanistan and the subsequent barrage of requests from non-Arabic readers, Al Jazeera launched an English-language version of its Arabic website, hosted by U.S. company DataPipe. The site was brought down almost immediately by hackers whose attacks took the form of "denial of service" and hijacking the domain name to redirect users to pages with U.S. patriotic slogans or pornography. While Al Jazeera attempted to solve these problems, many of their partners in the West left due to, some claim, political pressure from the U.S. government and private citizens. Later web hosts also declined to carry the site, and companies like Yahoo refused to carry ads for Al Jazeera programing and websites, citing sensitivities due to the war in Iraq. Al Jazeera eventually found a company to host the site in the fall of 2003.[19]

What began as a relatively simple English translation of the Arabic website has become the complex, sophisticated online news delivery platform of the AJE network. The website still remained relatively obscure until it came into sharp focus during the 2011 uprisings in Tunisia, Egypt, and other countries in the Middle East. Since late January, at the start of Egypt's revolution, AJE recorded more than 6.8 million views of its online video stream, 2.5 million of them from the United States. The network's website traffic increased by more than 2,500 percent, with half of that traffic originating in the United States.[20]

In addition to its popular website, AJE streams video content on a dedicated YouTube channel and several other satellite and Internet channels, such as Link TV, Livestation, Free TV, and Pacifica Radio KPFK 90.7 fm. Low-resolution video is available free of charge on the AJE website, while the high-resolution version by subscription through partner sites. The network also streams live video to Livestation (www.livestation .com/aje) for Internet-based broadcasting to viewers around the world, and the AJE YouTube site has more than 10,000 videos available for viewing. AJE's Facebook page has more than 530,000 fans as of May 1, 2011 and nearly 345,000 followers on Twitter.

During the crisis in Egypt, AJE used "Promoted Tweets," which are sponsored Tweets at the top of Twitter.com search results pages to drive viewers to the live video streams on its website and bypass the lack of cable coverage in the United States. By using the power of Twitter in this way, the network was able to work around major cable and satellite companies such as Comcast and DirecTV. *Twitter Media* reported that of "all Tweets mentioning Egypt or #Jan25, AJE's live stream is the single most-tweeted link."[21] AJE successfully used Twitter as a distribution platform for its news broadcasts and proved that broadcasters can draw large audiences using social media and new technologies.

AJE is also using its web site to put pressure on recalcitrant cable companies in the United States. The website features a "Demand Al Jazeera in the US" page, with instructions to tweet followers, organize a meetup to watch AJE, join a call-in day (March 23, 2011), read U.S. media coverage of AJE, find TV service providers and demand the service, and embed a free banner.

Barriers to Coverage in the West

There have been a number of analysts who have commented that AJE's lack of availability on the largest and most popular cable providers reflects hostility to the network following its sister network's broadcast of Osama bin Laden's post-September 11 videos condemning the United States as well as a fear of alienating advertisers and angering the former Bush administration and influential U.S. political leaders.[22]

Bush administration officials promoted the view that Al Jazeera was supporting Islamic terrorist groups and was anti-American. In advance of the Iraq invasion in 2003, the Pentagon hired consultants to target Al Jazeera reporters who did not stay "on message," and when the network broadcast violent images of the invasion, the administration said that Al Jazeera was inciting violence.[23] Former secretary of defense Donald Rumsfeld accused it of spreading "vicious, inaccurate and inexcusable" reports about U.S. activities in Iraq,[24] and as recently as February 2011, popular Fox News commentator Bill O'Reilly called Al Jazeera "anti-American" and "anti-Semitic."[25] Researchers Youmans and Brown cite the media advocacy group Accuracy in Media (AIM) and O'Reilly who have challenged AJE's efforts to obtain distribution agreements with dominant cable companies like Comcast and Time Warner. AIM circulated an online petition asking cable companies to refuse to carry AJE due to what it called propagandistic content. Smaller, less radical groups have made similar calls for AJE broadcasts to be banned in various locations.[26]

In an effort to make AJE more appealing to U.S. cable operators and audiences, Tony Burman, AJE's former managing director and current chief strategic advisor for the Americas, increased coverage of U.S. news, especially during the run-up to the presidential elections, and increased current affairs programing and investigative journalism.[27] In his new position, Burman has been tasked with accelerating expansion in the North American market and increasing the reach, reputation, and profile of AJE.[28]

Despite these efforts to reposition itself as a quality global media network, many in the United States continued to look at Al Jazeera as a supporter of terrorism. Exacerbating this misperception is a general lack of interest on the part of the American public in global news. Most cable carriers regard the news market as saturated and fail to see, in a purely commercial sense, the added value in another global news network.[29]

The strongly negative attitude toward AJE began changing in 2010. Secretary of State Hillary Clinton met with Al Jazeera's top executives during a visit to Qatar a year ago and cleared the air, according to Burman. "The cold war that existed between the Bush administration and Al Jazeera has totally ended. Now it's a professional relationship between an aggressive government and an aggressive news organization."[30]

Since then, high-ranking State Department officials, including Clinton, have been guests of both the Arabic and English networks, as have Defense Secretary Robert Gates, Gen. David Petraeus, and Adm.

Michael Mullen, chairman of the Joint Chiefs of Staff. In spring 2010, the State Department created a position of deputy assistant secretary for international media engagement to reach out to international media outlets and has assigned staff in media hubs like London, Dubai, and Brussels to lay out Washington's talking points and respond to requests from Arabic and other media organizations.[31]

But it wasn't until the January 2011 uprisings in the Arab world that AJE began attracting serious attention in the United States. With its coverage, particularly of the revolution in Egypt, the network distanced itself from the competition to become the primary source of information for American officials, media organizations, and audiences. AJE was the sole English-language media outlet with uninterrupted live video of the demonstrations in the Egyptian capital, and the network continued broadcasting even when government forces closed their offices and detained their reporters. Major U.S. networks were forced by necessity to replay Al Jazeera coverage of the events in Egypt, and Salon.com's Alex Pareene stated that "al-Jazeera's Egypt coverage embarrasses U.S. cable news channels."[32]

As demand for AJE's coverage of the events in the Middle East increased, online viewing, which was the only way for most Americans to watch the broadcasts, grew exponentially. U.S. officials, newspaper columnists, talk show hosts, and other influential citizens began questioning why the network was not available, as Fox News and MSNBC used AJE coverage when their reporters fled the turmoil. At a meeting of the Senate Foreign Relations Committee during the events in Middle East, Secretary of State Clinton criticized the superficiality of American media and particularly its coverage of international events. She then praised Al Jazeera and said, "You may not agree with [Al Jazeera], but you feel you're getting real news around the clock instead of a million commercials." She continued that media discourse in the United States "is not particularly informative to us, let alone foreigners."[33] "In fact," she said, "viewership of Al Jazeera is going up in the United States because it's real news."[34]

The challenge for AJE is to turn this newly favorable sentiment and customer demand into access to traditional and still dominant distribution channels in the United States—cable networks. A recent Arbitron study showed that cable television reaches nearly 6 in 10 U.S. adults aged 18–49 and more than 6 in 10 adults aged 25–64. This is clearly the audience that AJE needs to reach to expand its U.S. viewership. In addition, cable viewers closely mirror the age and gender profile of the average American.[35] AJE has sought to do this by launching a grassroots campaign to pressure cable companies to carry the network. AJE started an advertising campaign and designed a special webpage, IwantAJE.com, to increase public awareness and support. Viewers can enter their zip code that will lead them to a contact page for their local cable provider, where they are offered the option to send out a prewritten letter to their provider requesting the network become part of the cable package. The campaign has generated more than 40,000 letters. No distribution deals have yet been concluded, however, and AJE still faces an uphill battle, particularly given U.S. audiences' traditionally short attention spans.[36]

In their recent research study, Youmans and Brown concluded that it was unlikely that AJE will be able to penetrate the U.S. market to any large degree. They found that:

> the perception of AJE as biased is robust among American viewers in general, and especially among those politically conservative and suspicious of Arabs. Since these perceptions correlate highly with the more deeply held constructs of political ideology and prejudice, this "moment" is, at best, limited to a willingly receptive portion of the country. If those who remain prejudiced against AJE mobilize around this view and oppose cable carriage of AJE, it could offset gains in AJE's reputation. This would limit the network's market penetration and therefore the potential for educating or moderating the views of Americans who have little access to news and perspectives originating outside of the country's borders.[37]

The researchers note that, in this case, AJE's strategy should be to focus on niche audiences who watch AJE broadcasts on the Internet. By doing so, the network will be forced to stay ahead of the technological curve and will be, therefore, well-placed for an industry increasingly blurring the boundaries between platforms.

Another possible consideration is that, while the potential audience for AJE on cable might not be large, it could be highly targeted, which is appealing for advertisers. Although AJE does not specifically target Arab-Americans, there is the possibility of brand recognition that could draw this segment of the market. With more than 4 million Americans identifying themselves as Arab-Americans, a group with a median income of 19 percent higher than the national average and a rate of postgraduate education nearly double the national average,[38] this segment is potentially quite attractive. AJE managing director described recent meetings with executives at Comcast, Time Warner Cable, and Cablevision as "very positive" and is optimistic about striking a deal.[39]

Future Considerations

The stated mission of AJE is to "provide independent, impartial news for an international audience and to offer a voice to a diversity of perspectives from under-reported regions"[40]—to balance the traditional North-South flow of information with information that flows from the South to the North.

While audiences in the United States remain in large part suspicious of the network, segments of the global market are receptive to the network's broadcasts as they become increasingly available around the world.

Recent research has shown that the viewpoints of AJE's U.S. and international viewers were broadened by watching the network.[41] El Nawawy and Powers surveyed viewers in six countries and found that "viewers of AJE in Asia, the Middle East, Europe and North America all found AJE to work towards a conciliatory function, based on a typology of a conciliatory media developed and outlined here; and the longer viewers had been tuning into AJE, the less dogmatic they were in their cognitive thought."[42] The researchers argue that the study confirmed their hypothesis that AJE's model of journalism provides an alternative to the current style of news journalism that is premised on stereotypical attitudes toward cultural "others." The positive correlation between the length of AJE viewership and the viewers' level of dogmatic thinking is likely a result of the way that AJE reports the news, focusing on issues of culture and identity and drawing connections between different audiences where viewers might not have known connections exist.[43]

While news organizations are increasingly reducing their international coverage, Al Jazeera is expanding the number of its foreign bureaus. Its ability to collaborate with its Arabic sister network will mean that it will be able to keep control costs, adding another advantage over other networks. In addition, the U.S. government has adopted a more welcoming attitude toward the network, praising its coverage and comparing it favorably to U.S. media broadcasts. A U.S. State Department inspector general's report outlined the problem facing the government: "The network on occasion stakes out controversial and inflammatory positions on issues of interest to the United States. On the other hand, its reporting does support other U.S. objectives in human rights, democratization and environmental protection, among other issues."[44] So long as this removal of opposition to the network remains in effort, AJE's efforts to penetrate the United States and other markets will most likely meet with a great deal more success.

Al Anstey, AJE managing director, is optimistic about the future. "Remember, AJE is only 5 years old, and we competing with top world news networks now, and we would like to keep our position and strengthen it."[45]

The credibility of the network is enormously important as it expands internationally. Many viewers in the West are overcoming a perception of bias and anti-Americanism in the organization's broadcasts. If AJE is to remain successful, it must work hard to maintain its credibility and its focus on strict adherence to its professional ethics. It is a young network operating out of a relatively stable country that has not been a focal point of international news during the past five years. The network will be tested if the region's democracy movements gain ground in Qatar, whose leader supplies the vast majority of the network's funding. Whether or not AJE will be able to remain independent and impartial will be the true test of its growth and future.

Notes

1. Al Jazeera, "About Us: Corporate Profile," Al Jazeera, http://english
   .aljazeera.net/aboutus/2006/11/2008525185555444449.html.
2. Mohamed el-Nawawy and Shawn Powers, "A Conciliatory Medium in a Conflict-Driven Environment?," *Global Media and Communication* 6 (61) (2010), http://gmc.sagepub.com.library.aucegypt.edu:2048/content /6/1/61.full.pdf+html
3. Al Jazeera, "About Us: Facts and Figures," Al Jazeera, http://english
   .aljazeera.net/aboutus/2010/11/20101110131438787482.html
4. William Youmans and Katie Brown, "Can Al Jazeera English Leverage Its 'Egypt Moment' into an American Audience?," *Arab Media and Society* 12 (Spring 2011), http://arabmediasociety.com/index.php?article =768&printarticle
5. Ibid.
6. Al Anstey, e-mail message with author, April 28, 2011.
7. Al Jazeera, "Middle East: Al Jazeera to Broadcast in India," Al Jazeera, Middle East Section, December 9, 2010, http://english.aljazeera.net /news/middleeast/2010/12/201012762555877955.html.
8. Ibid.
9. CBC News, "Al Jazeera English Launches in Canada," CBC News, Arts & Entertainment Section, May 4, 2010, http://www.cbc.ca/news/arts /media/story/2010/05/04/al-jazeera-english-launch.html.
10. Canada NewsWire, "Al Jazeera English Launches on Shaw Cable," *Digital Journal*, Press Release, June 6, 2010, http://www.digitaljournal .com/pr/57597.
11. CBC News, "Al Jazeera English Launches in Canada."
12. Joe Garifoli, "Link TV Carries Al Jazeera English Egypt Coverage," *San Francisco Chronicle*, February 4, 2011, http://articles.sfgate.com /2011-02-04/news/27100778_1_cable-network-viewpoints
13. Carol Edwards and Diane Williams, "The Arbitron Cable Television Study: Exploring the Consumer's Relationship with Cable TV," Arbitron, http://www.arbitron.com/downloads/cabletvstudy.pdf
14. Al Jazeera, "Watch AJE: How to Watch Al Jazeera English on TV," *Al Jazeera*, March 9, 2011, http://english.aljazeera.net/watchaje/.

15. Lorraine Ali and Melissa Guthrie, "Why American Cable Systems Won't Carry the Al Jazeera Network," *Hollywood Reporter*, March 13, 2011, http://www.hollywoodreporter.com/news/why-american-cable-systems-wont-168953.
16. Garifoli, "Link TV Carries Al Jazeera English Egypt Coverage."
17. Pacifica Radio KPFK 90.7 fm, "Pacifica Radio KPFK 90.7 fm to Broadcast News from Al Jazeera English," Pacifica Radio KPFK 90.7 fm Los Angeles News Release, February 2, 2011, http://www.kpfk.org/press-release/4504-al-jazeera-english-broadcasts-on-kpfk-907-fm-html.
18. PR Newswire, "Free Speech TV to Broadcast Breaking Al Jazeera English Coverage of Middle East and Japan," *PR Newswire*, March 20, 2011, http://www.prnewswire.com/news-releases/free-speech-tv-to-broadcast-breaking-al-jazeera-english-coverage-of-middle-east-and-japan-118952449.html.
19. Philip Auter, "Meeting the Needs of Multiple Audiences: An Examination of the Aljazeera and English Aljazeera Websites from the Public Relations Perspective," *Global Media Journal* (3)(5)(Fall 2004), http://lass.calumet.purdue.edu/cca/gmj/fa04/gmj-fa04-auter.htm.
20. Ali and Guthrie, "Why American Cable Systems Won't Carry the Al Jazeera Network."
21. Paul Hoffman, "Al Jazeera Attracts Massive Audience through Twitter," *editorsweblog.org*, World Editors Forum, February 9, 2011, http://www.editorsweblog.org/web_20/2011/02/al_jazeera_attracts_massive_audience_thr.php
22. Youmans and Brown, "Can Al Jazeera English Leverage Its 'Egypt Moment' into an American Audience?"
23. Elizabeth Flock, "'Demand Al-Jazeera in the USA' Campaign," *Washington Post*, Blog Post Section, February 4, 2011, http://voices.washingtonpost.com/blog-post/2011/02/al-jazeera_on_us_television.html
24. Brian Bennett, "U.S. Mends Frosty Relations with Al Jazeera," *Los Angeles Times*, World Section, February 7, 2011, http://articles.latimes.com/2011/feb/07/world/la-fg-al-jazeera-20110207.
25. Garifoli, "Link TV Carries Al Jazeera English Egypt Coverage."
26. Youmans and Brown, "Can Al Jazeera English Leverage Its 'Egypt Moment' into an American Audience?"
27. Eric Pfanner, "Al Jazeera English Tries to Extend Its Reach," *New York Times*, May 19, 2008, http://www.nytimes.com/2008/05/19/business/media/19jazeera.html?pagewanted=print.
28. CNW, "Tony Burman to Assume New Position at Al Jazeera to Accelerate Expansion in North America," *CNW*, May 2010, http://www.newswire.ca/en/releases/archive/May2010/17/c4333.html.
29. Youmans and Brown, "Can Al Jazeera English Leverage Its 'Egypt Moment' into an American Audience?"
30. Bennett, "U.S. Mends Frosty Relations with Al Jazeera."
31. Ibid.

32. Flock
33. Pittsburgh Post-Gazette, "Media Critic: Al-Jazeera's Coverage Garners Praise from Clinton," *Pittsburgh Post-Gazette*, March 7, 2011,
34. Kirit Radia, "Sec. of State Hillary Clinton: Al Jazeera Is 'Real News,' U.S. Losing 'Information War,'" ABC News, Political Punch, March 2, 2011, http://blogs.abcnews.com/politicalpunch/2011/03/sec-of-state-hillary-clinton-al-jazeera-is-real-news-us-losing-information-war.html#.
35. Edwards and Williams, "The Arbitron Cable Television Study: Exploring the Consumer's Relationship with Cable TV."
36. Youmans and Brown, "Can Al Jazeera English Leverage Its 'Egypt Moment' into an American Audience?"
37. Ibid.
38. Ali and Guthrie, "Why American Cable Systems Won't Carry the Al Jazeera Network."
39. Ibid.
40. Al Jazeera, "About Us: Corporate Profile."
41. El-Nawawy and Powers, "A Conciliatory Medium in a Conflict-Driven Environment?"
42. Ibid.
43. Ibid.
44. Bennett, "U.S. Mends Frosty Relations with Al Jazeera."
45. Anstey, e-mail message with author, April 28, 2011.

CHAPTER 3

Content: The Messages of AJE's News

Tine Ustad Figenschou

In promotional presentations, Al Jazeera English's (AJE) mission is described as to provide "independent, impartial news for an international audience and to provide a voice of diversity of perspectives from under-reported regions."[1] "In addition," the promotional text continues, "the channel aims to balance the information flow between the South and the North. The channel of reference for the Middle East and Africa, AJE has unique access to some of the world's most troubled and controversial locations. AJE's determination and ability to accurately reflect the truth on the ground in regions torn by conflict and poverty has set our content apart."[2]

Along the same lines, AJE is portrayed on the official channel website as "balancing the current typical information flow by reporting from the developing world back to the West and from the southern to the northern hemisphere." Moreover, the channel aims "to give voice to untold stories, promote debate, and challenge established perceptions" and to "set the news agenda, bridging cultures and providing a unique grassroots perspective from under-reported regions around the world to a potential global audience of over one billion English speakers."[3]

To *balance, report back,* and *challenge* mainstream western international news, the channel has employed a number of editorial strategies:[4] first, AJE aims to cover the world without a domestic agenda, as a *truly global* news channel, in contrast to Western national and international news media that have become increasingly domesticated and localized in their coverage of international issues. Second, AJE aims to report forgotten stories from the *perspective of the voiceless*—the Global South, the under-privileged, the subaltern, the underdog, and the disenfranchised. To find and cover the stories of the voiceless, the channel has a policy of hiring local correspondents, instead of sending in Western correspondents. In addition, AJE has an extensive network of bureaus and correspondents around the world, particularly in the Global South where its competitors are scarcely represented. Third, the channel intends to cover the *other opinion* in international news, those diverging, oppositional, controversial views and voices that are rarely invited onto mainstream news media programs. To do this, channel staff highlight the competitive advantage of being part of the Al Jazeera Network.

Like the major Western news channels, AJE exhibits a high level of cyclicity in its schedules and a preference for half-hour or one-hour programs, with a repetitive news-on-the-hour format rolling 24/7, in combination with a variety of factual programs.[5] AJE has not introduced especially innovative or interactive news formats. Its distinctiveness from its Western rivals is most clearly expressed in its editorial perspective.[6] AJE's editorial distinctiveness and southern perspective can be analyzed in a variety of ways. With its editorial agenda and production strategies as a point of departure, this chapter discusses the news geography, the news sources, and the visual profile of AJE news.

At most times, AJE broadcasts from one of its four news centers, so that Kuala Lumpur anchors from 04.00 to 08.00 GMT, Doha from 11.00 to 17.00, London from 20.00 to 22.00 and Washington, DC, from 23.00 to 02.00.[7] At certain times of the day, it links up news centers to co-anchor the news shows. The flagship news program for the channel is the AJE *NewsHour* at 18.00 GMT, linking up the Doha headquarters with the London broadcasting center and the Washington broadcasting center (the Kuala Lumpur broadcasting center is not included due to the time difference), arguably making *NewsHour* a particularly interesting program to analyze in order to discuss the channel's coverage of world events.[8]

THE GLOBAL SOUTH: NEWS GEOGRAPHY ON AJE

With the geographical South as a point of departure, AJE informants emphasize that the Global South encompasses more than just the Southern Hemisphere, though there is an overlap between the two. Informants use notions like "philosophical South,"[9] "South with a capital S"[10] or "political South"[11]

A Doha-based news anchor gave the following illustration of his understanding of the South:

If a husband is the North, his wife is the South. If the politician is the North, his driver is the South. If I am the North in this office, the coffee guy in a yellow jumpsuit, the one who come in to pick up my coffee cup and take it from me—he is the South [...] For me that is possibly the closest that I can imagine. If you were to define the voice of the South in a studio, you've got someone from the North and someone from the South. Give that person from the South more time [...] because most of the time, those with wealth or those with political power, or those who are celebrities get free reign and make headlines.[12]

A senior producer in Doha argued that the South is a state of mind and not just a geographical entity:

You can find the South in the North. You can find the South as individual people who feel not really represented by the system, or groups of people who feel the same, or areas and countries, which feel the same. [...] So, it's not a geographical thing, but it is based on geography because the biggest bulk of people who are disenfranchised and in disenchantment, are in the South. But that's why geographically; if you have a camera and you have to work somewhere, that's where you will go. Of course, you will have to go to the North as well. It's for the world; this is a channel for the world.[13]

In its ambitious editorial agenda AJE aims to cover the world *from* the South to the North, to be a truly global channel. In a quantitative content analysis,[14] AJE's southern perspective (the philosophical, political, and symbolic South) was operationalized in terms of news geography (the geographical South). This was done primarily to relate the findings to the existing news flow and contraflow literature. Notwithstanding its limitations, the news flow literature served as a point of departure for the analysis of the news geography of AJE.[15] First of all, numerous studies of the ways in which the world is reflected in the news media from the 1950s until today document the prominence of regionalism (geographical and cultural proximity) in media systems throughout the world. They also show a systematic emphasis on the Global North (Western Europe and North America) worldwide.[16] The key features of the news geography studies are largely confirmed and theorized by the international news determinant research, surveying the social psychology of the news professionals and the ways in which these characteristics affect news output (the gatekeeper perspective), and the socioeconomic components and physical logistics of international news flows (the logistical perspective).[17]

News flow studies have documented that the international flow of information has been overwhelmingly one way, a geographical pattern that AJE aims to reverse. Given the channel's intended Southern perspective, a key question in this discussion is whether the channel covers the

South more extensively than the North.[18] The quantitative analysis of the AJE *NewsHour* was, therefore, conducted from a North-South perspective, comparing the channel's coverage of the Global South (Africa, Asia, the Middle East, and Latin America) with its coverage of the Global North (Europe and North America). In an extensive quantitative study, Figenschou ("A Voice for the Voiceless?) analyzed two months of AJE newscasts, from October–December 2007 to May–July 2008. Some of the main findings of the quantitative study are highlighted here: first, the South was covered more frequently than the North (61–38 percent). Second, Europe and Asia were the most covered regions, closely followed by the Middle East, with each of these regions accounting for about one-fifth of all locations. Third, AJE covered the South with in-depth news formats (offering reflection, discussion, and background information) more frequently than it did the North. Fourth, by considering the world region in which news items originate, regional variations in news formats became apparent as Europe, North America, and Latin America were covered in briefer formats, whereas Asia and the Middle East were reported in greater depth. Taken together, these findings reveal that AJE's geographical emphasis is on the Global South.[19] This largely corresponds with Painter's 2008 comparative analysis of one week of AJE, CNN International, and BBC World news. He found that AJE had significantly more coverage of the developing world than the BBC World and CNN International, with 81 percent, 47 percent, and 53 percent respectively (Painter included Russia and Turkey in the "developing world" category, which may explain why his percentages were higher than those mentioned in the Figenschou study).

Another key finding in the quantitative study was the fact that channel had a greater presence on the ground in the South than in the North. AJE correspondents were present where the events unfolded in the South in almost half the news items originating in the South. These findings reflect AJE's decentralized production structure, compared to its main competitors.[20] More importantly, the differences between AJE and its competitors will only increase if the current location trends in global news continue. In contrast to the major mainstream Western news organizations, which are all reducing their global networks of correspondents.[21] AJE has an extensive network of bureaux and correspondents around the world, especially in the Global South, where its competitors are much more scarcely represented.

Regionalism has been a defining feature of international news since the first news geography studies in the 1950s. It is thus relevant to measure the extent to which AJE reflects its geographical home region or counters the localization trend in international news. The regional emphasis has been a key characteristic of the channels' Arabic sister channel Al Jazeera channel. The Arab orientation—an Arab channel broadcasting from the Arab and Muslim world in Arabic to an Arab audience—was highlighted in Zayani and Sahraoui's analysis of Al Jazeera Arabic's success factors.[22] Although the English channel has a broader editorial mission, it has a stated aim of being the "channel of reference" for the Middle East and Africa.[23]

In the Figenschou quantitative mapping of the channel's news geography, the Middle East was among the most covered world regions, together with Asia and Europe: first, the Middle East was overemphasized relative to its geographical size, population size, and GDP per capita. Second, it was covered in more analytical news formats. Among the three most covered regions, Asia and the Middle East were reported in greater detail, and the Middle East in particular was covered in analytical news formats indicating that AJE put special emphasis on its home region.[24] These findings provided initial evidence of regionalism in the coverage, although the documented regionalism was not as evident as in Painter's analysis, which identified a stronger regionalism in AJE's coverage. In Painter's survey, AJE had significantly more coverage of the Middle East than the BBC World (which had more coverage of Europe) and CNN International (which had more coverage of the United States).[25] Moreover, compared with its competitors in the global satellite news ecology, AJE had a stronger presence in the Middle East region than in other parts of the world. The results of the channel's Arab presence were also demonstrated in the channel's coverage of the Gaza war and the popular uprising across the Middle East and North Africa.

AJE's Southern perspective reflects the channel's editorial values and thus its concept of newsworthiness through a higher proportion of stories from the developing world. Furthermore, the quantitative findings show how the editorial strategy to establish a Southern presence contributes to a higher number of news stories from the South. AJE's Southern emphasis is a result of the channel's definition of newsworthiness as broadly articulated in its editorial core values. Moreover, it is a result of its organizational structure, demonstrated through its extensive news network in the South, its local correspondents, and its cooperation with the other channels in the Al Jazeera Network. These progressive production strategies seem to have counteracted the logistical factors that traditionally determine international news, such as a nation's GNP, volume of trade, population, geographic size, regionalization, elite domination, communication resources and infrastructure, and cultural affinity.[26]

News Sources: Alternative Source Hierarchies in AJE

The critical investigation of the "smallest interactional setting of journalism,"[27] the source-journalist relationship, considers journalism in the context of other institutions. AJE management and staff aim to redress the elite domination of international news by consciously redirecting attention from the "corridors of power" to the margins.[28] This has two potential influences on the sourcing strategy. First, the channel aims to be systematically critical of authorities and elites and to invite all sides of the story into the studio. Second, it aims to invite ordinary people who are touched by the story to express their views and experiences. A senior AJE correspondent described the channel's sourcing strategy in the following words:

> This is a channel that will give a voice to those that have not been heard for whatever reason; be it geographical, be it political oppression, whatever the reason; you should go out of your way to liberate those voices. So certainly, that's a very strong editorial position. No, I don't think its Arab, and it's not very much an underdog thing. You know, some of the voices that we are giving voices to are not underdogs; that's patronizing and actually simply that they have been cut out of the news flow which being run by northern, western interests for decades. And there has not been an international forum where those voices can be heard unless what they do impacts someone of those [Northern] countries.[29]

For AJE informants, the sourcing strategy requires extra resources and effort. A Doha-based manager explains the challenges of finding and recruiting outside the established elites:

> So, I'll say, "voice of the voiceless" is probably the most useful way of describing what we are attempting to do, not exclude any opinion, any valid opinion should be able to be aired on AJE. Not just the people who shout the loudest, speak the best English or have the best PR machine. We'll go further and seek out people who have not gotten their message across.[30]

Other AJE informants go further and argue that giving a voice to marginalized groups means going beyond the balancing norm in mainstream journalism, toward alternative sourcing strategies. A Doha-based correspondent with background from Arab news elaborated further on Al Jazeera's progressive sourcing:

> For us at Al Jazeera, we don't identify with the West and we don't identify with the enemies of the West. We pose as a neutral side, but we think there

is a gap in the news and we want to fill this gap, this void. If there is a conflict, why do we listen to only one side? Why do we focus on the details only on one side? Why don't we listen to the viewpoint of the other side? Even if we see it as a demon, even if you see him as a monster, we, I think we have the obligation to let him at least speak and listen to him and make the world listen to him. Maybe he has something to say.[31]

A Doha-based news anchor extended the argument in the following way: "I believe that we need to give more voice to the voiceless and back the underdog. I am against the idea of giving equal airtime to both sides in a conflict if one is occupying the other, if one has invaded the other, if one has the bottle on the other's neck."[32] Informants further emphasize the challenges of interviewing ordinary people on television and particularly the linguistic barrier that favors elite sources. An interview producer with experience from both Doha and London explicated this dilemma:

> The big issue is more often than not language, and it's unavoidable. Like, we cannot put someone on air who speaks bad English. Immediately it limits our guests, it limits the number of alternative views we can put out. That's just the limit of the language we broadcast in, and there is nothing we can do about it. We cannot put someone with broken English on to the screen if someone in Jamaica or someone in Kuala Lumpur is not going to understand what they are saying. It has to be balanced. One of the jobs as an interview producer is to judge someone's English and their accent when we talk to them, and we let the editor know if it is suitable for air or not. A lot of times I have to say "I'm sorry. I understood about 50 percent of what you said, although the 50 percent I did understand sounded great."[33]

How do these sourcing strategies influence AJE's sourcing patterns in its daily newscasts? In a quantitative content analysis Figenschou found that AJE, like most transnational/global media, is elite-oriented. The main findings in the quantitative survey of sources are summarized here: Only 11 percent of the total number of news items have ordinary people as the main source. However, the elite sources represent a broader spectrum of elites than just government. To map this diversity, the elite sources were sorted into two subcategories: "Independent elites," such as the political opposition, international organizations, nongovernmental organizations (NGOs), media or cultural personalities and analysts and/or academics, and "Establishment elites," such as government officials, diplomats and/or ambassadors, military and/or armed forces, business leaders and religious leaders, who are more obligated to defend the status quo. Furthermore, the quantitative mapping found that independent elites were accorded more authority: they were invited more often on AJE, given greater visibility, and invited to more analytical news formats. Over time, the systematic authority accorded to the independent elites gave them a platform that was often not given to ordinary people.[34]

This sourcing pattern provides an interesting parallel to the "alternative hierarchy of sources" described by Atton and Wickenden.[35] In their investigation of sourcing practices in alternative, activist media, they found that the primary sources in the activist newspapers were the groups that the editorial staff identified closely with—radical activists as well as the reporters themselves. At the bottom of the alternative sourcing hierarchy were the nonactivist, nonpoliticized "ordinary citizens." On top were the activist sources involved in direct action and campaigning. These activist sources constituted a *counterelite* of "activist intellectuals" or "nonestablished intellectuals,"[36] which are given power, legitimacy, and authority in the alternative media as significant as that given to establishment elites in their mainstream competitors. This alternative hierarchy did not challenge the notions of hierarchical sourcing or sourcing relationships or even the elite notion of sourcing.[37]

AJE's alternative source hierarchies were demonstrated in practice during the Gaza war in 2009. In a comparative analysis, the sourcing patterns during one constructed week of evening news[38] on AJE, BBC World, and CNN International were surveyed quantitatively[39] The Israeli-Palestinian conflict was selected for analysis because it has been a primary example of global sourcing imbalance, as most Western mainstream news media have had a tendency to systematically subscribe to the Israeli government's framing of the conflict. The body of literature on the conflict has documented the systematically unequal information resources of Israel's professional, multifaceted information apparatus when pitted against the underdeveloped, uncoordinated Palestinian voice.[40] The resources and influences of the pressure and/or interest groups involved in the conflict echoed the structural inequality in communication resources. Whereas the pro-Israeli lobby in the United States was a powerful pressure group, its pro-Palestinian counterpart was significantly less influential.[41]

Israeli government officials have represented "the insider side" in global news, whereas Palestinian officials have been more or less marginalized. Analyzing insider groups, Manning found that the news interest of these sources was associated with their insider status and that they have opportunities to exploit the interaction between the political and media environment. All in all, the insiders are afforded higher authority and credibility and thus are better able to shape processes of primary definitions. Furthermore, since they possess information with exchange value and have greater bargaining power vis-à-vis journalists, insider groups are more able to control information flows emerging from within organizations. They control a concentration of material and symbolic resources, and they have the capacity to influence other organizations by virtue of their structural position and capacity to mobilize material and symbolic resources.[42] According to Manning's approach, the politically marginal groups more or less lack the media insight and communicative resources listed above. During the Gaza war, the editorial management of AJE explicitly set out to counter these mechanisms: the editorial management briefed the channel staff to acknowledge the structural inequalities between the two parties. They also made an extra effort to include Palestinian officials and voices in their coverage, even though they were not as professional, soft-spoken, or accessible as the representatives of the Israeli government information apparatus.[43]

AJE's proactive strategy was reflected in the channel's sourcing of the conflict: AJE had a higher number of Palestinian sources than the CNN and the BBC, and the most Palestinian officials invited to express their views in studio statements and studio interviews. Second, AJE had the fewest official government sources on all sides of the conflict and had the most civilian voices and greater source diversity than the two other channels. And, third, the channel invited a broader group of independent elite sources (analysts, legal experts, international organizations and international nongovernmental organizations) to provide other perspectives on the coverage.[44] This gave initial evidence that AJE may also include more marginalized groups than its competitors, but that issue requires further empirical investigation.

The role of government officials as news sources in the alternative sourcing hierarchies is also crucial here. All in all, alternative media include official sources to set the terms of reference so that the reporters may recontextualize these voices by criticizing them, where the criticism is aligned with the "native voices."[45] This sourcing practice includes official sources so as to demonstrate that the official representatives are ignorant, self-contradictory, or false. This editorial strategy of exposing the contradictions and spin of official sources is characteristic of AJE's sourcing practices, perhaps again best demonstrated in their critical interviews with and framing of Israeli government officials during the Gaza war in 2009. AJE's systematic emphasis on the ways in which the official Israeli information campaign diverged from the realities inside Gaza exposed the political spin of Israel's information campaign and distinguished the channel from its Western counterparts.[46]

AJE's approach to official spokespersons exemplifies the ways in which media professionals actively and critically countered the framing by the political and military elites during the war. By frequently inviting officials to give interviews and make statements, while placing the official narrative in a very critical context, AJE's editorial approach fundamentally undermined the Israeli media campaign. This inclusive, yet critical, sourcing strategy echoed the channel's aim of inviting "every angle, every side" on its newscasts.[47]

In conclusion, in addition to fundamentally altering the sourcing structures in global news in international conflicts located in the Middle East, AJE has altered the perception of *which elites* may be accorded credibility in its news. By authorizing other elites beside those on the Western satellite news channels, AJE has broadened the scope of elite views on the air. Though AJE had more ordinary people as main sources in their Gaza coverage than the BBC and CNN International, again in accordance with Painter's finding that AJE included more ordinary people than its competitors,[48] the channel remains elite-oriented: in AJE's alternative source hierarchies, ordinary people are still at the bottom of the hierarchy, whereas independent elites and AJE editorial staff hold the definition power more than official government sources.[49]

As a new channel, AJE affords much time and credibility to its correspondents on the ground in their newscasts. The strategy to brand the channel through promoting its correspondents was reflected in the broader quantitative study, finding that that AJE editorial staff were the only source in one-third of the news items studied.[50] They were often used as analysts in studio interviews and in two-way dialogues with the studio. As a compromise between professional news values and the southern agenda, AJE highlights the situation and problems of the voiceless. However, these marginalized groups remain silent and are spoken for and represented by male counterelites and channel staff. On AJE, the critical situation for the disenfranchised and voiceless masses is narrated mainly through the "visualization" of civilian suffering, as discussed in the following section.

PEOPLE-ORIENTED JOURNALISM: DRAMATIC VISUALIZATION

In stark contrast to the sanitized images in mainstream Western news, AJE's editorial distinctiveness is characterized by a dramatic visualization of civilian suffering. The channel's documentation of the situation on the ground is founded on its production strategies. For the AJE informants, it is an obligation to document the consequences of war and conflict and to expose underreported suffering. They express an ambition to document and reveal the atrocities that powerful political and military elites want to keep out of sight. Informants argue that strong images are needed to have an impact, but at the same time they argue that strong images should not be used gratuitously. A London-based senior correspondent with long experience in British news explained:

> I think it's important if war is being waged in the name of the people of this country, in America, or in whichever country it is that you see the consequences of what they support, what their government support is doing. And that will upset governments, because seeing dead bodies implies that things aren't going terribly well for them or that they've gone too far or that's there's an element of bloodshed in that. So they will always try and discredit, dissuade, or persuade people not to watch it, to look away from what they're seeing, and I think we should continue to do that....Al Jazeera is very good at it: it shines a light where many people would like to keep a little bit of dark.[51]

Al Jazeera Arabic has faced strong criticism for its graphic images of war and suffering.[52] AJE sources argue that the criticism against the Al Jazeera Network is mainly politically motivated and that the term "graphic images" itself is being misused for political purposes. Drawing on his experience with AJE and Arab satellite news channels, a Doha-based correspondent explained why it is imperative for the channel to document atrocities. He asked, "Do you show these things or do you cover it under the pretext that it is graphic? Well, one has to weigh out the risks and benefits....I don't want to go and cover up stories so as not to upset others. I need to show the world these things. A lot of atrocities took place in this part of the world."[53] AJE broadcasts from Britain and is thus regulated under Ofcom, and informants emphasize that the channel aims to take a middle road, between the most sanitized Western images and the goriest images broadcast on the Arab satellite channels. As explained by a news anchor in Doha,

> We definitely have some standards and guidelines because obviously we are broadcasting to a much bigger part of the world than simply Al Jazeera Arabic. I think here, in this part of the world, the tolerance level for seeing bloody and graphic images is much higher than, for example, in the West, where people don't have much stomach for that kind of pictures on their TV. They don't want to see that. So, I think that we would be cautious about, maybe more cautious than [AJA] in showing graphic pictures. But at the same time, I think maybe we will go further than some of the western networks in what we do decide to show or not to show. I think sometimes there are other reasons involved, [...] for why other organizations decide not to show pictures of destruction and death of civilian, properties and life, than simply that it's not something the audience wants to see. I think we would be somewhere in between.[54]

In the current global news ecology, visual framing in the media has become ever more difficult for geopolitical actors to control.[55] AJE's dramatic visualization was most prominent in the channel's coverage of the war in Gaza in 2009. The channel's visual framing of the war provided extensive documentation of the civilian suffering inside a war-torn Gaza. AJE's visualization provided a strong argument against the Israeli war and the ways in which its visual framing undermined the underlying premise of the Israeli core frame—that Israel was fighting a "just" and "proportional" war. AJE's visual framing thus exemplified what Kennedy has described as "a global information sphere that can swiftly expose and interrogate contradictions of declared values and apparent policies and actions."[56]

AJE's massive documentation of civilian suffering inside Gaza challenged the Western media coverage of the war and symbolized the channel's alternative approach to international conflicts, but further comparative, empirical investigations are needed. More profoundly, the channel's visual framing countered what has been characterized as the creeping image conservatism in the mainstream Western media.[57] In Western media, the mediation of suffering has become more cautious after the economic downturn accelerated ongoing changes in the news economy. AJE's visualization of civilian victims thus demonstrates what has been characterized as a *journalism of attachment*—"a journalism that cares as well as knows; that is aware of its responsibilities; that will not stand neutrally between good and evil, right and wrong, the victim and the oppressor"[58]—in contrast to the journalistic ideals of distance and detachment in the mainstream Western media. This strong visualization of civilian suffering during the war in Gaza distinguishes AJE from its mainstream competitors.

In its first years on air AJE has emphasized new parts of the world through its Southern news perspective, broadened the range of elite sources invited to express their views on air, and documented civilian suffering, anger, and protest on the ground in its coverage of wars and catastrophes. These key characteristics of the channel's news output have been AJE's most important contribution to international news reporting.

Notes

1. Al Jazeera Network, *Al Jazeera Network—Media Pack 2009* (2009), 4.
2. Ibid.
3. Al Jazeera Network, *Corporate Profile, about Us* (2009), http://english .aljazeera.net/aboutus/, November 10, 2009.
4. These strategies were identified in qualitative interviews with members of the channel management in Doha (September–December 2007) and London (January–September 2008).

5. The news-on-the-hour structure bears a stronger resemblance to the strict news schedules of the BBC than to CNN's longer periods of rolling news combined with hourly headline news updates. It thus echoes Al Jazeera Arabic's adaptation of the BBC style.

6. James Painter. *Counter-hegemonic News: A Case Study of Al-Jazeera English and Telesûr* (Oxford, UK: Reuters Institute of the Study of Journalism, University of Oxford, 2008), 22.

7. Ibid., 28.

8. An earlier version of this study (Figenschou 2010a) is published in *Global Media and Communication* 6 (1). Please consult the article about the methodological procedures, data sample, in-depth analysis, and graphic presentation of the findings. Tine Ustad Figenschou, "A Voice for the Voiceless? A Quantitative Content Analysis of Al Jazeera English's Flagship News," *Global Media and Communication* 6 (2010): 85–107.

9. Interview, London, May 16, 2008. All interviews by author: for a complete list of critical methodological discussions on interviewing Al Jazeera informants, see Tine Ustad Figenschou, "Young, Female, Western Researcher vs. Senior, Male, Al Jazeera Officials: Critical Reflections on Accessing and Interviewing Media Elites in Authoritarian Societies," *Media, Culture & Society* 32 (2010): 961–978; Tine Ustad Figenschou, "The South Is Talking Back—Al Jazeera as a Strategic Contra-Flow" (PhD diss., Oslo University, 2010).

10. Interview by author, London, April 24, 2008.

11. Interview by author, Doha, December 15, 2007.

12. Interview by author, Doha, December 1, 2007.

13. Interview by author, Doha, December 4, 2007.

14. Ustad Figenschou, "A Voice for the Voiceless? A Quantitative Content Analysis of Al Jazeera English's Flagship News," 85–107.

15. See, among others, Jaques Kayser, *One Week's News: Comparative Study of 17 Major Dailies for a Seven-Days Period* (Paris: UNESCO, 1953); James. F. Larson, Television's Window on the World: International Affairs Coverage on the U.S. Networks (Norwood, NJ: Ablex, 1984); Annabelle Sreberny-Mohammadi, et al. "Foreign News in the Media: International Reporting in 29 Countries" (Reports and Papers on Mass Communication, No. 93. Paris: UNESCO, 1985); Robert. L. Stevenson and Donald Lewis Shaw, *Foreign News and the New World Information Order* (Iowa: Iowa State University Press, 1984); Roger Wallis and Stanley. J. Baran, *The Known World of Broadcast News* (London and New York: Routledge, 1990), and Jürgen Wilke, "Foreign News Coverage and International News Flow over Three Centuries," *International Communication Gazette* 39 (1987): 147–180.

16. Ibid.

17. For systematization and theorization, see Denis H. Wu, "Investigating the Determinants of International News Flow: A Meta-Analysis," *International Communication Gazette* 60 (1998): 493–512; Denis

H. Wu. "Homogeneity around the World: Comparing the Systematic Determinants of International News Flow between Developed and Developing Countries," *International Communication Gazette* 65 (2003): 9–24. Denis H. Wu. "A Brave New World for International News? Exploring the Determinants of the Coverage of Foreign Nations on US Websites," *International Communication Gazette,* 69 (2007): 539–551.

18. Crude categorizations such as "North" and "South" can obviously be problematized and debated as they can be criticized of reflecting a Western-centric worldview. The terminology is maintained in this chapter because it is used both in the news flow literature, in Al Jazeera English's strategic communication and by Al Jazeera English informants.

19. Ustad Figenschou, "A Voice for the Voiceless? A Quantitative Content Analysis of Al Jazeera English's Flagship News," 91–98.

20. Ustad Figenschou, "The South Is Talking Back—Al Jazeera as a Strategic Contra-Flow," 98–101.

21. James T. Hamilton, "The (Many) Markets for International News: How News from Abroad Sells at Home," *Journalism Studies* 11 (2010): 650–666; John Maxwell Hamilton and Eric Jenner, "Redefining Foreign Correspondence," *Journalism: Theory, Practice & Criticism* 5 (2004): 301–321; Ulf Hannerz, *Foreign News: Exploring the World of Foreign Correspondents* (Chicago and London: University of Chicago Press, 2004); Susan. D. Moeller, *Compassion Fatigue: How the Media Sell Disease, Famine, War and Death* (New York and London: Routledge, 1999).

22. Mohamed Zayani and Sofiane Sahraoui, *The Culture of Al Jazeera: Inside an Arab Media Giant* (Jefferson, NC, and London: McFarland, 2007), 64–68.

23. Al Jazeera Network, *Al Jazeera Network—Media Pack 2009.*

24. The *NewsHour* at 18.00 GMT is coanchored from the Middle East (Doha), Europe (London), and North America (Washington), and the regional bias of international news may explain the high number of stories from the Middle East and Europe. Considering the fact that AJE aims to "follow the sun" in their reporting and highlight those regions where potential audiences are awake and watching, and the intended emphasis on the regions falling under each of the coanchoring bureaux, the relatively high number of Asian stories is more unexpected. The global time difference may influence these findings however: At 18.00 GMT, it is 14.00 in Washington, DC, 15.00 in Buenos Aires, 19.00 in London, 21.00 in Doha and Nairobi, and 02.00 in Kuala Lumpur. Although the Kuala Lumpur news center is closed and the regional audience small during the *NewsHour,* the high number of Asian stories most probably reflects the number of news stories accumulated from the region over the course of a long day. Moreover, the relatively limited reporting out of North America is interesting as Washington cohosts the *NewsHour*

and because North America has been historically overrepresented in international news, although this finding may also be influenced by the time difference, as it is still early in the day in North America when the *NewsHour* is aired.

25. James Painter, *Counter-hegemonic News*, 29.

26. Ustad Figenschou, "The South Is Talking Back—Al Jazeera as a Strategic Contra-Flow," 114–117..

27. Barbie Zelizer, *Taking Journalism Seriously: News and the Academy* (Thousand Oaks, London, and New Delhi: Sage, 2004), 150.

28. Ustad Figenschou, "The South Is Talking Back—Al Jazeera as a Strategic Contra-Flow," 97–98.

29. Interview by author, Doha, October 3, 2007.

30. Interview by author, Doha, October 2, 2007.

31. Interview by author, Doha, November 29, 2007.

32. Interview by author, Doha, December 1, 2007.

33. Interview by author, London, April 24, 2008.

34. Ustad Figenschou, "A Voice for the Voiceless? A Quantitative Content Analysis of Al Jazeera English's Flagship News," 98–101.

35. Chris Atton and Emma Wickenden, "Sourcing Routines and Representation in Alternative Journalism: a case study approach," *Journalism Studies* 6 (2005): 357.

36. Chris Atton, *Alternative Media* (Los Angeles, London, New Delhi and Singapore: Sage, 2002), 106.

37. Atton and Wickenden, "Sourcing Routines and Representation in Alternative Journalism: A Case Study Approach," *Journalism Studies* 6 (2005): 357.

38. Ustad Figenschou, "The South Is Talking Back—Al Jazeera as a Strategic Contra-Flow," 207–209.

39. Ibid., 201–223.

40. See, among others, Annelore Deprez and Karin Raeymaeckers, "Bias in the News? Representation of Palestinians and Israelis in the Coverage of the First and Second Intifada," *International Communication Gazette* 72 (2010): 91–109; Marda Dunsky, *Pens and Swords: How the American Mainstream Media Report the Israeli-Palestinian Conflict* (New York: Columbia University Press, 2008); Greg Philo and Mike Berry, *Bad News from Israel* (London/Sterling, Virginia: Pluto Press, 2004); Barbie Zelizer, David Park, and David Gudelunas, "How Bias Shapes the News: Challenging The New York Times' Status as a Newspaper of Record on the Middle East," *Journalism: Theory, Practice & Criticism* 3 (2002): 283–307.

41. Marda Dunsky, *Pens and Swords: How the American Mainstream Media Report the Israeli-Palestinian Conflict* (New York: Columbia University Press, 2008), 10.

42. Paul Manning, *News and News Sources: A Critical Introduction* (London, Thousand Oaks, and New Delhi: Sage, 2001), 150.

43. Ustad Figenschou, "The South Is Talking Back—Al Jazeera as a Strategic Contra-Flow," 203.
44. Ibid., 211.
45. Chris Atton and Emma Wickenden, "Sourcing Routines and Representation in Alternative Journalism: A Case Study Approach," *Journalism Studies* 6 (2005): 353.
46. Ustad Figenschou, "The South Is Talking Back—Al Jazeera as a Strategic Contra-Flow," 211–220.
47. Ibid.
48. Painter, *Counter-hegemonic News: A Case Study of Al-Jazeera English and Telesûr*, 43.
49. Ustad Figenschou, "The South Is Talking Back—Al Jazeera as a Strategic Contra-Flow."
50. Ustad Figenschou, "A Voice for the Voiceless? A Quantitative Content Analysis of Al Jazeera English's Flagship News," 100.
51. Interview by author, London, February 13, 2008.
52. Shahira Fahmy and Thomas J. Johnson, "Show the Truth and Let the Audience Decide: A Web-Based Survey Showing Support among Viewers of Al-Jazeera for Use of Graphic Imagery," *Journal of Broadcasting & Electronic Media* 51 (2007): 245–264.
53. Interview by author, Doha, October 3, 2007.
54. Interview by author, Doha, October 2, 2007.
55. Paul Frosh and Amit Pinchevski, "Introduction to *Media Witnessing, Why Media Witnessing? Why Now*," ed. Paul Frosh and Amit Pinchevski (Houndmills: Palgrave Macmillan, 2009), 1–22
56. Liam Kennedy, "Securing Vision: Photography and US Foreign Policy," *Media, Culture & Society* 30 (2008): 27.
57. Ibid.; Folker Hanusch, *Representing Death in the News: Journalism, Media and Mortality* (New York: Palgrave Macmillan, 2010); Kennedy, "Securing Vision: Photography and US Foreign Policy," 279–294; Carolyn Kitch and Janice Hume, *Journalism in a Culture of Grief* (New York and London: Routledge, 2008).
58. Martin Bell, "The Journalism of Attachment," in *Media Ethics*, ed. Matthew Kieran (London: Routledge, 1998), 16.

CHAPTER 4

AJE after the Arab Spring: The Politics of Distribution in the United States

Will Youmans

The first global news channel based in an Arab country built an international audience quickly after its launch in late 2006. Struggling to gain distribution on American television sets, the network managed to build only a small web audience through streaming video and other online means. After political uprisings started in Tunisia in December 2010 and took off in Egypt and followed by those in Libya, Syria, Yemen, and Bahrain, many Americans turned to Al Jazeera English (AJE) via its website, YouTube page, and social media. The news operation established a superior on-the-ground reporting presence in Egypt, especially in relation to other English-language news media.

AJE's absence from American TV became especially stark as media figures and government officials praised the network and interested members of the public sought it out. Soon, its availability became a public question. Before this "Arab Spring," such debates were largely restricted to the few localities where AJE was carried. Early 2011 saw something of a turning point for American discourse about the channel and whether or not it belongs as an option in the media environment for Americans. It underwent a transformation from being largely regarded as a terrorist mouthpiece to gaining backers and supporters, even at the levels of the political elite. While it remained controversial among some, its reputation and image shifted considerably.

For AJE, expanding into the American TV market was a goal, given its size, spending power, and political influence; the prestige of being there was an incentive. Getting into cable was especially important as it was the best chance at reaching a new and large audience in America.

Being politically controversial, the network did not gain wide cable carriage, and it continued to struggle even after its image started to change during the Arab Spring. This chapter considers the changing politics of AJE's distribution efforts in the United States after the 2011 Arab Spring.

Politics Defined and Key Actors

Politics, for the purposes of this chapter, is both broadly and narrowly defined. Borrowing on a distributional understanding of politics, "who gets what, when and how for a society,"[1] this chapter considers how AJE's availability in the United States is structured. Allocative decisions under this definition are primarily taken by formal organizations in societies.[2] The pressures and contestations around the decision of the availability of AJE in the United States constitute "politics" under this definition, even if they do not seem to fit under definitions that focus narrowly on politics as the activities of governments and office-seekers. AJE's carriage in the United States was politicized, and access to and the circulation of information generated by a news organization presenting a different take on the news was at stake. Interested parties sought to impact AJE's availability at TV, likely because it presented the best way to reach new audiences. Programers, AJE included, the government, and the public responded to the question of carriage through social action, public statements, and pressure on companies, thus comprising the politics of distribution. The following paragraph outlines the key parties or sectors, how they fit into the process of operators' TV programing, and what types of influence they exercise.

In media distribution, the chief decision makers are telecom agencies and companies, as well as the programers, such as AJE: negotiations between the two are determinant. Generally, new programers pursue carriage vigorously, while carriers select, and thus tend to hold the bargaining advantage. The cable company is essentially the gatekeeper since programers need access to their customers. Their power is far from absolute. Since they are a middle man, they are subject to several industrial pressures that shape the politics of distribution. Though carriers generally have a bargaining advantage over programers, this is not the case with the most powerful content providers, the high demand channels. Usually, they are part of some conglomerate. Distribution deals with them often entail higher carriage fees going back to the stronger programers, and/ or the bundling of lesser sister channels. For example, to carry ESPN, which garners one of the highest carriage fees, cable carriers must also offer the less popular ESPN Classic. For smaller programers without such economic power, the carriers have the leverage. This also means that pro-gramers could have tacit and explicit influence to pursue the exclusion of competitors. AJE as a programer itself can bring some pressure to bear on companies, as well.

Second, governmental pressure and influence, or the threat of it, could come into play. In the United States, the government has mandated some distribution decisions, for example, by requiring cable companies carry certain public access and local channels. The U.S. government has also prohibited the carriage of channels affiliated with designated ter-rorist groups, such as Hizbollah's Al-Manar channel, under legislation passed after the September 11, 2001, attacks. Al Jazeera is not banned under these provisions. Its sponsor, Qatar, is an ally of the United States. With cable deregulation, however, the government's largely hands-off role meant that formally, distribution decisions belonged to the compa-nies, contingent on their ability to secure viable agreements with content providers. Still, cable as an industry has no desire to incur the wrath of legislators who could be encouraged to reassert their regulatory author-ity through acts of Congress, or simply find other ways, for example, through hearings, investigations, meetings, and public statements, to pressure companies or the industry. The government can also place con-ditions on industry mergers, such as the 2011 deal between NBC and Comcast, which can be used as leverage.[3] Therefore, even with deregu-lation, there is an industrial interest in maintaining good relations with the government.

Third, public preferences are important. In the United States, private interests run the primary television carriage industry, cable. A few large companies plus thousands of small, localized ones make the allocative decisions of channel availability. Their underlying concern is profit, which carries with it a need to secure more customers, prevent the loss of current ones, and gain as much revenue from them and advertisers as possible. Even if the companies function as gatekeepers, they are restricted by their customers"—current and potential—preferences to some degree. Consumer power is limited in that cable television for a long time had few substitutes and competitors: satellite was not an option for many, and over-the-air broadcasting was limited in channel selection. As alternatives and industry competition increase, traditional gatekeepers may be forced to offer more options. Consumer pressure is possible through complaints, boycotts, and negative publicity. Issue publics, or groups of citizens who advocate for certain policies or causes, try to influence public opinion and political decisions. They also mobi-lize to affect corporate decisions, in this case whether cable companies should carry AJE.

AL JAZEERA AND THE UNITED STATES: BACKGROUND

AJE gained scant access to television audiences in the United States. By early 2011, AJE was fully[4] accessible in cable systems only in three cities, Washington, DC, Toledo, OH, and Burlington, VT, which make up a very small proportion of American households. Significant obstacles stood in the way of American TV market penetration. A main one was AJ's depiction as a terrorist-affiliated network by the George W. Bush administration.[5] This led some to speculate that U.S. carriers refused to include AJE in their offerings "out of fear of alienating themselves from advertisers and angering the Bush administration and other American political leaders."[6] Despite the channel's efforts to position itself as a global media outlet, many in the United States continued to associate AJE with Al Qaeda and Osama bin Laden, America's adversaries in the "war on terror." Even in the absence of the heavy criticism of AJE by American policymakers and opinion leaders, the majority of Americans do not demonstrate an interest in global news[7]—a significant commercial hurdle. Cable carriers also see the news market as saturated, questioning the value of adding yet another news channel to the mix. The cable industry is inclined to suggest the decision is a purely commercial, apolitical one. Following talks between AJE and Comcast, the country's largest cable carrier, reports cited an anonymous insider source that claimed AJE's noncarriage "is strictly a business decision."[8] However, the political history of American-Al Jazeera relations suggests otherwise.

As a pan-Arab news organization initiated by the emir of Qatar and given the mandate, functional independence, and resources to shake up the Arab news landscape, Al Jazeera's Arabic news channel was bound to make political waves in the region. Its sharp departure from the region's largely servile state media shook up a semistatic Arab body politic. Long-reigning regimes, whether heavy state bureaucracies or seemingly entrenched monarchs, dominated Arab politics. By giving airtime to dissidents and the uncensored public, reporting on taboos, and questioning authority figures not used to such challenges, the young network represented something new, the beginning of a transnational Arab public sphere.[9]

Given the centrality of the Middle East in world affairs, Al Jazeera's impact grew global in scope fairly quickly. It was the leading journalistic outfit on the ground in Afghanistan, and was positioned to cover the U.S.-led invasion in Afghanistan before any other TV news agency. With Afghanistan and Iraq, the young network stepped on the toes of world powers, earning American animus.

The opposition was not just discursive. In 2005, Frank Gaffney, head of the Center for Security Policy, a Washington-based think tank, described Al Jazeera as "fair game" on the grounds that it promoted beheadings and suicide bombings.[10] Separately, AJ reporters were arrested and detained by American and allied forces. Whether intentional or not, the bombings of AJ bureaus in Kabul and Baghdad furthered the sense that the news operation was a villain in the American-led war. This antagonism reached absurd proportions with the leaked details of a 2004 meeting between U.S. president George W. Bush and UK prime minister Tony Blair. Bush apparently proposed bombing AJ's headquarters in Doha, Qatar.[11] Spokesmen for the government dismissed his suggestion as an off-color joke. The network's director-general, Wadah Khanfar, did not find it funny; he wrote in 2010 that the proposed plot was suggested in earnest, even if quickly and gently repudiated by others in the meeting.[12]

If one looks at American relations with AJ since 1996, when the network began operating, the Bush-era antagonism has not been characteristic. During the Bill Clinton presidency, AJ was both praised as a force for reform initiated by an American ally in the region, and assailed in some quarters for its critical coverage of American foreign policy in Israel-Palestine and Iraq. In fact, AJ made its name in the Arab world for its hard, critical coverage of the 1998 "Desert Fox" operation, in which the United States bombed Iraq, and the attacks on Sudan and Afghanistan that targeted Osama bin Laden. It was only with the war on terror that AJ was directly accused of being linked to America's enemies by those in power.

Being hated by the Bush administration probably helped the network's visibility. Its global reputation spread, although most outside its regional home could not understand its Arabic language news. Like action films, it enjoyed international appeal because of a visual power that transcended language barriers. In countries such as Indonesia, non-Arabic speakers watched AJ for the compelling images of war-torn places far away. It brought them pictures and footage other global news media did not. Other media watched AJ, retransmitted its images, and translated its stories.[13] The network had a global brand and notoriety, but not a directly global audience. There was clearly a bigger, global market for AJ's reportage. It presented a narrative and information that ran against the prevailing discourses found in the global English language media, namely the CNN and the BBC. AJ started with an English-language website, but soon planned the launch of another news channel, one that would communicate directly with the English-speaking audiences dispersed throughout the world.

Given its Arabic sister channel's footprint on the geopolitical landscape and vilification by American leaders, how could an English-language "version" *not* be rife with political significance? Leading up to the network's launch, the anxieties and speculation about the channel bespoke of this. A 2006 *New York Times* article, out six months before launch, questioned if the channel would "provide an Arab and Muslim point of view to the rest of the world."[14] Many asked whether AJE would function as a translation of the original network, an inquiry sometimes based on war-on-terror-infused concerns such as larger fears of the spread of proterrorist propaganda. Ultimately, AJE's identity was distinct from the Arabic news division's even as they shared a common mission and were part of the same network.

AJE framed itself as a novel addition to the global news media. While it did proffer journalistic platitudes about balance and so on in its marketing, what really stuck out was that its announced identity was couched in critiques of the various centricities of the main global news media. The BBC was British and headquartered there. CNN was American and based in Atlanta. AJE was Qatari only by sponsorship, and was headquartered there, but was signaled as dispersed, decentered, and highly diverse in terms of staff's national origins and the use of broadcasting centers in London, Washington, DC, and Kuala Lampur (which have since been downsized). This, the network argued, became manifest in a different perspective on the world's events and what the day's news, as a construction, would be according to new standards.

AJE was to "set the news agenda," implying it would be a new one, in which celebrities and certainly celebrity-reporters were not newsworthy—an implicit admonishment of Western media. AJE sought to overturn the standing international news networks' stark undercoverage of certain parts of the world, which it called "the global South" in its official communications—the places that normally get reporters flying in when there are "coups and earthquakes."[15] AJE spokespeople disavowed such "parachute journalism," and asserted that its reporters possessed local and lingual familiarities, promising a sort of authentic representation of news subjects. A slogan that emerged was that AJE would give "voice to the voiceless," meaning marginalized people would have their stories told through AJE's brand of journalism.

AJE was quite explicit about trying to reverse the prevailing directionality of global informational flows, which headed generally from the political and media capitals of the advanced industrial states to the parts of the world said to be developing and underdeveloped. Even as most news production in the world is locally or regionally produced and consumed, AJE offered itself as a new and somewhat subversive player in world news.

The Arab Spring: AJE's Moment in America

On several major stories, AJE could be portrayed as counterhegemonic. It challenged American power, for example, in its coverage of the Wikileaks release of the 2010 Iraq War Logs. As one of the only networks in Gaza when Israel launched its "Operation Cast Lead" offensive in December 2008–January 2009, it undermined Israel's ability to control the strategic narrative around events in Gaza. AJE, along with the Arabic network, proved itself to be a significant annoyance to regimes the world over, north and south. Historically, the network has been more critical of Arab regimes. Especially during the Arab Spring in early 2011, AJE challenged the heads of "global South" states. It arguably subverted Arab leaders such as Libya's Muammar Gaddafi, Tunisia's Zine El Abidine Ben Ali, and Egypt's Hosni Mubarak by covering closely, and helping advance, the uprisings in their respective countries. By getting out information and analysis critical to the revolutions in Egypt and Libya, and to a lesser extent Tunisia, AJE was vital for observers in other countries, including their governments. AJE helped to put and keep Arab movements for change in the international limelight. AJE practiced a type of networked journalism that let protesters and local reporters share their views and information with the rest of the world. This offset somewhat governments' strictures on reporters and efforts to control news flows.

The Arab Spring demonstrated the "Al Jazeera Effect," referring to the power of new forms of media, such as AJE, to re-create and reformulate political identities, networks of affiliation and structures in global politics.[16] AJE helped internationalize an Arab Spring reform movement that called into question traditional modes of state power and facilitated lines of solidarity between different populations. It also arguably privileged online activists by giving them coverage and rebroadcasting their content, which empowered them to define and frame the uprisings in their terms. This broke through government propaganda aims, as well as the impulse of outside experts and advocates to impose their own interpretations on the events. It was a powerful on-the-ground presentation that piqued the world's and America's interest. Some Americans who had long opposed the network, suddenly changed their stances. Increasingly, political elite, media figures, and public intellectuals turned to the network for news, and declared so publicly. Tony Burman, AJE's chief strategic adviser for the Americas, said that the story of the uprising against Egypt's president "Hosni Mubarak did in 18 days what I thought it would take two years to do," referring to AJE's new prominence in the United States. He noted that the "impact and importance of Al-Jazeera seems to be visible to all, particularly people in Washington."[17]

Al Jazeera did experience a warming of relations with the United States in the early Obama years. Certainly, the tone of the relationship shifted remarkably, just as Obama's rhetoric toward Arab and Muslim countries showed signs of greater sensitivity. However, the Arab Spring led to unprecedented public displays of affection. American president Barack Obama and his staffers kept up on news in Egypt by watching the CNN and AJE.[18] In apparently candid remarks to political donors, Obama was quoted as saying about his meeting with Qatar's emir that the country and the network were a force for democracy in the region. "Reform, reform, reform—you're seeing it on Al Jazeera," he said.[19]

Further legitimation came from other government officials. Significantly, national figures House Minority Leader Nancy Pelosi and Sen. John McCain "praised Al Jazeera's role as a catalyst in the Arab Spring uprisings before a room of journalists" at the inaugural Al Jazeera U.S. Forum in mid-May, 2011.[20] Juliette Kayyem of the Department of Homeland Security wrote a pro-AJE op-ed in the *Boston Globe*.[21] She directly urged cable companies to carry AJE, arguing that AJE's exclusion "sends a message to the Arab world about America's willingness to accept information, unfiltered, from the very region we spend so much time talking about." This appeared to be a green light to the cable industry. Even before that, governmental agencies warmed relations with the network. The State Department fundamentally shifted its policy after a review was completed in December 2010.[22] Dana Shell Smith, the State Department's deputy assistant secretary for international media engagement, said that there was a new more constructive relationship:

> They are a really important media entity, and we have a really great relationship with them. This administration has empowered those of us who actually do the communicating to be in a close relationship with Al-Jazeera. They understand that the relationship can't consist of complaining to each other about the differences we have.[23]

This new relationship included a greater willingness by officials to associate publicly with the network. For the 2011 Congressional Correspondents' Dinner in Washington, DC, Al Jazeera brought as its guests staffers from the White House, State Department, and the CIA.[24] Later, on-air appearances by General Stanley McChrystal, Secretary of State Hillary Clinton, and U.S. Ambassador to the United Nations Susan Rice on AJE indicated a new era. A multitude of officials followed suit.[25] This is different from the political liability that appearing on AJE once meant for American public figures. Steve Clemons witnessed Howard Dean, chairman of the

Democratic Party, refuse to go through a scheduled interview with AJE at the 2008 party convention.[26]

Even with the new opening at official levels, the American position toward AJE is still nuanced. During a U.S. Senate committee meeting on American foreign policy priorities and budgeting in early March, Secretary of State Hillary Clinton praised AJE—an unprecedented endorsement that was widely reported. She said it was gaining an online audience in the United States because it was "real news." Secretary Clinton asserted, "Al Jazeera has been the leader in that they are literally changing people's minds and attitudes. And like it or hate it, it is really effective."[27] The nuance is located in the motive of the statement. The secretary was seeking more funding for America's own informational activities abroad by playing up a rivalry. Significantly, she used the term "information war," referring to the state of competition between her government and the young news network, among others. While American officials have lavished some praise, there is also a tacit acknowledgment that it is a foreign news media source that challenges American communication power even if belonging to an ally.

Voices within the mainstream media, including AJE officials, began to refer to this sea-change as "AJE's moment."[28] This is a reference to "CNN's moment" during the 1990–1991 Gulf War. CNN's novel brand of 24-hour news coverage, with continual reporting and dramatic visuals made it an international news leader. Supporting the notion that AJE might enjoy such a breakthrough, opinion leaders and public figures endorsed the channel. Lee Bollinger, the president of Columbia University, wrote an op-ed calling for AJE's carriage in the United States, and even outlined how the government's telecom regulator, the Federal Communications Commission, could encourage cable operators—especially Comcast—to carry AJE.[29] Media personalities such as MSNBC program host Rachel Maddow, Sam Donaldson of ABC News, *New York Times* columnist Frank Rich and NBC News' chief foreign affairs correspondent Andrea Mitchell also publicly praised the channel.[30] These notes of support suggested a turning point in the news network's standing and popularity.

Political discourse about AJE, often framed around the question of cable carriage, became increasingly polarized as an opposition emerged. High-profile pundits and various organizations claimed in response that AJE has no place on American televisions, citing allegations that AJ is supportive of terrorists and is fundamentally anti-American and antidemocracy. The Washington, DC-based media advocacy group Accuracy in Media (AIM) and Fox News program host Bill O'Reilly directly opposed AJE's efforts to sign distribution deals with large cable companies, such as Comcast and Time-Warner.[31] AIM launched an online petition calling for cable companies to shut out AJE due to what it deemed propagandistic content.[32] AIM called on Comcast, and all cable and satellite companies to "not help to provide Al-Jazeera English the audience and the exposure that they seek" because "America is at war with radical Islam."

During its Egypt coverage, criticism that the network was biased and driven by an anti-American agenda continued. For instance, charges of AJE bias circulated after a *Washington Post* columnist argued that AJE buried the story about CBS News reporter Lara Logan, who was sexually assaulted in Egypt after the overthrow of President Hosni Mubarak.[33] AIM put out more material deeply critical of AJE and relaunched a web-based campaign against the network. One public opponent was Judea Pearl, father of the *Wall Street Journal* reporter, Daniel Pearl, who was beheaded in Pakistan by militants. In an earlier *New York Times* op-ed, he warned that AJE was dangerous due to "the growing number of social misfits in society, and the growing confusion between 'information' and deception in the news media." He argued the station would provoke anger, even if the station had well-respected Western anchors.[34] During the Arab Spring, he recirculated the op-ed, adding that "even if Al Jazeera English waters down its sister network's alarmist content, it should still be seen as a potential threat."[35]

A similar argument was put forward in a lengthy piece put out by the Washington Institute for Near Eastern Policy (WINEP). David Pollock argued that compared with the Arabic channel, AJE has "a greater internationalist bent to its reporting."[36] The biases are apparent and strongly in favor of Qatar's interests, he argued, to such a degree that Al Jazeera is in total not a force for reform despite the new image. The piece implicitly acknowledges AJE's "freedom to report on regional developments," but concludes that the gap in messages across the network as a whole must be considered.

These criticisms had strong currency with some members of the public. In some localities, groups and individuals lobbied to have AJE removed from places where it or its news bulletins were carried, including in Daytona Beach, Florida, where a local college TV station that carried AJE news bulletins was criticized.[37] When the progressive radio network Pacifica signed a deal with AJE to retransmit the channel's news bulletins, a board member protested publicly. This deal spawned protests in Houston, TX, where Pacifica has an affiliate station. Many took issue with taxpayer-supported stations offering AJE, saying that the people should not pay to support a foreign government's broadcasting channel, especially one they argued was biased. They are targeting government funding of any entity broadcasting or carrying AJE.

These kinds of protests occurred before the Arab Spring, of course, and they were not always just about its availability on their airwaves. In 2008, at the time of the Democratic National Convention in Denver, Colorado, citizens of a small nearby town held a march and protest against the presence of AJE reporters who put together a small panel of citizens to talk about the elections in a local tavern.[38]

Other members of the American public wanted to see AJE on their television screens. As AJE became the primary news source for many Americans following Arab protest movements in Egypt, Tunisia, Libya, and other Arab countries in early 2011, demand for AJE grew. Online viewing, the primary means for Americans to watch AJE, skyrocketed. Of those watching online around the world, around half were Americans.[39] AJE sought to parlay its new online popularity into a grassroots-style campaign to pressure cable companies through demonstrated demand. Using a specially designed webpage, social media, and e-mails, they generated tens of thousands of letters to American cable companies demanding AJE be made available.[40] It also took out print and web ads in the prestige press to promote the network and encourage demand to sway cable companies. In grassroots fashion, student activists and community groups began letter-writing campaigns, national call-in days and Facebook groups asking their local cable operators to carry AJE.[41] The social meeting site Meetup.com became a place for AJE viewers to gather and advocate for the channel's carriage. "Demand Al Jazeera" became a slogan for its advocates, many of whom were involved in other campaigns pertaining to changing American foreign policy.

The segments of the American public attentive to international affairs and issue publics were divided over AJE after the Arab Spring. Among the power elite in Washington, AJE was embraced publicly. However, what about the less attentive public, those who make up the mass of TV audiences? In the weeks after Egyptian leader Hosni Mubarak stepped down, when accolades for AJE were at their height, the author co-conducted an online experiment with 177 Americans from around the country.[42] This study gauged whether Americans were generally open-minded toward AJE's news or if they were prejudiced in their assessments. The participants were randomly assigned to three groups. Two of the three groups of participants watched an AJE-produced news clip about the Taliban's position toward peace talks. One of those groups watched the original clip, which carried AJE's original branding. Another saw the same news piece reedited to carry CNN International's (CNNI) logo. And a third, the control group, viewed no clip. This served as the baseline to determine how the groups differed in their evaluations of the network based on the clip.

The participants rated how biased they thought AJE and CNNI were in general after viewing their respective clips. Those who watched the AJE piece did not differ in their ratings of the network compared to those who didn't watch a clip. When the story carried the CNNI branding, however, participants rated CNNI as less biased than did those in the control group. This suggested that Americans, on average, were still unfair in their evaluations of AJE even during the Arab Spring and the new fanfare for the network. Some participants watched with an open mind. They either held no predispositions against the network or were willing to change their views with exposure to even one news report from AJE. These individuals, along with those favorably predisposed, are AJE's target audience.

Who were most open toward changing their assessments or welcoming AJE? The study found that liberal political ideology and attitudes toward Arab-Americans were important factors. By the same token, opposition to AJE was linked to conservative political views and suspicion of Arab-Americans generally. Public views toward AJE likely fit within a polarized American political landscape, where U.S.-Arab relations is one issue of division. Though this was not asked in the study, it is likely that those pushing for a stronger foreign policy against Arab states and a more intense engagement in the war on terror are more likely to oppose AJE.

In terms of the cable carriage question, which was asked about in the survey, there was a normally distributed split. The largest group (40 percent) was indifferent as to whether AJE should be available on their televisions. There was relative parity in preferences among those wanting and not wanting it on air. That kind of breakdown is expected of any channel. However, the range of support and opposition was wide. Some (7 percent) said they would actively oppose carriage by contacting cable companies, while nearly the same number indicated they were willing to contact companies to call for its carriage. A debate around this issue of carriage and cross-cutting pressures on cable companies was already taking place in the public realm.

CARRIAGE PROSPECTS AFTER THE ARAB SPRING

While prior negotiations with the largest companies failed to produce results, AJE reentered negotiations in late February 2011. It carried the momentum of heightened, positive publicity stemming from its Arab uprisings coverage, the transformation in the government's position toward AJE, and a new political elite admiration for the network. Its executives met with the nation's largest cable operators, Comcast[43] and Time Warner, and others. Despite delivering the 13,000 letters from Comcast subscribers, AJE executives could not announce a deal after the meetings. A letter sent by Comcast to an opponent of AJE carriage months later stated that no agreement was reached with AJE and that the company was "not currently in active talks to complete such an agreement."[44] Smaller deals were signed with local operators in Rhode Island and Massachusetts by late April 2011, however. The transformation of AJE's image among policymakers and media figures did not immediately translate into greater carriage.

There are several plausible explanations for cable's reluctance. An industry source suggested the cable industry's leader, Comcast, wanted to see if interest in AJE lasted beyond the period of Arab uprisings.[45] One industry insider suspected the threat of pressure had an effect: "Some people would attack some of the distributors like Comcast and others who would carry it for being un-American for carrying Al-Jazeera," said Jeff Zucker, who stepped down as CEO of NBC at the end of January 2011. He added that some news channels "would go after some of those distributors if they were to put Al-Jazeera on."[46] Others suggest that news in general is in such decline that the money-making window for TV news networks has already closed.[47] Taken together, these suggest a commercial rationale deeply impacted by tumultuous post-9/11 politics in America.

On prior occasions, political considerations were seen bearing directly on carriage decisions. For example, before AJE's launch, Comcast mysteriously nixed a near-deal to carry AJE in Dearborn, MI, which houses a large Arab-American population, a natural constituency for the network.[48] AJE officials involved believed that a fear of backlash and active pressure caused the last-minute change. More explicitly, AJE's cable carriage in Burlington, VT, was subject to a lively local debate, which involved townhall meetings and a vibrant discussion in the local media. AJE was available on Burlington Telecom, a municipally financed company's fiber-optic system. That upset some of the town's residents, who turned it into a local issue. Burlington's citizens mobilized for and against the station's carriage. Advisory committees considered the issue, held public meetings, and eventually passed a resolution in favor of AJE's continued carriage. The mayor, city council, and the telecom head agreed that AJE would stay on.[49] In one of the few other cities where AJE was carried, Toledo, OH, a private cable operator, Buckeye Cable, unilaterally chose to offer AJE. They received some angry correspondence from subscribers, but reported no substantial loss of subscribers, and the opposition eventually quieted.[50] Reasons given by protesting subscribers and members of the public who would mobilize against AJE are largely political—ranging from the fear of promoting terrorism to resentment of what they perceive is an anti-American bias.

These episodes suggest that carrying AJE risks some backlash. Alienating subscribers, even just 7 percent of them, could harm business, especially as cable television generally fears a declining subscriber base. This forms the basis for the *risk* of AJE's carriage for distributors. Until companies perceive the benefit of offering AJE as being great enough to assume the risk of a backlash, it does not make clear commercial sense. Even without the risk of backlash, the level of demand and advertiser interest would need to suggest the possibility of positive revenues greater than the next best programing alternative for carriers. While some carriers point to limits on bandwidth as an obstacle to a deal, it is clear that some channels with very small audience shares could easily have been replaced.[51] Still, operators see channels as "real estate" and want to make sure they maximize revenue potential.[52]

There is no reason to conclude the cable industry has any other basis for exclusion. In the public statements made by cable and satellite carriers about the prospects of AJE, none dismissed it out-of-hand. In often guarded, public-relations language, they kept open the possibility of eventual deals without suggesting one was imminent.[53] Time Warner's spokesman said, "We remain willing to talk with them, or any other programing provider, for carriage of their network." Charter Communications acknowledged meeting with AJE staff on occasion, but not on a "regular basis." Verizon stated that its FiOS digital cable TV service receives "requests for many channels, including Al Jazeera English, and we make those requests part of our decision-making process." It added that it evaluates additions to the lineup "against expressed customer interests as well as other factors." As strategic communication, these are not the best gauges of actual positions, however, because companies closely guard their actual programing decision-making processes. There is not clear evidence of ideological exclusion by the industry.

AJE's managing director Al Anstey maintains that its cable penetration is a matter of "when, not if."[54] There were reasons for this optimism after the Arab Spring. Although the study cited above found a linkage between ideology and prejudices against AJE, Republican lawmakers increasingly appeared on AJE. The political divide was not then clearly a partisan one at the level of the elite, a sentiment that could spread to the public. A *Politico* story noted that a Republican-run lobbying firm that worked to advance Qatar and Al Jazeera's standing with the party may have paid off. It quoted Suhail Khan, who was in the White House Office of Public Liaison during the George W. Bush administration: "The PR campaign, to a certain degree, was successful. They just began booking

Republican guests." AJE, it should be noted, has the ability to lobby and impact public perceptions through publicity and marketing. It was difficult in the months following the Arab Spring to find Republicans willing to openly criticize Al Jazeera. It quoted a spokeswoman, Rep. Paul Broun (R-Ga.), and noted the conditionality of the warning that "If Al Jazeera English hopes to establish itself more so on American soil, it must prove to the United States that their intentions are primarily improving our relations with the Middle East—rather than promoting anti-American rhetoric."[55] Elite-level views may spread to the public in due time.

AJE began making strides toward greater acceptance in the United States. It announced its intention to open two new domestic bureaus in 2011, one in Chicago and another in Miami. It launched a journalism fellowship in partnership with Columbia University. In May 2011, it held its first U.S.-based media forum in Washington, DC, where it attracted opinion leaders. *Time* magazine recognized one of the network's correspondents who reported from Egypt, Ayman Mohyeldin, as one of the top 100 most influential people in the world in 2011.[56] News junkies and those interested in international affairs, particularly in areas underreported by cable and network news, now recognize AJE as a primary source. Its newsgathering apparatus is increasingly seen as superior to those of American news networks. In contrast with AJE's 400 journalists and 65 bureaus around the world, CNN, the most international of America news channels, pales in comparison with only 33 bureaus.[57]

The gains of greater legitimation after the Arab Spring became apparent in one big international story. After U.S. forces raided Osama bin Laden's compound in Pakistan and killed him, media and government officials relied on AJ as a source. Joe Scarborough of MSNBC interviewed an AJ correspondent on "Morning Joe," a weekday morning talk show on MSNBC the morning of May 3, 2011. Going to reporters from AJ had happened in the past, but Scarborough later referred to the interviewee as "our friend from Al Jazeera"—a significant departure in tone from the Bush administration years. In a White House press conference later that day, John Brennan, the deputy national security adviser for homeland security and counterterrorism, responded to a reporter's question by citing what he watched on AJ. The press conference was aired live on several news networks, giving this type of high-level validation wide publicity.

At the level of the public, anecdotes hinted at a normalization of AJE. A bar full of Americans, including veterans, in Sierra Madre, CA, asked that the bartender change the TV to AJE after news broke about bin Laden's killing—and everyone there agreed.[58] A high school student in New York City in a class discussion brought up the subject of bin

Laden after watching AJE all night.[59] These anecdotes signify the transformation of Al Jazeera's brand from that of a vilified, alleged terrorist mouthpiece into a reliable and reputable source of information on news events. When news of the bin Laden assassination began breaking roughly before midnight on May 2, web traffic to AJE's site increased tremendously, showing increases similar to the news of Hosni Mubarak's resignation. The vast majority of the web traffic came from the United States. Interestingly, the death of bin Laden coincided with the reformation of the AJ brand in the minds of many Americans—the death of the perceived connection between AJ and Al Qaeda.

CONCLUSION: THE CALCULUS OF CABLE

It is impossible to show there was a concerted effort to exclude AJE, but it was alo hard to prove a purely apolitical commercial logic laid behind the cable companies' disinclination to offer their customers the choice to view AJE on their televisions. Going back to the notion of cable companies as the primary gatekeepers, it is worth weighing how the parties and sectors that pressure and influence them changed during the Arab Spring. The greatest conversion was among the political elite, especially within the government. A network that was largely shunned by those in power was increasingly welcomed by officials in 2011. Also, other media and programers, especially CNN, MSNBC, and the networks, grew more favorable publicly. Fox News did not, suggesting some polarization in American news responses to AJE. Former NBC CEO Jeff Zucker considered this of central importance in shaping the risk of carrying AJE. This point must be made with the caveat that behind-the-scenes machinations of the news business and cable industry are largely kept out of the public's eye, so one cannot confirm nor deny whether programers actively lobby distributors about the accessibility of AJE to the American market. It seems natural that competitors for what is widely seen as a declining audience for TV news would do that, but it cannot be proven.

In terms of the public, the study on viewer responses provided a snapshot in the weeks following the substantial attention paid to AJE's coverage of the uprising in Egypt. It pointed to a greater overlap between reactions to AJE and general political polarization. While the average American was indifferent to the question of whether AJE should appear on American TV sets, she was also more likely to gauge AJE as more biased than CNN International for the same exact news package. Being linked to deeper values, such as suspicion toward Arab-Americans, as well as political ideology, suggests the question of AJE taps into deeper currents within American society. Even if Republican political leaders were not willing to oppose AJE publicly, those activelyagainst AJE presented cable companies with a degree of risk, particularly as groups such as Accuracy in Media maintained pressure campaigns.

Cable companies, which are at the focus of the decision, are bottom-line-driven and as risk averse as other corporations. Their mandate is primarily to make money, to maximize revenues, and minimize costs and risks. Lack of interest in AJE is likely not based on some ideological exclusion, but on their estimation of the impact on their balance sheets. They have the legitimate concern of profitability. With the political class no longer as opposed to Al Jazeera after the Arab Spring, the companies did not have to fear political backlash from them as much as they had in the past. However, the companies remain apprehensive that some Americans, issue publics, and pundits see AJE as an anti-American terrorist mouthpiece and so carrying it could be bad for business. This is why AJE's goal of gaining wide entry through cable required it to demonstrate a large, sustained audience. It had to assure cable that the gains of carriage would compensate for the perceived risks of carriage.

There are alternatives to big cable deals, such as online streaming, which will likely get less expensive over time. The media environment is too dynamic to make concrete conclusions. TV-watching, like journalism and news consumption, is changing structurally due to new technologies. As AJE picks up more piecemeal deals in localities, larger companies could be persuaded. Advertisers may seek out placement on AJE to reach its audience, which should happen over time as it becomes normalized within the news scape. However, enhancements in digital cable have led to further proliferation of channels with smaller niche audiences—something programers, advertisers, and others fear. If cable news and the broadcasting networks lose audiences, they could lose revenues and see their budgets shrink, giving state-subsidized AJE an even bigger competitive advantage (which in theory should eventually encourage its carriage because it faces less journalistic contenders).

If cable eventually faces more competition from online video service, or "over-the-top," providers, this could pressure cable to prevent customer loss by carrying AJE—as long as they do not lose more as a result of carriage. AJE's deal with Roku, an Internet-based video service that provides a set-top box for channel-viewing is an example of such a direction.[60] Current consumer behavior suggests that "cable-cutting," or online watching of video as a substitute for TV in the United States, is a long way off.[61] Ironically, by the time the politics of distribution evolves to support AJE, and demand becomes persuasively demonstrable, the utility of cable TV as the key to building a large audience may end anyways.

NOTES

1. Samuel Huntington and Jorge Dominguez, "Political Development," in *Handbook of Political Science*, vol. 3, ed. Fred I. Greenstein and Nelson W. Polsby (Reading, MA: Addison-Wesley, 1975), 1–98; quoted in Timothy Cook, *Governing with the News: The News Media as a Political Institution*, (Chicago: University of Chicago Press, 1998), 66.

2. Ibid.

3. Lee Bollinger, "Al Jazeera Can Help U.S. Join Conversation," *Bloomberg*, March 15, 2011. http://www.businessweek.com/news/2011-03-15/al -jazeera-can-help-u-s-join-conversation-lee-c-bollinger.html, May 1, 2011.

4. Some of AJE's programs, including its hour-long news bulletin, are carried on various public and local access channels, as well as by Pacifica radio, in a patchwork of places around the country.

5. David Marash, "Why Can't You Watch Al Jazeera English?" *Television Quarterly* 37 (3/4) (Spring/Summer 2007): 47; Anthony R. Dimaggio, *Mass Media, Mass Propaganda: Examining American News in the "War on Terror"* (Lanham, MD: Lexington Books, 2008), 241; Hugh Miles, *Al Jazeera: The Inside Story of the Arab News Channel That Is Challenging the West* (New York: Grove Press, 2006), 320, 395.

6. Dimaggio, *Mass Media, Mass Propaganda*, 246.

7. Sahar Khamis, "The Role of New Arab Satellite Channels in Fostering Intercultural Dialogue: Can Al Jazeera English Bridge the Gap?," in *New Media and the New Middle East*, ed. Phil Seib (London: Palgrave Macmillan, 2007), 48.

8. David B. Wilkerson, "Al Jazeera English Makes Case to Comcast," *MarketWatch*, March 1, 2011. http://www.marketwatch.com/story/al -jazeera-english-makes-its-case-to-comcast-2011-03-01

9. Lynch Marc, *Voices of the New Arab Public: Iraq, al-Jazeera, and Middle East Politics Today* (New York: Columbia University Press, 2007).

10. Sarah Baxter, "Rumsfeld's Al-Jazeera Outburst," *Times* (London), November 27, 2005. http://www.timesonline.co.uk/tol/news/world /article597096.ece

11. Kevin Sullivan and Walter Pincus, "Paper Says Bush Talked of Bombing Arab TV Network," *Washington Post*, November 23, 2005, http:// www.washingtonpost.com/wp-dyn/content/article/2005/11/22 /AR2005112201784.html

12. Wadah Khanfar, "They Bombed al-Jazeera's Reporters. Now the US Is after Our Integrity," *Guardian*, UK, December 10, 2010, http://www .guardian.co.uk/commentisfree/cifamerica/2010/dec/10/al-jazeera-us -integrity-wikileaks

13. Lorraine Ali and Marisa Guthrie, "Why American Cable Systems Won't Carry the Al Jazeera Network," *Hollywood Reporter*, March 17, 2011, http://www.hollywoodreporter.com/news/why-american-cable -systems-wont-168953

14. Lorne Manly, "Translation: Is the Whole World Watching?" *New York Times*, March 26, 2006, http://www.nytimes.com/2006/03/26/arts /television/26manl.html?pagewanted=1&_r=1

15. Mort Rosenblum, *Coups and Earthquakes: Reporting the World for America* (New York: Harper & Row, 1979).

16. Philip Seib, *The Al Jazeera Effect: How the New Global Media Are Reshaping World Politics* (Washington, DC: Potomac Books, 2008).

17. Keach Hagey and Byron Tau, "Al-Jazeera Has Fans in Obama W.H.," *Politico*, April 17, 2011, http://www.politico.com/news/stories/0411 /53339.html

18. Glyniss MacNicol, "Even President Obama Is Watching Al Jazeera," *Business Insider*, January 29, 2011, http://www.businessinsider.com /egypt-crisis-obama-al-jazeera-2011-1

19. David Jackson, "Obama: 'No Big Move toward Democracy in Qatar,'" *USA Today*, April 16, 2011, http://content.usatoday.com/communities /theoval/post/2011/04/obama-no-big-move-toward-democracy-in -qatar/1

20. Keach Hagey, "Pelosi, McCain Salute Al Jazeera," *Politico*, May 17, 2011. http://www.politico.com/blogs/onmedia/0511/Pelosi_McCain _salute_Al_Jazeera.html?showall

21. Juliette Kayyem, "Let US See Al Jazeera," *Boston Globe*, February 14, 2011, http://www.boston.com/bostonglobe/editorial_opinion/oped /articles/2011/02/14/let_us_see_al_jazeera/

22. Brian Bennett, "U.S. Mends Frosty Relations with Al Jazeera," *Los Angeles Times*, February 7, 2011, http://articles.latimes.com/2011/feb /07/world/la-fg-al-jazeera-20110207

23. See note 17.

24. Ibid.

25. Also on were the State Department's chief spokesman Philip J. Crowley, Assistant Secretary for Near Eastern Affairs Jeffrey Feltman and Sen. John F. Kerry (D-Mass.), chairman of the Senate Foreign Relations Committee (Bennett, "U.S. Mends Frosty Relations with Al Jazeera"). Defense Secretary Robert M. Gates, Army Gen. David H. Petraeus, and Adm. Michael G. Mullen, chairman of the Joint Chiefs of Staff, were on the network's Arabic and English channels (ibid.). One-time presidential candidate and Republican Senator John McCain (R-AZ) appeared on AJE's *Frost over the World* program on March 4, 2011, and gave a one-on-one interview with AJE's Tony Harris in late April.

26. Steve Clemons, comment on "Al Jazeera's Rise," *Washington Note*, comment posted February 9, 2011, http://www.thewashingtonnote.com /archives/2011/02/al_jazeeras_ris/

27. Kirit Radia, "Sec. of State Hillary Clinton: Al Jazeera Is 'Real News,' U.S. Losing 'Information War,'" *ABC NewsOnline*, March 2, 2011. http://blogs.abcnews.com/politicalpunch/2011/03/sec-of-state -hillary-clinton-al-jazeera-is-real-news-us-losing-information-war.html;

David Bauder, "Clinton Media Criticism Buoys Al-Jazeera," *Washington Post*, March 5, 2011, http://www.washingtonpost.com/wp-dyn/content/article/2011/03/04/AR2011030405714.html.

28. David D. Kirkpatrick and Robert F. Worth, "Seizing a Moment, Al Jazeera Galvanizes Arab Frustration," *New York Times*, January 27, 2011, http://www.nytimes.com/2011/01/28/world/middleeast/28jazeera.html; Mark Robichaux, "Can Al-Jazeera's CNN Moment Last?" *Multichannel News*, February 4, 2011, http://www.multichannel.com/article/463499-Can_Al_Jazeera_s_CNN_Moment_Last_.php; Bauder, "Clinton Media Criticism Buoys Al-Jazeera"; Tony Burman, "The 'Al Jazeera Moment'?," *Toronto Star*, February 4, 2011, http://www.thestar.com/opinion/editorialopinion/article/933097--the-al-jazeera-moment.

29. See note 3.

30. John Hudson, "Andrea Mitchell: What I Read," *Atlantic Wire*, April 19, 2011, http://www.theatlanticwire.com/business/2011/04/andrea-mitchel-what-i-read/36797/; Frank Rich, "Wallflowers at the Revolution," *New York Times*, February 6, 2011, WK8; Marty Kaplan, "Al Jazeera English vs. the Charlie Sheen Channel," *Huffington Post*, March 7, 2011, http://www.huffingtonpost.com/marty-kaplan/al-jazeera-english-vs-the_b_832343.html.

31. Steven Loeb, "Naturally, Bill O'Reilly Thinks Al Jazeera Is Both 'Anti-American' and 'Anti-Semitic," *Business Insider*, February 2, 2011, http://www.businessinsider.com/bill-oreilly-al-jazeera-anti-american-video-2011-2; Cliff Kincaid, "How Al-Jazeera Kills Americans," *Accuracy in Media*, February 28, 2011, http://www.aim.org/aim-column/how-al-jazeera-kills-americans/.

32. http://www.aim.org/al-jazeera-english/

33. Jonathon Capehart, "Al-Jazeera's Silence on Lara Logan," *Washington Post*, February 17, 2011, http://voices.washingtonpost.com/postpartisan/2011/02/al_jazeeras_silence_on_lara_lo.html; Jonathon Capehart, "More on Al-Jazeera's Silence on Lara Logan," *Washington Post*, February 18, 2011,http://voices.washingtonpost.com/postpartisan/2011/02/update_on_al-jazeeras_silence.html

34. Judea Pearl, "Another Perspective, or Jihad TV?," *New York Times*, January 17, 2007, http://www.nytimes.com/2007/01/17/opinion/17pearl.html?pagewanted=print.

35. Judea Pearl, "A Statement of Observations concerning Al Jazeera," *America's Survival*, February 23, 2011, http://www.usasurvival.org/alj.ck30111-2.html

36. David Pollock, "Aljazeera: One Organization, Two Messages," *Washington Institute for Near East Policy: PolicyWatch #1802*, April 28, 2011, http://www.washingtoninstitute.org/templateC05.php?CID=3355.

37. Deborah Circelli, "DSC's Airing of Al Jazeera Raises Concerns," *Daytona Beach News-Journal*, August 8, 2010, http://www.news-journalonline.com/news/local/east-volusia/2010/08/08/dscs-airing-of-al-jazeera-tv-raises-concerns.html

38. Dana Milbank, "Live, from Golden, Colo., It's Al-Jazeera," *Washington Post*, August 28, 2008, http://www.washingtonpost.com/wp-dyn /content/article/2008/08/27/AR2008082703977.html

39. See note 13.

40. Bauder, "Clinton Media Criticism Buoys Al-Jazeera."

41. Leah Buletti, "SADAC Campaigning for Al Jazeera Broadcast," *Campus Times*, February 24, 2011, http://www.campustimes.org/2011/02/24 /sadac-campaigning-for-al-jazeera-broadcast/; Keach Hagey and Byron Tau, "Al-Jazeera Has Fans in Obama W.H.," *Politico*, April 17, 2011. http://www.politico.com/news/stories/0411/53339.html, May 1, 2011.

42. William Youmans and Katie Brown, "Can Al Jazeera English Leverage Its 'Egypt Moment' into an American Audience?," *Arab Media & Society* 12 (2011), http://www.arabmediasociety.com/?article=768

43. Bob Fernandez, "Al-Jazeera Seeks TV Distribution Deal with Comcast," *Philadelphia Inquirer*, February 25, 2011, http://articles.philly.com /2011-02-25/business/28629801_1_mouthpiece-for-osama-bin-al-jazeera-officials-al-jazeera-english

44. Cliff Kincaid, "Good News, Comcast Slams Door on Al-Jazeera," *GOPUSA*, April 22, 2011, http://www.gopusa.com/commentary/2011/04/22 /kincaid-good-news-comcast-slams-door-on-al-jazeera/

45. See note 8.

46. "Talking Heads Block Al-Jazeera TV in U.S.-Zucker," *Reuters*, February 7, 2011, http://blogs.reuters.com/mediafile/2011/02/07 /talking-heads-block-al-jazeera-tv-in-u-s-zucker/

47. See note 13.

48. Tal Samuel-Azran, *Al-Jazeera and US War Coverage* (New York: Peter Lang, 2010), 106.

49. Shakuntala Rao, "Adding Al Jazeera," *American Journalism Review* (August/September 2007), http://www.ajr.org/Article.asp?id=4397

50. Linda Moss, "Tempest Brews over Al Jazeera English," *Multichannel News*, May 24, 2007, http://www.multichannel.com/article/talkback /128891-Tempest_Brews_Over_Al_Jazeera_English.php

51. Aaron Barnhart, "Cable's Least Wanted: 10 Channels that Could Be Replaced by Al Jazeera and No One Would Care," *Kansas City Star*, February 15, 2011, http://www.kansascity.com/2011/02/15/2656461 /10-channels-that-could-be-replaced.html

52. See note 13.

53. Brian Stelter, "Al Jazeera Finds New Paths in U.S.," *New York Times*, February 1, 2011, http://mediadecoder.blogs.nytimes.com/2011/02 /01/al-jazeera-finds-new-paths-in-u-s/

54. See note 13.

55. See note 17.

56. Dan Rather, "The 2011 Time 100: Ayman Mohyeldin," *Time*, April 21, 2011, http://www.time.com/time/specials/packages/article /0,28804,2066367_2066369_2066506,00.html.

57. Sherry Ricchiardi, "The Al Jazeera Effect," *American Journalism Review* (August/September 2011), http://www.ajr.org/Article.asp?id=5077.

58. John Stephens, "Sierra Madre Residents Gather to Celebrate and Discuss the Death of Osama Bin Laden," *Sierra Madre Patch*, May 2, 2011, http://sierramadre.patch.com/articles/sierra-madre-residents-react-to-death-of-osama-bin-laden

59. Sharon Otterman, "Students Take Time to Reflect on Bin Laden," *New York Times*, May 3, 2011, http://cityroom.blogs.nytimes.com/2011/05/03/students-take-time-to-reflect-on-bin-laden/

60. Josh Levy, "Al-Jazeera, Roku and the Future of Online Video," *GigaOM*, February 9, 2011, http://gigaom.com/video/al-jazeera-roku-online-video/

61. Brian Stelter, "Ownership of TV Sets Falls in U.S.," *New York Times*, May 3, 2011, http://www.nytimes.com/2011/05/03/business/media/03television.html

CHAPTER 5

Covering and Reaching Africa

Amelia Arsenault

Even before its first live broadcast, Al Jazeera English (AJE) sought to set itself apart from other global news organizations. Although headquartered in the Middle East, it eschewed any domestic or regional agenda. It promised that unlike its primary competitors CNNI and BBC World, who often privilege stories and speakers from their countries of origin, AJE would give previously unheard news and views from the global south equal weight and equal time.

Not only would AJE broadcast more news *about* the disenfranchised, it would report news from *their* perspective, thereby acting as an ambassador for the entire global south upon the world news stage. By establishing bureaus in forgotten regions of the world and drawing upon local reporters and sources, AJE promised to ameliorate decades of imbalance in information flows between north and south. Its reporters would not simply parachute into famines and wars and transmit superficial news bites that reinforced stereotypes and shallow understandings of deeply complex problems. Rather, AJE would bring voice to the formerly "voiceless" through its unique focus on the developing world in good times and in bad, in periods of conflict and crisis and of birth and renewal. In doing so, AJE cast itself as "the channel of reference for the Middle East and Africa"[1] and as a "counterhegemonic" force, a corrective to over a century of Western dominance over the production and dissemination of news and information around the world.

Central to this vision, AJE promised that its outreach to and coverage of sub-Saharan Africa,[2] typically relegated to the margins of global news flows, would be "unparalleled,"[3] going well beyond stories about war, famine, and disease to those about political and social developments.

The expansion of satellite networks and direct-to-home broadcasting has enabled organizations like AJE to transform into a global presence. As Beer and Thompson stress, the use of common technology, language, and professional norms have facilitated the rise of a common global communication space into which media elites, increasingly freed from geographic boundaries, can expand.[4] While they share common norms, they distinguish themselves and attract new audiences by drawing upon the individualized cultures and contexts out of which they originate. AJE has made privileging the voices of the historically disenfranchised global south into the global media narrative a principal building block in its branding strategy. But what is the reality behind the rhetoric in regard to sub-Saharan Africa? Has AJE served as a counterhegemonic force challenging the dominance of Western media flows that gives voice to the African voiceless?

Politicians, development workers, and academics have debated the implications of global news actors for developing countries for decades. Particularly during the 1970s, scholars began to equate the presence of global news actors in developing countries with "electronic colonialism," and "cultural imperialism."[5] In the wake of rapid changes in the available communication technologies and the rise of media and creative centers in far-flung corners of the globe, these structural theories of southern dependency on northern media have slowly been discarded. A number of scholars, most prominently Daya Thussu, have turned to studying the implications of the interaction of dominant flows originating from the north and "contraflows" emanating from areas of the globe traditionally considered to be on the periphery of the global media system. Both Al Jazeera Arabic and AJE have been evaluated according to this framework. Thussu, for example, argues that Al Jazeera Arabic represents "a prominent example of contra-flow in global media products."[6] Hartmut Wessler and Manuel Adolphsen concurred but were doubtful about the extent to which this contraflow had actually influenced dominant discourses on the global level.[7]

There has been considerably more debate about whether AJE plays a similar role. Scholars remain divided about whether AJE represents a credible contraflow or simply another global news organization that happens to be headquartered in the Middle East. Mohammed el-Nawawy and Shawn Powers assert that AJE "presents a challenge to the existing paradigms guiding international news broadcasters."[8] Adel Iskandar remains skeptical, maintaining that AJE is "structurally on par with its Western mainstream counterparts in terms of organization and planning" and that characterizing it as an alternative media and does not apply outside of the Middle East.[9] Writing in 2008, James Painter concluded that "it is too early to tell if AJE...will have an impact on reversing traditional information flows from the north to the south."[10]

As Naomi Sakr stresses, "for the contra- flow concept to have explanatory value in respect of a phenomenon like Al-Jazeera, it has to refer to changing power relations in the production and dissemination of media messages and not just superficial changes in the geography of media flows. Directional change alone can only tell part of the story."[11] As an international broadcaster headquartered in the Middle East with bureaus across Africa, AJE has the geographic credentials, but can it be considered as a contraflow in the African context? In other words, does AJE represent something new for international broadcasting vis-à-vis sub-Saharan Africa? In order to answer this question, this chapter assesses AJE's successes and failures in covering the continent. In doing so it examines three dimensions: first, it evaluates the extent to which AJE's coverage of sub-Saharan Africa can be deemed qualitatively different. Second, it examines AJE's ability to reach and engage with African audiences. And, finally, it contextualizes AJE's efforts in the context of the larger evolution of media and communications flows in and about sub-Saharan Africa.

Bringing Africa to the World

In the lead up to the launch of AJE, Managing Director Nigel Parsons promised a South African audience that "our reporting from Africa will be unparalleled. We will have more bureaux and resources dedicated to Africa than any other global broadcaster." Parsons' words evoked age-old complaints about Africa's position within the global media sphere. Traditionally, foreign news correspondents based in one country (most often Kenya or South Africa) have been tasked with covering untenably large sections of the continent. Provided with limited resources, correspondents must triage stories according to their accessibility and "newsworthiness." Thus international news coverage about Africa has generally been limited to famines, wars, and crises, presenting a monochromatic worldview of the continent. As Charles Okigbo lamented, "there are many positive developments in Africa, but unfortunately these are not covered by the international media. It is in the nature of journalism to focus on the unusual."[12]

In 2006, AJE Africa Bureau Chief Andrew Simmons promised that AJE would be of an entirely different journalistic nature:

Large swathes of Africa have been uncovered by television news for too long. And so many parts of this beautiful continent suffer from what

I would term reactive coverage. We want to carve out a news agenda that is pro-active. I believe that in doing so the outside world's perception of this continent could gradually change.[13]

AJE launched on the premise that localization of newsgathering would foster diversity of content and bring new stories about Africa to light. This included a three-prong strategy: (1) broader representation on the ground; (2) diverse coverage; and (3) the incorporation of everyday African voices and experiences.

AJE does have more bureaus in sub-Saharan Africa than any other international broadcaster. It maintains permanent operations in Abidjan, Ivory Coast; Nairobi, Kenya; Johannesburg, South Africa, and Harare, Zimbabwe, and shared bureaus with Al Jazeera Arabic in Ndjamena, Chad; Nouakchott, Mauritania; Dakar, Senegal; Mogadishu, Somalia; and Khartoum, Sudan. AJE's decision to locate one of their first bureaus on the African continent in Zimbabwe, whose president Robert Mugabe has been at odds with the West since 1998, raised eyebrows both within in and outside of Africa. However, the decision to set up operations in Harare was strategic. CNNI, Reuters, the BBC, and just about every other major world news organization had been expelled from the country. By negotiating an operations license in Zimbabwe, AJE sent a message that it was willing and able to cover countries outside the Western fold. It also highlighted that AJE had the financial resources to expand its footprint at a time when news organizations were cutting back and consolidating bureaus. In contrast, CNNI maintains only three bureaus in Lagos, Nairobi, and Johannesburg. BBC has four major bureaus in East Africa (in Nairobi, Kenya), West Africa (in Dakar, Senegal), and Southern Africa (Johannesburg, South Africa). However, despite the number of bureaus operated by AJE on the continent, the BBC still has a much larger reach. In addition to BBC News Television, the BBC World Service radio has services in English, Arabic, French, Hausa, Kinyarwanda, Kirundi, Portuguese, Somali, and Swahili spanning the continent. In February 2008, perhaps in an effort to compete with AJE and BBC, CNNI broadened its presence in Kenya, Nigeria, and South Africa and appointed additional Africa-based correspondents. It also ramped up its regionally focused programing, adding *African Voices* and *CNNI Marketplace Africa* to its lineup.

Despite the expanding Africa initiatives of BBC and CNNII, AJE highlights the fact that it includes more coverage of African news and events when compared to other global news actors. AJE has featured numerous in-depth explorations of African issues. It has commissioned and screened award-winning documentaries such as *Photographing the*

Exodus, an AJE-commissioned documentary about asylum seekers from Mali, and *Mitumba, the Second-Hand Road*, which followed the path of secondhand clothes donated to an African charity. In 2009, it also commissioned an eight-part documentary series on the emergency room in South Africa's biggest hospital. It is hard to imagine BBC World or CNN International committing a total of four hours of programing time to a story largely outside the mainstream news agenda.

However, quantitative evidence suggests a more mixed record in incorporating African news into its broadcasts. A content analysis conducted by BBC Monitoring after the first month of AJE broadcasts concluded that "during its first month on air Al-Jazeera English has kept its pledge to be the voice of the South" but "news from Africa is not quite so frequent."[14] In 2007, Media Tenor concluded that AJE includes only marginally more coverage of news about countries outside of the Middle East and West than Al Jazeera Arabic (23 percent versus 18.6 percent). The major difference in content between the two networks is that AJE contains more news stories focusing on Western countries than Al Jazeera Arabic (30.6 percent versus 19.3 percent).[15] More recently, Figenschou conducted a content analysis in 2009 and found that stories about Africa constituted 10 percent of reporting compared to 20.8 percent for Asia, 19.6 percent for the Middle East, and 38.2 percent for Europe and North America.[16] Moreover, news about Africa largely focused on political crisis and armed conflict. As Figenschou concluded, this may be because there are more such events in the global south, but may also suggest that AJE mirrors many of the same criteria for news-worthy events that it aims to counter.[17]

However, all of these studies include countries of the Maghreb region as African as opposed to the Middle East. While no quantitative data is available, it is unlikely that given Al Jazeera's ground-breaking coverage of events in the Middle East and North Africa that its coverage of sub-Saharan Africa, Latin America, and Asia have increased. It has most likely declined. As a small indication, approximately 30 percent of news labeled as African by the AJE website between January 1 and March 1, 2011, featured stories about sub-Saharan Africa. The remainder focused on events in Tunisia, Morocco, and Libya. Further complicating matters, news about the countries of the Maghreb region are irregularly labeled as African or Middle Eastern.

Conflating coverage of North Africa with sub-Saharan Africa in many ways obscures a full appreciation of the depth and breadth of AJE's sub-Saharan African coverage. The countries of the Maghreb region partially isolated from the rest of the continent by the Atlas Mountains and the Sahara desert have had much closer relationships with southern Europe and the Middle East. While Libya and Tunisia have participated in discussions about pan-African movements, the northern Africa media landscape has largely been divorced from that of sub-Saharan Africa. They also boast much higher media and Internet penetration rates than sub-Saharan Africa and have more frequent access to European and Arab satellite providers than their southern counterparts.

The third component of AJE's African coverage included featuring a diversity of African voices. As Nigel Parsons explained, "we [AJE] want Africans to tell us about Africa and Asians to tell us about Asia." However, AJE's incorporation of diverse voices has been ambiguous at best, both in terms of its selection of correspondents and of sources. The majority of AJE staff, while talented, can hardly be counted as new voices. Indeed, AJE has used its considerable financial resources to cherry pick the best staff from its direct competitors. For example, Africa Bureau Chief Andrew Simmons spent 20 years working for the BBC and Sky News. In another example, while both Zimbabwean, neither journalist chosen to lead the Zimbabwean bureau were radical choices. Both men had worked with various Western media organizations for years. Farai Sevenzo served as a Channel 4 newscaster in the UK. Cyrus Nhara had worked for Reuters for the previous four years, and before that as a stringer for organizations like CNNI, BBC, and CBS. Similarly, Mohammed Adow came to AJE after years of service as the BBC East Africa correspondent.

AJE's original corporate profile promised to "set the news agenda, bridging cultures and providing a unique grassroots perspective from underreported regions around the world."[18] Although the grassroots element was dropped on December 5, 2010, to read, "to provide independent, impartial news for an international audience and to offer a voice to a diversity of perspectives from under-reported regions."[19] Perhaps a meaningless change of phrasing, the removal of the "grassroots perspective" from the corporate profile statement underscores a broader trend in AJE coverage. AJE privileges elite sources over the man on the street to much the same degree as its competitors. Figenschou found that AJE, like its competitors, is dominated by elite sources; only 11 percent of sources cited during the period under analysis could be characterized as the "man on the street."[20] Stories about the global South featured more ordinary people than stories about the global North, but only slightly (13 percent versus 8 percent).[21] She also concluded that

> Overall, independent elite sources [were] given more authority and more frequently invited to analyze news events...if the channel has a 'grassroots perspective', this has been voiced by independent elite sources

and Al-Jazeera correspondents rather than by ordinary citizens on the ground.[22]

The evidence presented above suggests that the reality of AJE coverage of Africa, while still more expansive than its competitors, does not measure up to its rhetoric. The following section evaluates the extent to which AJE has been successful in reaching African audiences.

BRINGING THE WORLD TO AFRICA

The proliferation of Western-based global media platforms in Africa, a paucity of news bureaus based on the continent, and a reliance by African media outlets on Western news wires means that mediated images abroad are inextricably tied to mediated images circulating within the African continent. Historically speaking, because the African consumer market was not considered lucrative, most global news organizations rarely considered domestic African audiences. African countries could either buy foreign news about the African continent from Western news agencies or go without. Covering Africa ranked low on the priority list for all global news organizations, reaching African audiences rated lower still. Consequently, as Dhyana Ziegler and Molefki Assante argued, global news gatherers "operate in an African country with little regard for the home-country...The aim is to outdo the competition, where there is competition" in more lucrative markets.[23] Thus, assessing AJE's reach within the African continent is particularly an important criteria for its transformative power.

By most accounts AJE has achieved only limited success with African audiences. Although no statistics are available for its reach continent-wide, individual country studies suggest that CNNI and BBC still far outrank AJE in terms of viewership. For example, a 2009 survey found that in the past 12 months only 5 percent of Nigerians had watched AJE, lagging well behind the BBC (13 percent) and CNNI (11 percent).[24] Similarly, a 2009 Synovate study of 12 cities across Nigeria, South Africa, Kenya, Morocco, and Cameroon found that CNNII was by far the most popular international media platform.

AJE's ability to connect with the sub-Saharan African population at large has been hindered by somewhat contradictory trends in African media consumption and platform availability. On the one hand, low media penetration rates preclude many Africans from accessing AJE programing. On the other hand, the proliferation of new communication platforms has facilitated the rise of an ever-increasing number of domestic and international competitors that cut into its audience share. AJE's difficulties in reaching African audiences can be subsumed under four broad trends.

First, radio remains the dominant medium, although this is slowly changing. According to the most recent Afrobarometer survey of sub-Saharan Africa, approximately 42 percent of citizens regularly access television a few times a week for news, compared to 80 percent for radio. These general figures also hide vast variation across the continent; 72 percent of South Africans and more than half (56 percent) of Cape Verdeans get news from television on a daily basis compared to 11 percent of Liberians and 13 percent of Malawians who access television a few days a week.[25] In Sierra Leone, only 16 percent of the population has ever watched television.[26] Access is also widely disparate within countries; 55 percent of urban respondents in a 19-country survey reported accessing television on a daily basis compared with 17 percent of rural inhabitants. In fact 57 percent of rural dwellers have never used a television.[27] Statistics for Internet penetration are the lowest of any region in the world. Continent-wide, Internet penetration is estimated at around 10 percent, ranging from 0.5 percent in Sierra Leone to 28.9 percent in Nigeria.[28]

Second, the majority of Africans can ill-afford satellite access. While 42 percent of Africans have weekly access to television, the number of individuals who actually own a television is estimated to be only around 35 million total across all of Sub-Saharan Africa. Of these 35 million, only 11 percent are satellite subscribers.[29] In more developed countries like Kenya, it is estimated that 42 percent of Kenyans have access to cable or satellite, but only 1.4 percent of satellite TV viewers have home subscriptions (8.3 percent in Nairobi). Table 5.1 provides an overview of AJE's availability in sub-Saharan Africa as of March 2011.

When the station launched in 2006, it had distribution deals with terrestrial stations in Ghana, Kenya, Uganda, and South Africa. Over the past four years it has expanded to Zambia, Tanzania, and Uganda. Unless accessed over the Internet, AJE is available to the rest of the continent only for a price. Satellite and cable television are prohibitively expensive for the majority of citizens living in sub-Saharan Africa. AJE is available continent-wide on DSTV Africa a satellite subscription service based in South Africa. However, DSTV subscriptions begin at US$45 per month, a hefty sum particularly when per capita gross national income (GNI) ranges from US$145 in Burundi to US$6,260 in Botswana.[30]

Third, although penetration numbers remain low when compared with other regions, the information revolution has prompted a diversification of media sources throughout the continent. Domestic private news organizations—not AJE or its rivals—have emerged as clear winners among

Table 5.1 Al Jazeera Availability in Sub-Saharan Africa in 2011

	Mobile/ Internet	Satellite[1]	Freeview	Syndication
Angola		Zap TV, Channel 14		
Benin, Botswana,[2] Burkina Faso Burundi, Cameroon, Cape Verde, Central African Republic, Chad, Congo Côte d'Ivoire Democratic Republic of Congo Equatorial Guinea Ethiopia, Gabon Liberia, Mali, Niger, Senegal, Somalia, Zimbabwe		DS TV		
Gambia				Gambia Radio & Television Services
Ghana		Infinity TV, SKYY,[3] WICE Net	Multi TV	Metro TV, TV3
Guinea				
Guinea-Bissau				
Kenya		Nation TV Star Africa[4] Zuku		Citizen TV, GBS, Kiss TV Stella
Madagascar		TVF		
Malawi				Malawi TV (2009)
Mozambique		TIM Soico TV		
Namibia				Namibia Broadcasting Corporation
Nigeria (2009)		Delta Cable, Disc, Multi Mesh, My TV, Hi TV and Infinity TV, Star Africa		
Rwanda		Star Africa		
Sierra Leone (2009)	Africell	ABC TV Africa		
South Africa	Strike Media Int: News 24	DS TV, Top TV, Multi Choice		Soweto TV and Cape Town TV (2009), Bay TV
Tanzania				Cloud TV
Uganda		Pearl Digital TV Smart TV		Nation TV
Zambia (2009)				Zambia National Broadcasting Corp., CBC TV

[1] Unless otherwise noted, Al Jazeera English is available continent-wide on DSTV Africa, a satellite-subscription service based in South Africa.
[2] AJE had a deal with MABC TV, a satellite provider whose license has been revoked.
[3] Eight hours each of CNNI, DW, and AJE
[4] Owned by Chinese company.

the expanding competition for news audiences. Throughout Africa, the liberalization of media spaces has led to the increase in consumption of private domestic broadcast television stations rather than international actors such as AJE or the BBC. Domestically speaking, a 2009 Africascope Study stresses the importance of domestic versus international news sources.

As table 5.2 illustrates, domestic private television stands out as the preferred media in almost every news bracket. Only in Cameroon do audiences turn to international television stations rather than domestic sources for global news events.[31]

The popularity and accessibility of domestic over international news sources is likely behind AJE's recent push to expand syndication deals to major domestic cable and terrestrial channels (as depicted above). Not surprisingly, Aljazeera is most popular in areas where it has syndication agreements with private and public national broadcasting channels. In 2006, the Kenyan Nation Media Group (owned by the Aga Khan Foundation) dropped its contract with CNNI in favor of a syndication deal with AJE. In 2009, slightly more than 5 percent of Kenyans watched AJE on satellite in the past 12 months compared to over 40 percent who watched Nation TV and 58 percent who watched Citizen TV (which also carries AJE syndicated content).[32]

Fourth, AJE's successes have been impeded by language barriers. Not surprisingly, in Francophone Africa, Canal followed by EuroNews far

Table 5.2 Primary Source of News When Events Happen

	Senegal			Cameroon		
	In Senegal	In Africa	In the World	In Cameroon	In Africa	In the World
Domestic Radio	32	15	13	16	4	2
International Radio	5	18	18	12	36	25
Domestic Print	2	1	1	2	1	0.3
International Print	0	2	2	0.1	1	0.4
Domestic State TV	4	7	7	7	4	2
Domestic Private TV	**57**	**42**	**38**	**58**	**28**	**18**
International TV	1	14	22	4	25	51
Internet	0.4	1	1	0.3	1	1

Source: Africascope 2009[1]

[1] Data reprinted in Anne Geniets, "The Global News Challenge: Assessing Changes in International Broadcast News Consumption in Africa and South Asia," Reuters Institute for the Study of Journalism, Oxford, UK. http://reutersinstitute.politics.ox.ac.uk/about/news/item/article/the-global-news-challenge-assessin.html (accessed December 10, 2010): 51.

outreaches AJE. For example, 62 percent of Senegalese watch Canal on a weekly basis, while only 13 percent watch AJE.[33]

In recognition of the challenges reaching African audiences, beginning in 2009 AJE began to experiment with mobile delivery methods. The program was piloted in two different markets via Africell in Sierra Leone and via Strike Media in South Africa. Phil Lawrie, Al Jazeera Network's director of Global Distribution, framed the program as a means for African audiences to access a "new perspective on their region and on world news."[34] However, as of yet, AJE remains just one of many international news platforms within the continent with a limited audience.

African Media in Transition

The first two sections of this chapter examined AJE's ability to integrate African news and African audiences into the global news flows. This section primarily examines how historical legacies of foreign media intervention and recent changes in the African media sphere have conditioned its African Agenda.

The sub-Saharan African media environment has been a source of contestation for almost a century. Beginning in the late 1920s, the first broadcasts in Africa targeted Europeans, not Africans. The BBC Empire Service broke the radio silence for the first time in 1932. Radio Moscow began broadcasting in 1929 in English, French, and German. The first broadcasts originating in Africa similarly targeted the colonial population. Kenya launched its first radio station in 1927 and Senegal in 1939. As African independence movements took hold, the targets of these broadcasts changed, but they were colored by cold war contestations for influence over fledgling African nations between Russia, the West, and increasingly white South Africa. Writing in 1964 on the state of the media in Africa, Rosalynde Ainslie referred to the

> "the propaganda war of the air," in which external services of the leading African states compete with those of white South Africa on the one hand and of foreign countries on the other, to influence the thinking of the continent.[35]

As the cold war came to a close and the information revolution began to reach Africa, if slowly, as in virtually every facet of African affairs, external influence over domestic media platforms were equally contested.

The formal end of colonialism did not lead easily to the independence of airwaves, screens, and communication networks. The long history of inequitable distribution of ownership, access, and content colors the extent the participation of external actors, even those originating from other former colonies, in the contemporary African information sphere. In the late 1970s, many African countries were active supporters of the New World Information Communication Order (NWICO) movement within UNESCO, a movement by nonaligned countries to protest Third World dependence on Western sources of news and information.[36] Against the backdrop of the NWICO controversy, the Organization of African Unity (OAU) launched the Pan-African News Agency (PANA), an organization that promised to combat that dependency:

> As a strategic telecommunications network, PANA will enable African countries to communicate with each other without recourse to non-African channels. Thus through PANA's work, the voice of Africa will be heard proclaiming and defending the collective interest of the nations and people of Africa.[37]

The excitement surrounding PANA quickly faded, however, as it earned a reputation as a mouthpiece for various governments rather than a credible news source. In the years that followed, sweeping calls for independence and pluralism in the information sector have regularly resurfaced.

Thus, in 2006 AJE entered a region historically sensitive to foreign broadcasts. There is little evidence that African elites perceive AJE as different from organizations like CNNI and BBC World. In fact the three are often mentioned in the same breath as indicative of "international media." For example, head of A24 African news portal, Salim Amin, labels AJE as part of the "big three."[38] Zimbabwean minister of state for national security Sydney Sekeramayi goes so far as to include AJE as part and parcel of the anti-Zimbabwean Western agenda:

> The purpose of this global information warfare, fought by CNNI, BBC, Sky News and Aljazeera [English], is aimed at discrediting the Zimbabwe land reform (programme) by assaulting the morality behind the noble exercise.[39]

Ironically, Al Jazeera Arabic's success in the Middle East helped to create additional challenges to AJE's entry into Africa. Until the launch of Al Jazeera Arabic in 1996, almost all major players in transnational broadcasting were based in the global north. It was soon joined by a panoply of other Arab news organizations such as Al Arabiya (launched in 2003), and the American government-funded Al Hurra (launched in 2004). Al Jazeera Arabic's launch had three major ramifications for African news. First, Al Jazeera Arabic illustrated that regional news organizations could be financially lucrative. Many credit the expansion of Africa-focused news channels to unfolding economic opportunities. Gary Alfonso, chief operating officer of CNBC Africa, explained the timing behind the channel launch: "there is a specific time in the curve of the economic development of all emerging markets, which is the best time to invest."[40] As media markets in other regions of the world reach saturation point, Africa looms as the next big opportunity.

Second, as Philip Seib noted, Al Jazeera Arabic played a pivotal role in establishing "Arab media as a viable alternative to Western news organizations" and attracting "global recognition of Arab media voices."[41] Al Jazeera Arabic's apparent success in promoting pan-Arab identity and garnering global recognition for the Middle East provided new fuel to the fire for the establishment of a pan-African news organization first that would promote African unity. These calls peaked in 2003 when speaking before the South African Editors Forum (SANEF) in Johannesburg in April 2003, Thabo Mbeki stressed the importance of a continent-wide African-run, African-focused broadcaster that would promote pan-African identity and information-sharing; "If Al-Jazeera can succeed, there is no reason why an African Al-Jazeera cannot succeed."[42]

Several contenders have moved into position. Launched in 2004, Africable is a pan-African francophone news station headquartered in Mali with a focus on Francophone Africa. Africable stresses that it is 100 percent African owned and highlights programing that focuses on African unity. Its motto is "La Chaîne du Continent," which can be loosely translated as "the network of the continent." Also in 2004, Salim Amin,[43] the head of the Kenyan company Camerapix, began gathering investors for a 24-hour news channel—Africa 24 or "A24"—what he referred to as "an Al Jazeera for Africa." According to the business plan, the network would feature 44 two-person bureaus located across Africa, staffed by African journalists producing news and features, and discussion forums using the latest in low-cost digital technology. Television networks across Africa would have free access to A24 content and it would also be available via Internet and mobile phones. Using the tagline "An African Voice Telling an African Story," A24 finally launched in September 2008 as "the first Pan-African online agency for Video, Pictures & Texting," a more modest endeavor than originally planned. As Amin told a press conference at the launch, "Africa can only be covered by Africans. (There is a story) beyond the starving children with flies in their eyes, beyond executions and genocide. Ours is a new and balanced agenda."[44] While the site features African-made content commissioned from journalists around the continent, it also syndicates content from BBC World Service and AJE.

Several African-led attempts at beginning a pan-African news channel followed. Propelled in part by Mbeki's calls for an African Al Jazeera SABC, South Africa's public service broadcaster launched SABC International

(SANI) in 2008 with bureau in Nairobi, Kinshasa, Dakar, Washington, and London. Its stated goal was to deliver African news made by Africans to Africa and ultimately compete with other international channels in the market for global news. Despite SABC's investment of millions of rand into the project, SANI failed to secure distribution on Multi-choice, the largest satellite provider in Africa, headquartered in South Africa. The channel closed on January 1, 2010. Another South African organization, ETV, launched a 24-hour news channel in 2008. In 2009, it expanded its presence to Namibia, Zimbabwe, Mozambique, Botswana, Lesotho, Swaziland, Zambia, and Malawi on the DStv southern African bouquet. Africa 24 (unrelated to the Kenyan A24 project) based in Paris, but targeting the African continent, and founded by Cameroon-born Constant Nemale launched in May 2009.

Processes of globalizing media and localizing strategies are mutually interdependent. AJE sought to bring Africa into the global conversation, but it has thus far failed to localize its content for African audiences. In contrast to AJE, CNBC Africa, although an African version of the American business news channel, is rarely referred to as a foreign organization. CNBC launched CNBC Africa in partnership with the South African company African Business News (ABN) in May 2007. It is available on freeview and satellite providers across Africa. CNBC, not AJE, broke new ground by including live broadcasts from the African continent. CNBC Africa set up bureaus in Cape Town, Abuja, Lagos, and Nairobi and broadcast headquarters in Johannesburg punctuated by a lavish launch attended by African heads of state and celebrities. Rather than focusing on bringing Africa to the world or the world to Africa,[45] CNBC has focused on framing itself as a locus for "the ongoing inter-African discussion on globalization, employment, career, business and investment opportunities, living standards, and infrastructure development."[46] The channel provides full coverage of events that would otherwise receive marginal coverage among global broadcasters. For example, it signed a deal with the World Economic Forum to be the sole broadcaster of the annual WEF on Africa. CNBC, not AJE, has risen as a major challenger to CNNI and BBC in terms of audiences and has been well received across the continent.

CONCLUSION

As Naomi Sakr cautions, contraflows must by definition change "power relations in the production and dissemination of media messages." Although AJE has made laudable attempts to incorporate African coverage into its news broadcasts, its efforts to cover and reach Africa are more like than unlike those of its global news competitors. There is little evidence that its African coverage has effected systematic changes in news and information flows about and into Africa. In AJE as in most global news organizations, sub-Saharan African news, reporters, and voices account for a disproportionately small amount of total news coverage.

AJE has in many ways been a victim of its own rhetoric. The station set a high bar when it cast itself as "counterhegemonic" and a "voice for the voiceless." In regard to Africa, it has yet to fulfill these promises, and in its current configuration most likely cannot. This is said not to detract from AJE's efforts, because even moderate improvements in incorporating Africa into global news flows are admirable and should be encouraged.

It might be said that AJE entered the right place at the wrong time. Although AJE highlights its African coverage, its ability to reach African audiences and cover African stories has been challenged by the unique set of political, economic, and communications challenges characterizing the African continent. Limited television penetration and even more limited satellite television penetration present a major barrier to reaching African audiences. At the same time, the exponential rise in news and information sources within the continent presents greater challenges to soliciting viewers who are able to access AJE content. Its 2006 launch followed on the heels of numerous other broadcasters focused on bringing African news produced by Africans via African platforms.

While AJE is respected, and increasingly recognized within the sub-Saharan Africa, it is one of the many "other continents' voices" that crowd the African airwaves.[47] It may feature more content about Africa than other global broadcasters; however, it remains first and foremost a globally oriented network. Its efforts to include more African news remain laudable, but in an environment populated by pan-African news start-ups, what would have been revolutionary a decade ago is today merely adequate. However, while the AJE network may have had limited success in covering and reaching Africa, the Al Jazeera stable of channels played an instrumental role in invigorating the market for pan-African news and information by suggesting that regionally focused media could prove both politically and economically viable.

Notes

1. Al Jazeera English, "Our Corporate Profile," http://english.aljazeera.net/aboutus/2006/11/2008525185555444449.html
2. This chapter focuses on AJE's coverage and reception of sub-Saharan Africa only. While the Maghreb countries (Morocco, Tunisia, Libya, Algeria, and Egypt) are located within the African continent, they are

more closely related—politically, religiously, and socially—to the Middle East. Moreover, media offerings available in the Middle East are commonly available in North Africa and vice versa.

3. "Press Release: African Line Up Al Jazeera English Announces African Line Up—A Full Line Up of Bureaux and Correspondents Unveiled," Al Jazeera English, 2006, http://english.aljazeera.net/aboutus/2006/11/200852518541361384.html

4. Francis A. Beer, and G. R. Boynton, "Globalizing Media and North-South Initiatives," in *North and South in the World Political Economy*, ed. Rafael Reuveny and William R. Thompson (Oxford: Blackwell, 2009).

5. See, for example, Herbert Schiller, *Communication and Cultural Domination* (White Plains, NY: International Arts and Sciences Press, 1976); Thomas L. McPhail, *Electronic Colonialism: The Future of International Broadcasting and Communication*, Sage Library of Social Research, Vol. 126 (Beverly Hills, CA: Sage, 1981).

6. Daya Thussu, "Mapping Global Media Flow and Contra-Flow," in *Media on the Move: Global Flow and Contra-Flow*, ed. Daya Kishan Thussu (New York: Routledge, 2006), 24.

7. Hartmut Wessler, and Manuel Adolphsen, "Contra-Flow from the Arab World? How Arab Television Coverage of the 2003 Iraq War Was Used and Framed on Western International News Channels," *Media, Culture, and Society* 30 (4) (2008): 439.

8. Mohammed el-Nawawy and Shawn Powers, *Mediating Conflict: Al-Jazeera English and the Possibility of a Conciliatory Media* (Los Angeles: Figueroa Press, 2008), 60.

9. Adel Iskandar, "Is Al-Jazeera Alternative? Mainstreaming Alterity and Assimilating Discourses of Dissent," *Transnational Broadcasting Studies* 15 (2005).

10. James Painter, *Counter-Hegemonic News: A Case Study of Al-Jazeera English and Telesur* (Oxford: Reuters Institute for the Study of Journalism, 2008).

11. Naomi Sakr, "Challenger Or Lackey? the Politics of News on Al-Jazeera," in *Media on the Move: Global Flow and Contra-Flow*, ed. Daya Kishan Thussu (New York: Routledge, 2006), 117.

12. Charles Okigbo, "National Images in the Age of the Information Superhighway: African Perspectives," *Africa Media Review* 9 (1995): 105–121.

13. "Press Release," Al Jazeera English, 2006, http://english.aljazeera.net/aboutus/2006/11/200852518541361384.html

14. Steve Metcalf, "Analysis Al-Jazeera English and Al-Jazeera Arabic News Coverage Compared," *BBC Monitoring*, December 14, 2006.

15. Roland Schatz and Christian Kolmer, "Widening the Perspective: Al Jazeera International Enriches Media Landscape" (Powerpoint Presentation delivered at the launch of the Emory University Arab Media Center, Atlanta, GA, 2007).

16. Tine Ustad Figenschou, "A Voice for the Voiceless?: A Quantitative Content Analysis of Al-Jazeera English's Flagship News," *Global Media and Communication* 6 (1) (2010): 93.

17. Ibid., 98.

18. Al Jazeera English, "Our Corporate Profile," http://www.facebook .com/group.php?gid=19670224596

19. Al Jazeera English, "Our Corporate Profile," http://english.aljazeera .net/aboutus/2006/11/2008525185555444449.html

20. Ustad Figenschou, "A Voice for the Voiceless?," 99.

21. Ibid.

22. Ibid., 101.

23. Dhyana Ziegler and Molefi K. Asante, *Thunder and Silence: The Mass Media in Africa* (New Jersey: Africa World Press, 1992).

24. Anne Geniets, "The Global News Challenge: Assessing Changes in International Broadcast News Consumption in Africa and South Asia," Reuters Institute for the Study of Journalism, Oxford, UK. http:// reutersinstitute.politics.ox.ac.uk/about/news/item/article/the-global -news-challenge-assessin.html (accessed December 10, 2010), 77.

25. Zenobia Ismail and Paul Graham, "Citizens of the World? Africans, Media and Telecommunication," *Afrobarometer Briefing Paper No. 69,* May (2009).

26. AudienceScapes, "Television Access and Use in Sierra Leone," InterMedia, 2009.

27. Ibid., 4.

28. In comparison, internet penetration is estimated to be 77.6 percent in North America, 58.4 percent in Europe, 39.8 percent in the Middle East, 39.5 percent in Latin America, and 21.56 percent in Asia.

29. "The Market for TV Services in Africa is Developing at a Fast Pace," *Balancing Act: Telecoms, Internet, and Broadcasting in Africa Broadcast* (2011).

30. World Bank, "Gross National Income Per Capita 2009, Atlas Method and PPP," http://siteresources.worldbank.org/DATASTATISTICS /Resources/GNIPC.pdf, February 15, 2011.

31. Ibid.

32. Geniets, "The Global News Challenge," 70.

33. Ibid.

34. "Al Jazeera Expands Reach in Africa," Press Release posted on AMEInfo.com, May 12, 2009, http://www.ameinfo.com/196187 .html, February 1, 2011.

35. Lebona Mosia, Charles Riddle, and James Zaffiro., "From Revolutionary to Regime Radio: Three Decades of Nationalist Broadcasting in Southern Africa," *African Media Review* 8 (1) (1994): 6.

36. According to then director-general of UNESCO, Amadou Mahtar M'Bow, the NWICO would counter "the systematic conditioning of minds and mentalities by information which is conceived and produced

by people who are not only sometimes ignorant of Third World realities, but who also consider that the Third World should think and see things in a certain way" (quoted in Kevin Cavanagh, "Freeing the Pan-African News Agency," *Journal of Modern African Studies* 27 [2] [1989]: 355).

37. Cavanagh, "Freeing the Pan-African News Agency," 355.

38. Ferial Haffajee, "Newly-Launched Media Agency Plans 'Changing' Reporting on 'African Story,'" *Mail & Guardian* (South Africa), August 1, 2008.

39. John Manzongo, "Zimbabwe: Security Minister Accuses West of Funding Regime Change Agenda," *Zimbabwe Herald Online,* October 22, 2009.

40. Edward West, "Scramble for African TV News," *Business Day* (South Africa), May 24, 2008, Economy, Business, and Finance Section, 10.

41. Philip Seib, "Hegemonic No More: Western Media, the Rise of Al-Jazeera, and the Influence of Diverse Voices," *International Studies Review* 7 (2005): 603. Al Jazeera Arabic also provided new fuel to the fire for calls for pan-African news organization first vocalized during the New World Information Communication Order. See also Marc Lynch, "Watching Al-Jazeera," *Wilson Quarterly (1976)* 29 (3) (2005): 36–45; Kai Hafez, "Arab Satellite Broadcasting: Democracy without Political Parties?," *Transnational Broadcasting Studies* (Fall) (2005).

42. Rapule Tabane, "We Need an African Al-Jazeera," *IOLNews.com,* April 23, 2003.

43. Salim is the son of Mohamed Amin—founder of the Nairobi-based photo and video agency Camerapix in the 1960s. Mohamed Amin is widely considered to be Africa's most prominent photographer and his pictures are credited with drawing world attention to the Ethiopian famine in 1984 and inspiring Live Aid and the worldwide relief effort.

44. "Idea of Pan-African TV Channel Long Overdue, Kenyan Media Session Told," *Daily Nation* (Kenya) (2006).

45. Although it does rebroadcast several popular NBC programs including Jay Leno and Meet the Press.

46. Issa Sikiti da Silva, "Milestone in African Broadcasting History," *Biz-Community,* June 4, 2007.

47. "Idea of Pan-African TV Channel Long Overdue, Kenyan Media Session Told," *Daily Nation* (Kenya), May 5, 2006.

CHAPTER 6

Covering and Reaching South Asia

Michael Kugelman

On November 2, 2007, Al Jazeera English's (AJE) *Frost over the World* program aired an interview with Benazir Bhutto, the former Pakistani prime minister. Just several weeks earlier, she had returned home after eight years of political exile, and narrowly escaped death when a bomb exploded near her motorcade.

Bhutto told her interviewer, the venerable British journalist David Frost, that she had recently sent a letter to Pakistani president Pervez Musharraf. The missive, she explained, identified three people she thought should be investigated in the event of her assassination. In describing the first of these individuals, she said something shocking. This man, she told Frost, "had dealings with Omar Sheikh, the man who murdered Osama bin Laden."[1]

What happened next was also stunning. Bhutto did not elaborate, and Frost did not demand clarification. Nothing else was said about Bhutto's reference to bin Laden's alleged killer. However, soon thereafter, the BBC—which had an agreement with AJE to share news content—aired the interview with the comment mysteriously edited out. The broadcaster offered no explanation.

Even more surprising was the muted response to Bhutto's seemingly bombshell revelation. It was not until nearly two months later, just after Bhutto was assassinated, that the blogosphere began to crackle with debate about the AJE interview. Conspiracy theorists alleged that by outing bin Laden's "killer," she had signed her death warrant. Others reasoned that she had simply misspoken, and that Frost had fallen asleep at the switch for not catching the error. The great majority of this discussion took place on American and British blogs; virtually none of it transpired within the Pakistani English-language blogosphere or broader media.[2]

Such silence is striking. Pakistanis are notorious for attributing all manner of misfortune to sinister external forces; one newspaper editor in the country has quipped that conspiracy theories constitute Pakistan's only growth industry. Hard-line media have accused the United States of triggering Pakistan's devastating 2010 floods by "manipulating weather patterns."[3] Not to be outdone, the Supreme Court Bar Association in Islamabad declared that the failed 2010 Times Square bombing was executed not by the Pakistani-American Faisal Shehzad, but by an unnamed American "think tank."[4] How surprising, then, that Pakistanis hardly weighed in on a media story rife with juicy conspiratorial implications, particularly a story revolving around one of the country's most famous women and public figures.

In due course, the controversy subsided. Several years earlier, Omar Sheikh had been sentenced to death for the murder of *Wall Street Journal* reporter Daniel Pearl, and most observers concluded that Bhutto had simply meant to say Pearl's name, not bin Laden's. The BBC justified its decision to edit the interview by saying that Bhutto quite clearly misspoke, though it did apologize for editing it and later broadcast the original version. Similarly, Omar Chatriwala, an AJE journalist, disclosed on his blog that he declined to pursue the story because Bhutto's comment was merely the result of a "slip of the tongue."[5]

In the end, what resonates the most about this strange tale is not the interview itself, but rather the fact that Pakistanis did not latch on to it. The most logical conclusion is that few of them saw the interview—an illustration of AJE's poor penetration in Pakistan, which has persisted in that country and in the broader South Asia region to the present day. Though the region's media climate provides great opportunities for AJE to flourish, a combination of factors—from viewer preferences and perceptions to access and distribution issues—has so far constrained the channel from doing so.

To be sure, AJE executives are well aware of these challenges and are actively tackling them, suggesting that AJE could still one day make a big splash in the region. For the time being, however, AJE's presence in South Asia is more a story of producing regional coverage for a global audience, and less one of taking a regional audience by storm.

SOUTH ASIA'S SEEMINGLY WELCOMING MEDIA ENVIRONMENT

At first glance, South Asia's historic experiences with foreign satellite media would appear to portend great things for AJE.

Until the 1990s, the South Asian television media environment was dominated by terrestrial, state-run broadcasters—Pakistan Television

(PTV), Nepal Television (NTV), India's Doordarshan, and the like. Such channels were watched not necessarily because they were popular, but because there were few other options. Many South Asians were, and still are, turned off by their staid, party-line tone.

However, in the early 1990s, the AsiaSat-1 satellite was launched, enabling South Asians to watch a rapidly proliferating array of new and independent foreign channels (many of them, like Star and Zee, were beamed from Hong Kong). According to David Page and William Crawley, authors of a comprehensive book that details the history of satellite media in South Asia, India was located particularly advantageously to reap the benefits of the international satellite revolution. While in much of the region new satellite offerings could be viewed only by those fortunate enough to own a dish, India enjoyed the early presence of a large number of cable providers, thus enabling viewership of satellite television offerings to intensify. India also boasted high levels of access. By the late 1990s, it was home to more than 80 percent of the households with television sets, and to nearly 95 percent of the households with cable and satellite, in all the major countries of South Asia (India, Pakistan, Bangladesh, Sri Lanka, and Nepal). In 1999, 40 percent of homes with TVs in India enjoyed cable and satellite facilities.[6]

Early Perceptions of Satellite Television Channels

Though India may have been an early pioneer, by the dawn of the new millennium, satellite programming was making great strides throughout South Asia. Page and Crawley gauge South Asians' public reactions to the explosion of satellite television across the region. Their polling, undertaken in the late 1990s, captures two major trends, both of them promising for AJE's prospects. One is support for the channels' independent and foreign programming. The other is criticism that centers on issues that largely do not figure in AJE's output.

Proponents of satellite television stations praised them for providing counterpoints to dominant state-owned channels, and for bringing different viewpoints and cultures into their living rooms. Viewers spoke of now "being part of the world" and of learning about foreign cultures that had previously been unknown to them. Since many of the early satellite offerings in the region featured Hindi films and other Indian programming, one might expect Pakistani viewers to have been less favorable. However, many Pakistanis praised satellite channels for playing a humanizing role. By deepening their exposure to so many things Indian, the programming "demystified the differences" between the two rivals.[7] AJE, with its 60 worldwide news bureaus and intensive coverage of nearly every corner of the world, would appear to play right into regional viewers' appreciation for reportage emanating from abroad.

South Asian opponents of satellite television took the opposite view. They argued that such channels amounted to cultural imperialism, with their foreign (mostly Indian) and perceived violent and crass material threatening local cultures. Others complained that satellite media failed to "go local." Still other viewers alleged that satellite TV stations were too biased in their reportage—thus undermining the claim of such outlets that they embodied "independent" media, free from the strictures of state-run channels. Pakistanis expressed outrage at what they deemed an overtly anti-Pakistan tone in satellite networks' reportage of two major regional events in 1999—the conflict in Kargil, and the hijacking of Indian airplanes by Kashmiri separatists.

Such criticism should not concern AJE. While some of the station's cultural coverage of South Asia—such as its stories on Bollywood—could perhaps be construed negatively by more sensitive viewers, AJE is for all intents and purposes a news channel, not a cultural affairs network, and is hardly characterized by crass reportage. Similarly, AJE may well favor coverage of the Middle East and wider Muslim World, yet with its bureaus in Islamabad and New Delhi and ample coverage of South Asia (discussed in detail below), it could never be accused of ignoring local affairs. In the words of Tony Burman, a former AJE managing director, the station aspires to be "of the region, and a part of the region," and seeks to cover South Asia "from within."[8] Finally, AJE has never been accused of bias toward any one nation in South Asia.

Today, satellite television stations—both international and domestic—proliferate across the region. Most South Asian countries boast dozens, if not more, of such channels, with many of them being news outlets—an illustration of the strong market for news media across South Asia. In an indication of how dramatically the region's media environment has changed since the days of terrestrially based, state-run media monopolies, the Cable & Satellite Broadcasting Association of Asia announced in 2010 that "pay TV" in Asia had reached "the tipping point" of 50 percent penetration of all Asian homes with television—and that two South Asian nations, India and Pakistan, have demonstrated some of the highest growth in such penetration.[9]

GREAT EXPECTATIONS: THE CASE OF PAKISTAN

Perhaps no other nation in South Asia would appear to be more receptive to AJE than Pakistan, a Muslim-majority country with about 100 private cable and satellite television stations (most are domestic, and were established in the early 2000s during an unprecedented period of media liberalization). Pakistan boasts not only of a cosmopolitan English-speaking elite, but also of a young population (two-thirds of the country is less than 30 years old) more sophisticated and globally minded than it typically gets credit for. Illiteracy figures are admittedly high among the general population, yet more than two-thirds of Pakistanis between the ages of 15 and 24 are literate. In addition, every second Pakistani is a mobile-phone subscriber—one of the highest rates in South Asia.[10] Internet use is also growing, particularly among young users. For an English-language channel that appeals to young viewers, is drawn to stories of interest to Muslims, and offers a variety of resources to complement its television output (from a YouTube channel and Facebook page to blogs and an iPhone application), such statistics are most encouraging.

A Taste for News

A survey on Pakistani media preferences undertaken by the BBC in 2008 gives additional reason to believe that AJE would fare well in the country.[11] It concludes that news constitutes one of the preferred forms of media content in Pakistan (indeed, in Pakistan, the most-watched television stations are news channels, not entertainment stations). In addition, those who watch the most news tend to be urban, wealthy, and well-educated—characteristics that describe the English-speaking elite likely to tune into AJE. This demographic cohort—unlike more low-income, rural Pakistanis—was also found to prefer satellite television offerings over those of terrestrial, state-run media. Finally, household access to cable and satellite television is considerable. Survey data found that nearly 70 percent of urban residents have home access to cable and satellite. Thanks to the fact that most local satellite TV channels are free-to-air (i.e., requiring no subscription fees), even low-income urbanites enjoy home access to such options.

Opportunity for a Balancing Act

Another reason to be optimistic about AJE's prospects in Pakistan is the discomfort expressed by some English-speaking Pakistanis about private Pakistani television programming. Television journalists—and particularly talk show hosts—are often described as brash and crude ideologues. Irfan Husain, a columnist for the English-language newspaper *Dawn*, writes of "ill-informed and poorly educated anchors who amplify and perpetuate myths and prejudices," and of how private TV channels have added little but "sound and fury" to public discourse.[12] Consider Meher

Bukhari, a frequently watched anchor, who berated and bullied the late Punjab Province governor Salman Taseer, an outspoken supporter of religious minorities, in a November 2010 interview. A post on the *Pak Teahouse* blog later concluded that Bukhari's interview whipped up such hatred among Pakistanis that it played an indirect role in Taseer's assassination several weeks later.[13]

There is also criticism about the country's poor media standards. Coverage of rape cases often identifies the names (and sometimes even the addresses) of victims, while reportage of tragedies often appears to exploit human suffering. In 2010, English-language bloggers lambasted aggressive television reporters for chasing after relatives of survivors of an Islamabad plane crash while wreckage smoldered nearby—all in an effort to get exclusive quotes and scoop their competitors.[14] Television executives claim that viewers relish such sensationalism—and probably many do—yet a small but vocal viewership (one that includes in great part, interestingly, other journalists) deplores it in the strongest terms.

Such uneasiness and criticism does not at all suggest that Pakistanis are turning away from their domestic stations. On the contrary, Pakistani television viewers—including the critics—are deeply addicted to these networks, warts and all. What it does suggest is an opportunity for a station of AJE's ilk to serve as a balance to the angry, polarizing, and sensationalist rhetoric emanating from the local channels.

An Encouraging Start

Indeed, one could argue that AJE, with its polished and professional tone, should theoretically come across as a breath of fresh air. Gayatri Murthy, who monitors Pakistani media for the AudienceScapes project at Intermedia, contends that the station "has a great opportunity" in Pakistan among those "tired of the nonprofessional nature of news" on domestic news channels.[15] And as a television network without a headquarters in the West—an important factor in a nation with strong anti-Western sentiment—AJE's prospects would seem to be heightened even more.

Indeed, in the early days of AJE, anecdotal evidence suggested that people were ready for a change. In January 2007, a survey of AJE viewers conducted by the *Nation* newspaper—incidentally, one of the few English dailies in Pakistan with an aggressively anti-West tone—found that AJE was "fast replacing" Western news channels as an information source, and was "in great demand," particularly among affluent residents of Karachi. Cable providers claimed that conservative Muslims and moderates alike were requesting the channel. Nearly every featured AJE viewer praised the channel's balance, objectivity, and credibility—the very qualities that the BBC survey would identify a year later as Pakistani news consumers' most important criteria for high-quality news programming.[16]

These, however, were already AJE viewers, and their support for the channel differed significantly from opinions of the larger public.

DREAMS DEFERRED: THE CASE OF PAKISTAN

AJE executives often speak of the station's triumphs in Pakistan; managing director Al Anstey contends that AJE is "well-known" and "widely watched" in the country.[17] In reality, however, the station's footprint in Pakistan is tiny—a fact underscored repeatedly in conversations with Pakistani journalists and media experts in 2010–2011.

"Off the Radar"

Adil Najam, who manages the popular *All Things Pakistan* blog, says that the AJE's presence ranges from "nil to nothing." Tellingly, contributors to the *Café Pyala* blog—regarded as one of the most credible and well-informed English-language blogs about Pakistan media—describe AJE as "off the radar," and admit they cannot even identify AJE's Pakistan correspondents.[18] Others point out that most Pakistanis—particularly in rural areas—have never even heard of the station. Such comments dovetail with the findings of the 2008 BBC survey. The poll found that only 1 percent of television viewers had watched AJE over the past week of the survey, and that only 14 percent were familiar with it at all.

To the extent that AJE has a niche audience in Pakistan, it is what journalist and blogger Tazeen Javed describes as English-speakers who seek an alternative to both local and Western media—"a tiny tiny minority." Pakistanis are not fully convinced that this small subset includes Pakistan's English-speaking political and policymaking elite. According to the analyst Ayesha Siddiqa, foreign policymakers do tune in to AJE, but purely as a reference, and only after consulting CNN and the BBC to get a hand on the West's take on news.[19] A number of Pakistani journalists contend that politicians prefer to watch Urdu-language stations because such outlets provide the nitty-gritty local political information required to keep them informed, while AJE (and other international stations) do not. According to Syed Irfan Ashraf, a communications professor at the University of Peshawar, even the most highly educated politicians "hurriedly browse" through the likes of AJE before settling on the "24 hours pure political diet" of the local networks.[20] Huma Imtiaz, a journalist who has worked for Geo, arguably Pakistan's largest and most-watched news channel, says she has come across politicians who know of and occasionally view AJE, yet spend more time appearing on the channel than they do watching it.[21]

To be sure, poor connectivity in Pakistan prevents many who may want to watch AJE from actually doing so. Though access to cable and satellite TV has intensified in recent years, overall rates are still low (about 8 million households in a nation of roughly 180 million people have cable access, according to the Pakistan Electronic Media Regulatory Authority [PEMRA]). Also, Pakistan's crippling electricity shortages—in early 2011, the country was suffering, on average, from 10 hours of outages per day—compromise Pakistanis' ability to watch TV.

A related problem is that of distribution. Many Pakistanis based in the financial capital of Karachi—which boasts the highest cable and satellite access rates in the country—report that in 2010, their cable providers, which used to carry AJE, abruptly dropped it from their platforms. AJE does not have landing rights in Pakistan, though many cable providers—undoubtedly capitalizing on the early enthusiasm surrounding the launch of AJE back in late 2006—initially carried it anyway. However, in August 2010, a Supreme Court order demanded that all channels without landing rights be taken off the air.[22] Judging by AJE's disappearance on cable across Karachi, many providers complied. Some Pakistanis report they can still get the channel, though only as part of premium digital packages that cost more than most Pakistanis can afford.

Some Pakistanis can avoid this problem by tuning in to AJE online or via social media. Indeed, many Pakistanis who say they do not watch the station on TV admit to accessing it online. Afia Salam, a journalist who worked at *Dawn News* when it was English-language, and who follows AJE on Twitter, says that "for the Internet-savvy audience," AJE is a "preferred medium."[23] Several of Pakistan's most high-traffic English-language blogs post content from AJE fairly regularly. However, Pakistani bloggers underscore that they post AJE coverage not because it comes from AJE, but simply because it happens to focus on stories they wish to showcase—often dealing with Middle East issues with little direct relevance to Pakistan. Steve Manuel, who manages the *Journalism Pakistan* website, contends that English-language bloggers often post AJE material instead of material from Western English-language media simply to avoid being branded as pro-West. "No Pakistani journalist/blogger/website wants to be seen as supporting western channels," he says.[24] In general, AJE's web presence in Pakistan, while more extensive than its presence on TV screens, pales in comparison to that of local channels. *Café Pyala*, for example, posts material from AJE exceedingly rarely, but often contains clips from top Urdu-language news stations.

At any rate, most Pakistanis cannot view AJE online even if they wish to. Pakistan's Internet use rates, while relatively high, are also deceptive. Though more than 18 million Pakistanis were Internet users in 2009, a miniscule 413,000 enjoyed broadband—suggesting that the vast majority of Pakistani Internet users are stuck with dial-up connections that complicate efforts to view AJE's streaming video.[25]

Lack of Viewer Interest

Another consideration that explains AJE's minimal reach is that English proficiency does not necessarily translate to a desire to consume English-language news. Ahsan Butt, who blogs for the Five Rupees site, notes that English speakers prefer to watch Urdu-language stations because their coverage "by virtue of being local, is better."[26] And the Café Pyala bloggers speak of authenticity: a preference for getting "the original flavor of statements/quotes" as opposed to having them "parsed" in English. Not surprisingly, Pakistan's English-language television media have become a dying breed. For all the talk about the country's rapidly proliferating television media scene, there is only one domestic English-language television station—Express 24/7, a relatively unpopular outlet that likely survives only because it is the sister station of the more prominent Urdu-language channel Express News. Dawn News, Pakistan's first domestic English-language general news channel, failed to survive and has been reborn as an Urdu station. Earlier, CNBC Pakistan underwent a similar change. Even the mighty Geo was obliged to scupper a short-lived plan to launch an English-language companion station.

Some Pakistani media experts and practitioners argue that the audiences of the BBC and CNN, and not those of the domestic stations, may represent a more realistic target. Talib Qizilbash, an editor with *Newsline* magazine, asserts that many Pakistanis perceive CNN and BBC as "too West-centric," simplistic, and superficial. By contrast, AJE "has by its very nature a different worldview, and one especially sensitive and in touch with Middle East and Muslim cultures." Consequently, AJE is regarded as more balanced and honest.[27] Not surprisingly, Imtiaz contends that AJE is thought of by some as more credible than BBC or CNN, and could conceivably give these Western networks "a run for their money" if AJE were carried by more cable providers.

All the same, efforts to win over these audiences have been limited. BBC's viewers will not be easy to poach, particularly given the strong links many Pakistanis retain toward the station, which has a long presence in the nation that harkens back to colonial times. It is regarded as "the channel of choice" for those interested in international English channels. In addition, some Pakistanis contend that the country's obsession with the United States (and its perceived meddling in Pakistan's affairs) ensures that there will always be a strong interest in viewing news from

American broadcasters. Yet at the same time, according to Qizilbash, many Pakistanis have a stronger appetite for domestic than international news, given the endless array of crises playing out at home.

Unflattering Perceptions

A final factor likely accounting for AJE's limited reach in Pakistan is the prevalence of two contradictory perceptions about the channel. The first view, fueled by the strong presence of Western on-air talent, is that AJE is a BBC clone. The second view, undoubtedly driven by the branding power of the parent Al Jazeera network, is that AJE is essentially an Arab network that only cares about stories of the Mideast. Numerous Pakistanis recall their high hopes on the eve of AJE's launch, relishing the arrival of a non-Western news alternative. Such sentiments quickly faded, however, as people concluded that the station was a variety of things: too bland, too Western-like, or too excessively focused on the Muslim world.

Pakistanis betray much confusion about AJE's brand, which undoubtedly is a reflection of AJE's struggles to project a definitive identity either as a truly global news channel (which it pledges to be), or as a mere accessory to the Mideast-centric Arabic parent network (which many believe it to be). Such confusion has yielded some peculiar results. Ashraf, professor at the University of Peshawar, recalls a time in 2008 when local and international networks converged on South Waziristan to secure an interview with the late Pakistani Taliban commander Beitullah Mehsud. He opted only for AJE. Ashraf's conclusion is that in Pakistan, the station is closely associated with the Al Jazeera brand, its non-West bonafides, and its "Arab connections." Indeed, these strong associations likely caused Mehsud to mistake AJE for the parent network.

In some ways, AJE's identity crisis helps its prospects in Pakistan, because its association with the Al Jazeera brand has actually enhanced its credibility—at least among those Pakistanis who value the station's emphasis on Mideast and Muslim-world coverage. Yet when perceptions of AJE swing in other directions, the results are quite different. Some Pakistanis, explains Javed, regard AJE as a "Western-influenced if not exactly a Western channel," and the perceived lack of Pakistani on-air personalities turns people away.

AJE Coverage of Pakistan

AJE's failure to make a major imprint in Pakistan is lamentable given the high quality of its coverage of the country. This reportage is warmly praised by Pakistanis—even by those who claim to be put off by the station's perceived banality or overemphasis on Mideast affairs.

Limited Criticism

To be sure, there are critics who describe the station's coverage as limited and pedestrian. Wajahat Ali, a TV journalist who used to host a talk show on the now-defunct English-language *Dawn News*, believes this is a function of AJE's "limited resources" vis-à-vis those of local channels. He notes, for example, that AJE's reportage on Pakistan is often obliged to borrow freely from local television networks. To win over audiences—and to be taken seriously by the Pakistani media community—AJE must "shift its philosophy on news-gathering" in Pakistan, and focus less on big-ticket stories and more on micro-level ones.[28]

High Praise

Some Pakistanis, however, rave about the station's local reportage, from coverage of army operations in the northwest (it is "excellent," and "really gets down in the weeds," says Butt) to the catastrophic floods of 2010—which Pakistanis refer to as the best coverage by any international media. The biggest stories in Pakistan—whether those with currency mainly in Pakistan, such as the trial of suspected terrorist Aafia Siddiqui, or those of interest to the broader world, such as the assassination of Taseer—receive extensive coverage on AJE. Pakistanis also praise the diversity of expert commentators—who extend far beyond the usual (Western) suspects—featured in the channel's analytical reporting.

Critically, many Pakistanis insist that AJE's coverage of their nation is not restricted to big-picture stories like terrorism and natural disasters. It also focuses on the truly local. Imtiaz praises a story appearing on the *Witness* program about the endangered language of the Kalash, a small indigenous people based in the remote Hindu Kush mountain range of northern Pakistan. Of no less significance was Rageh Omaar's special series on military operations in the northwest. Produced in 2008, "Pakistan's War" chronicled the toll these efforts were taking on the lives of Pakistani soldiers and their families—at a time when few international media outlets were highlighting the sacrifices made by Pakistani armed forces in their campaign against militancy. AJE's focus on both national and local stories in Pakistan, in the views of many in the country, separates it from the likes of the BBC and the CNN, whose coverage of Pakistan is more limited. "Only when something really big happens here" do these two networks concentrate their reportage on Pakistan, according to Salam. On average, for every one story the BBC does on Pakistan, Ashraf estimates, AJE does two or more.

Perhaps most striking about AJE's Pakistan coverage is that, contrary to the claims of critics, it has produced a number of exclusives.

David Frost's interview of Pervez Musharraf in late 2010 was the first TV interview the former president granted after announcing his return to politics. In May 2009, an AJE crew—embedded with the Pakistani army—beamed the first images of Mingora, the major city in the district of Swat, after a military offensive against the Taliban. Such footage proved that the army had regained control of Swat. The three-minute story, which ran with "Al Jazeera Exclusive" emblazoned at the top of the screen, featured images of army personnel patrolling the quiet and largely deserted city, scenes of destruction and desolation, and a cache of weaponry captured from the Taliban. An AJE producer interviewed an army commander, residents of Mingora, and a person identified by the army as a captured Taliban fighter.[29]

Also standing out was AJE's March 2010 reportage on an immense landslide in the mountainous northern region of Gilgit-Baltistan. At the time, few, if any other media, had covered this story. The landslide created an artificial lake, which flooded villages in the Hunza Valley as well as the Karakoram Highway, Pakistan's only direct road to China. AJE's Islamabad correspondent, Kamal Hyder, traveled to the disaster site and interviewed both displaced villagers—who were critical of the government for its lack of assistance—and army engineers. His reportage underscored the continuing threat—another landslide hit while his crew was filming—yet few other news organizations would cover the issue until a few months later, when the artificial lake was nearly 20 kilometers long and 20,000 villagers had been displaced.

Links to AJE's coverage of the disaster were posted on *Pamir Times*, a community affairs blog focusing on the Hunza Valley.[30] Many of the viewer comments are worth quoting at length (for the sake of authenticity, they are transcribed in unedited form):

> *Rahim Khan:* Good job by Kamal Hyder & Al-Jazeera; why not Pakistani Media are doing this?
> *Gohar Shah:* Because Pakistani media are in slumber still now...
> *Zohra:* I would like to thank Mr. Kamal Hyder of Al Jazeera Tv for taking interest and sharing his findings...At a time when Pakistani media and journalists are showing least or almost no interest in capturing our difficulties, we are grateful to a foreign media to come forward and share our problems with the rest of the world...
> *Muhammad Karim:* it is a v good work by Al-jazira our media is still sleeping and nt take any part to uplift our government to take a serious actions against this disaster...
> *Dee Jay:* Gud Job Kamal...your contribution is commendable...at least you sensed the deprivation existing and tried to portray the ground realities. Keep going....

Such comments undoubtedly please AJE executives, and give credence to their claims that AJE covers events well and consistently in Pakistan without being guilty of parachute journalism. A former head of news, Ben Rayner, said in 2007 that the channel's Pakistan bureau is staffed by locals and those who have long resided in the country, and "who know exactly what the story is, whereas ITN are sending in people from Beijing who aren't based in Pakistan."[31] Given the breadth of AJE's Pakistan coverage, such boasts are difficult to dismiss.

To be sure, Pakistanis do not only rave about AJE's coverage of their own country. In fact, many claim to tune in to AJE only for information about the Middle East and broader Muslim world. They do so, on the one hand, because they believe such stories are covered without the bias that prevails in BBC and CNN coverage. Yet they also do so because the themes of such reportage resonate so deeply. Injustice, violence, poverty, dislocation, Western domination and oppression—these themes, says Qizilbash, are those "that Pakistanis can relate to easily given the turbulent and controversial history of their own nation."

THE REGIONAL CONTEXT

AJE has covered a variety of stories across South Asia, from civil war in Sri Lanka and Maoism in Nepal to the travails of India's poor amid rapid economic growth and child prostitution and environmental threats in Bangladesh. However, even though AJE's reportage extends across South Asia, only 3 of its 60 worldwide bureaus are located in this region. One is in Islamabad, and another in Kabul. The third one is in New Delhi.

AJE in India

Given India's influential role in South Asia's satellite media explosion, it is not surprising that AJE has long held high hopes for its prospects in the country. Both on and off the record, the station's Doha-based leadership, both past and present, attest to the country's vitality. Back in July 2007, just months after launch, the channel's head for global distribution identified India and the United States as the "two strategic markets that we need to develop."[32] In an interview with an Indian news site, the executive, Phil Lawrie, spoke glowingly of India's immense growth and noted that "it makes sense" for the "flag-bearer of free speech" to be present in the world's largest democracy. He gushed about the eagerness of cable distributors to pick up AJE's programming, and expressed his desire to tap into India's 180-million-strong mobile phone subscribers.

Alas, it was not to be. For several years after AJE's launch, New Delhi refused to allow the station to downlink into India, effectively keeping the station off Indian airwaves. Some Indians at this time surmised that their government was uncomfortable with AJE's feistiness (compared to the relatively docile local media). In actuality, the Indian government had succumbed to a view then—and still—prevalent in the United States: AJE was a hardline Islamist network, and hence a security threat. This was a strongly held perception in India that AJE was unable to shatter.

Unsurprisingly in a nation as vast and complex as India, public views about AJE varied. Those favoring AJE included Muslims interested in news from the Middle East and Muslim world. Some saw the case for broadcasting AJE as a logical extension of India's pluralistic and secular tradition. "It's totally unfair to not allow AJE from broadcasting in India," opined one English-language blog commenter in September 2009. "By not allowing this channel to be aired will tarnish our image of secularism. People have the right to view the channels and decide on what they have been informed [of], whether its biased like CNN, FOX or non-biased like AJE."[33]

In June 2008, one of India's most popular English-language blogs, *Churumuri*, published a post strongly in favor of AJE, contending that it offered "a much-needed respite from the stuffiness of its western competitors and from the itsy-bitsyness of their Indian counterparts."[34] The 15 posted responses ranged from supportive comments about AJE's status as a news alternative to a variety of criticism. Several feared access to AJE would replace Western "propaganda" with "Arabic imperial propaganda." Others wondered why India even needed another foreign news channel when global news could be easily obtained via the Internet.

In late 2010, AJE announced it had finally obtained landing rights to broadcast in India. Anstey, in an interview with the *Wall Street Journal*, promised to do what Indian channels do not: "Cover India for the world and then cover the world for India."[35] AJE, however, has many challenges to overcome—and not just the media environment, which, with as many as 30 English-language television stations alone (not to mention hundreds of vernacular outlets) is much more daunting to penetrate than Pakistan's. There will also be the difficulties of capturing a niche audience. Anstey has spoken of the "potential market" of India's 300 million English speakers.[36] Of these, Muslims may provide the most logical target. Yet India's Muslims are not a monolith. While some undoubtedly are drawn to the station's perceived Islamic bonafides, others surely are not. According to Intermedia's Murthy, Indian Muslims' affinities for "pan-national" Muslim identities—such as those attached to the Al Jazeera brand—are weaker than those of their coreligionists elsewhere in the Muslim world.

Another likely target—the globally minded political and strategic elite—will be a challenge to capture as well. As in Pakistan, the BBC tends to be a viewer default option for foreign news channels. There is also reason to wonder whether AJE will have any sort of impact on Indian policymakers. M. Obaid Siddiqui, a media expert at Jamia Millia Islamia University in Delhi, describes as a "myth" the idea that Indian political elites "have no brain of their own" and only formulate policies after viewing foreign news coverage. Perhaps this was true decades ago, in the immediate postcolonial era, when the Indian elite had few indigenous news options—yet not in the current era.[37] The implication is that if India's strategic thinkers watch AJE, they do so only casually.

However, perhaps the biggest challenge for AJE in India will be overcoming the lingering perceptions of the channel as an English-language incarnation of what Donald Rumsfeld famously described as "terror TV." To be sure, news of AJE's launch in India was greeted with enthusiasm about enhancing Indians' knowledge of the world and expanding the range of foreign media outlets in the country. Yet it was also denounced in withering terms that one would likely not hear anywhere else outside of the United States:

> Please get these people out of my country and for heaven's sake off my television screens. They are absolutely bias[ed] and all they are good [at is] broadcasting Osama bin Laden. How can they ever say see "the world through their eyes" which basically stands for only Islamic ideology and any other religion is considered an ill. How they can understand the secular society in India which allows all to live without anyone trying to harm the other by any means.[38]

Such invective likely helped spark AJE's decision to undertake an extensive marketing campaign across India in January 2011 to debunk misperceptions about the station.

Strategic Mistakes?

Former AJE staffers knowledgeable about the station's Asia activities, speaking off the record, argue that AJE's struggles in India are as much a function of the channel's ineffective strategies as of conditions endemic to the country. They speak of the sluggish manner in which the Delhi bureau began its operations, of poor personnel decisions, and of banal coverage about economics and politics that ignores the more grassroots, human-interest stories screaming to be told.

Such institutional considerations warrant some examination from a region-wide context as well. How does AJE conceive of South Asia and broader continental Asia? On the one hand, Asia is depicted by the station as a core target market imbued with high strategic importance (according to

Anstey, the India-Pakistan-Afghanistan region is one "very fast-moving, very hot news story"). AJE has a considerable presence throughout the region; as of January 2011, a fifth of the channel's bureaus were located in Asia. Yet at the same time, there are questions about the station's true commitment to Asia. Whispers abound about the pull of the headquarters in Doha, and about its desire to shift attention and resources away from Asia and more toward the Middle East—as well as Europe and the United States.

In 2010, AJE announced a "restructuring" of the Kuala Lumpur broadcast center, with numerous staff asked to relocate to Doha. Some obliged, while others resigned, and several were fired. Uncertainty reigns as to the true motivations of this move. Burman, the former managing director, depicts it as the first step in an effort to redistribute the channel's resources across the wider region, in which correspondents move out of KL and fan out in greater mass across Asia, with the prospect for new bureaus. Anstey describes it as an effort to become more regionally focused. Instead of broadcasting all of AJE's news for a four-to-five-hour daily block (as was done pre-restructuring), the KL facility now hosts all news emanating from Asia. This new model, he says, enables AJE to showcase the strength of its regionally based staff.

Others, speaking off the record, argue that AJE is effectively staging a modified withdrawal from Asia, in order to centralize resources in Doha—with an upsurge in Middle East coverage to follow. The once-mighty KL broadcast center, according to these observers, has become a shadow of its former self—it is now a mere bureau, left with a fraction of the staff and output that it enjoyed pre-restructuring. Significantly, as of early 2011, most talk of enhanced or new Asia bureaus centered on cities—Seoul, Hong Kong, Bangkok, and Sydney—outside the South Asian ambit. Anstey, however, says that AJE hopes to strengthen its India operations by deploying more resources in Mumbai.

The South Asia Balance Sheet

AJE's performance in South Asia has been mixed, mirroring its experiences in the wider continent. Due to negative perceptions, language barriers, limited cable and Internet access, and crowded media environments with no shortage of news channels (both domestic and foreign), the station's reach has been limited. On the other hand, the station's small regional audience praises its diverse and often exclusive coverage.

One striking conclusion about AJE's presence in South Asia is that it rarely exhibits the feistiness and confrontational tone that have become hallmarks of the parent network, as well as of AJE's own reportage on the Middle East (particularly Egypt's antigovernment protests in 2011). Such qualities have occasionally materialized elsewhere in Asia. One of AJE's signature moments was its broadcasting of footage of Malaysian security forces violently suppressing peaceful antigovernment protestors in 2007—images that put the Malaysian government on the defensive and that, according to some media experts, helped hasten the ruling party's ouster in elections several months later.[39]

To be sure, AJE has not shied away from controversy in South Asia. The station has found itself in hot water in Sri Lanka (after producing stories about civilian suffering in that country's civil war) and in Bangladesh (after its coverage of extrajudicial killings). However, Colombo and Dhaka have largely targeted their ire on AJE's Tony Birtley, who reported both stories, and not on the channel itself. According to Birtley, he has been unable to get a visa to enter either of these countries since the offending stories were aired, yet his AJE colleagues have experienced no such problems.[40]

In Pakistan, AJE has stayed out of trouble and rarely clashes with the government. One exception arose in 2007, when Musharraf declared a state of emergency and banned AJE from Pakistani airwaves. However, this move targeted television media on the whole, with domestic channels (and even the BBC and the CNN) also blocked.

Tellingly, some of the station's most memorable reportage—such as its coverage of Swat and Omaar's pieces on the army's offensive in the tribal areas—has been undertaken while correspondents and camera crews were embedded with army forces. One could argue such stories would not have been possible had the station's relations with Islamabad not been cordial enough to allow for these embeds. Pakistani media experts cite a number of reasons to explain the lack of conflict with Islamabad. One is the government's perception that AJE represents a non-Western news source. Another is Islamabad's close ties with the Gulf states, including Qatar. The prime reason, however, is that Pakistan's government has so many problems with indigenous media that it has no time to pick fights with AJE.

The latter factor explains why AJE has had such trouble penetrating the Pakistani media market. In Pakistan—unlike in Malaysia, and unlike in much of the Middle East—most domestic television outlets are openly confrontational and overtly antigovernment. They regularly provide platforms for government opponents and cover antigovernment protests, and are credited with having catalyzed the antigovernment fervor that exploded following Musharraf's decision to remove the country's chief justice in 2007. One can argue that Pakistan's local private channels have co-opted the reputational core of the Al Jazeera brand by demonstrating their own version of the vaunted Al Jazeera effect.

Despite this narrative, AJE's prospects in South Asia are not interminably bleak. The channel's upper management seems to understand the challenges. Burman, for example, fully acknowledges the negative perceptions. He expresses confidence that AJE's acquisition of landing rights in India will trigger a period of "diversification" that makes the station seem less Western. He also speaks of AJE's need to ensure that its Mideast coverage not dominate other regional reportage. In addition, Doha is responding to a suggestion made by many Pakistan media experts: institute an Urdu-language Al Jazeera service, or use Urdu subtitles on AJE broadcasts. According to Anstey, both arrangements, though not yet in the planning stages, are under consideration. An intensive marketing and advertising campaign, similar to the one launched in India, could go a long way toward enhancing AJE's reach in Pakistan—particularly if, as Anstey hopes, the station eventually receives landing rights in the country.

Finally, at least in the Pakistan context, there is some genuine admiration for the channel. When Pakistani journalist Saima Mohsin posted some questions about AJE on her public Facebook page in February 2011, the dozens of responses from her "fans" were telling. Even while many confessed that they did not (or could not) watch the channel, or contended that it was too Western or Mideast-centric, a significant portion portrayed AJE in glowing terms. Respondents—most of them young urbanites—depicted it as informative, credible, comprehensive, high-quality, and reliable. Some even resorted to superlatives, describing AJE as "one of the leading channels I have ever seen," while "cater[ing] to English-speaking Muslims like no other news channel does."[41]

AJE's South Asia Legacy: Refocusing the Geopolitical Lens for a Global Audience

Despite housing bureaus in two of South Asia's most important capital cities and garnering praise for its ample coverage of regional stories, AJE's audience in South Asia is a small one. In many ways, however, fixating on the station's modest regional audience misses the point. This is because AJE, with its 60 bureaus around the world, is above all a global news channel that appeals to a global audience.

Recall Anstey's comment about India: AJE seeks to "cover India for the world and then cover the world for India." Tellingly, he says nothing about covering India for Indians. Consider, also, the view of Kamal Hyder, AJE's correspondent in Islamabad. AJE "is not a local channel," he says bluntly. The station "covers stories that are of international importance as opposed to what may be important locally."[42]

He dismisses the suggestion of opening new bureaus in Pakistan, given that AJE "can readily deploy" Doha-based reporters on short notice. It is notable that even AJE's "local" coverage—such as its reportage on the Hunza Valley landslide—projects a global angle. To be sure, Hyder, true to AJE form, focused on the people—on the villagers with flooded homes, and on the internally displaced. Yet he also underscored the global significance of the landslide—such as how the Karakoram Highway flooded by the artificial lake constitutes a vital trade route linking Pakistan with China. Ultimately, AJE seeks not to capture a South Asian audience, but rather to capture South Asia for a global audience.

And capture South Asia it does. With its frequent coverage of the region, AJE is spotlighting a large geographic component of what may emerge as the most geostrategically significant region of the twenty-first century: the Indian Ocean Region, or IOR. (AJE's ample coverage of East Africa and the Persian Gulf rounds out its focus on this immense expanse.) Robert Kaplan, perhaps the most prominent articulator of the IOR's rising geostrategic value, argues that the region "may comprise a map as iconic to the new century as Europe was to the last one."[43] In the coming decades, an immense share of the world's people, wealth, and threats will be housed in this non-Western area spanning two continents and dozens of countries—a landscape that receives relatively little attention, particularly from Western media.

When AJE reports on the plight of the 400,000 inhabitants of Bangladesh's rapidly sinking Bhola Island—a location visited by few, if any, international media—it humanizes the realities of climate change threats, one of the biggest challenges of the new millennium, and which arguably afflict the IOR more than any other region. And when AJE files stories on piracy in the Indian Ocean, it highlights a major threat to the globe's most highly trafficked sea lanes—which play host to rising-power competition between India and China over precious sea-based energy resources.

Kaplan describes AJE, with its entrenched presence in and reportage on the IOR, as a reflection of the region's dynamism. AJE "constitutes a feast of vivid, pathbreaking coverage of the travails of the weak and the oppressed throughout the Indian Ocean region," he concludes in the closing pages of *Monsoon*, his 2010 book on the IOR. "Al Jazeera's reporters cry out for justice, even as they are honestly representative of an emerging middle-of-the-road, middle-class viewpoint in developing nations."[44]

In effect, relatively few South Asians pay attention to AJE. Yet AJE pays immense attention to them, their region, and the broader expanse that encompasses it. By training its cameras on the IOR, a region that is geostrategically vital yet heavily underreported by international news channels, AJE showcases an innovative approach that will surely be appreciated more and more in the decades to come.

NOTES

1. The interview, which has now generated hundreds of thousands of hits on YouTube, can be seen in full at http://www.youtube.com /watch?v=oIO8B6fpFSQ. Bhutto's comment about bin Laden is made about six minutes into the interview.

2. For a representative sample of the debate about the interview, see http:// littlecountrylost.blogspot.com/2008/01/benazir-bhutto-omar-shiekh -murdered.html. While much of the discussion occurred within the blogosphere, several newspapers weighed in as well. See, for example, "Benazir Bhutto Named Bin Laden's Killer Weeks Before Her Death," *Pravda*, January 15, 2008, http://english.pravda.ru/world/asia/15-01 -2008/103426-benazir_bhutto_osama-0/.

3. Chidandand Rajgatta, "Pak Hardliners Blame India, U.S. for Floods," *Times of India*, August 19, 2010, http://timesofindia .indiatimes.com/world/us/Pak-hardliners-blame-India-US-for-floods /articleshow/6335115.cms.

4. Sabrina Tavernise, "U.S. Is a Top Villain in Pakistan's Conspiracy Talk," *New York Times*, May 25, 2010, http://www.nytimes.com/2010/05/26 /world/asia/26pstan.html.

5. Omar Chatriwala, "Bhutto and bin Laden in the Rumor Mill," *Synthetic Jungle* blog, December 30, 2007, http://syntheticjungle.com /syntheticjungle-122.

6. David Page and William Crawley, *Satellites over South Asia* (London: Sage, 2001), 101–102.

7. Ibid., 236.

8. Tony Burman, interview by the author, Washington, DC, January 12, 2010.

9. "CASBAA Release—Pay-TV Now Taking 'Lion's Share' of High Networth Audiences," CASBAA, October 26, 2010, http://www.casbaa .com/media-and-resources/news-center/1304-casbaa-release-pay-tv -now-taking-qlions-shareq-of-high-networth-audiences-.

10. "Education for All: Mid-Decade Assessment, Country Report: Pakistan," Government of Pakistan, Ministry of Education, Islamabad, 2008, http:// planipolis.iiep.unesco.org/upload/Pakistan/Pakistan_EFA_MDA.pdf, and Population Reference Bureau, "2010 World Population Data Sheet," Washington, DC, 2010, http://www.prb.org/pdf10/10wpds_eng.pdf

11. Though the BBC survey is not available to the public, analyses of the poll can be accessed from the Pakistan page of Intermedia's AudienceScapes website, http://audiencescapes.org/country-profiles-pakistan-pakistan

-communications-profile-research. The article on Pakistani news television found on the website is particularly useful: Gayatri Murthy, "News Television in Pakistan: A Study in Socioeconomic Differences," http://audiencescapes.org/country-profiles-pakistan-news-television-pakistan-whos-watching-cable-state-run-access-rural-urban.

12. Irfan Husain, "The Ten-Decibel Rule," *Dawn*, January 12, 2011, http://www.dawn.com/2011/01/12/the-ten-decibel-rule.html.

13. Zia Ahmad, "Meher Bukhari Has Salman Taseer's Blood on Her Hands as Well," *Pak Teahouse* blog, January 11, 2011, http://pakteahouse.net/2011/01/11/meher-bukhari-has-salman-taseers-blood-on-her-hands-as-well/.

14. Sana Saleem, "Margalla Tragedy—Adding Insult to Injury," *Mystified Justice* blog, July 30, 2010, http://sanasaleem.com/2010/07/30/margalla-tragedy-adding-insult-to-injury/#more-1843. "None of these media channels for once thought of the implications of such irresponsible reporting," Saleem wrote. "Perhaps the only thing on their mind was to sensationalize the news and develop conspiracy theories."

15. Gayatri Murthy, interview (via e-mail) by the author, December 7, 2010.

16. Faheem Raza, "Al Jazeera Gaining Viewership," *Nation*, January 30, 2007, available from Adrian Monk's news blog, http://adrianmonck.com/2007/01/al-jazeera-english-in-pakistan/.

17. Al Anstey, telephone interview by the author, Washington, DC, February 7, 2011.

18. Adil Najam, interview (via e-mail) by the author, December 13, 2010, and Café Pyala, interview (via e-mail) by the author, January 2, 2011.

19. Tazeen Javed, interview (via e-mail) by the author, December 28, 2010, and Ayesha Siddiqa, interview (via e-mail) by the author, December 15, 2010. Throughout this chapter, "BBC" refers to the English-language service of the BBC World Service. It does not refer to the Urdu-language or other vernacular services of the BBC World Service available (and quite popular) in South Asia.

20. Syed Irfan Ashraf, interview (via e-mail) by the author, December 20, 2010. Some media observers perceive a different dynamic elsewhere in the region. The political analyst Faheem Haider, citing anecdotal evidence, argues that the Bangladeshi political elite, in need of objective facts on which to base their political moves, look to AJE (one of the few international media outlets to regularly cover the country) as an impartial news source that, unlike most local television channels in a heavily partisan media environment, has no incentive to skew the truth. Faheem Haider, interview (via e-mail) by the author, December 28, 2010.

21. Huma Imtiaz, interview (via e-mail) by the author, December 13, 2010.

22. Omer Farooq Khan, "Outrage in Pakistan as Court Blacks Out Indian Channels," *Times of India*, August 28, 2010, http://timesofindia.indiatimes.com/world/pakistan/Outrage-in-Pakistan-as-court-blacks-out-Indian-channels/articleshow/6449272.cms.

23. Afia Salem, interview (via e-mail) by the author, December 14, 2010.

24. Steve Manuel, interview (via e-mail) by the author, December 22, 2010.

25. This Internet data comes from the International Telecommunication Union. It is important to point out, however, that broadband subscribership increased significantly between 2008 and 2009—from 168,000 to 413,000. Pakistan's Information Technology Ministry is actively seeking to expand broadband further through subsidizing expansion service in remote areas. See "The Internet in Pakistan," Intermedia AudienceScapes website, http://www.audiencescapes.org/country-profiles-pakistan -country-overview-internet-research-statistics.

26. Ahsan Butt, interview (via e-mail) by the author, December 28, 2010.

27. Talib Qizilbash, interview (via e-mail) by the author, February 7, 2011.

28. Wajahat Ali, telephone interview by the author, December 29, 2010.

29. "Inside Pakistan's War Zone," Al Jazeera English, May 28, 2009, http:// www.youtube.com/watch?v=PfV6Nn9nFgc&feature=player_embedded.

30. "Al-Jazeera TV's Kamal Hyder Reports on Hunza Disaster," *Pamir Times*, March 14, 2010, http://pamirtimes.net/2010/03/14/al-jazeera -tvs-kamal-hyder-reports-on-hunza-disaster/.

31. Ian Burrell, "Al-Jazeera: It's No Hangout for Al-Qaida," *Independent*, November 17, 2007, http://www.independent.co.uk/news/media /al-jazeera-its-no-hangout-for-alqaida-400892.html.

32. Shuchi Bansal, "Al Jazeera's Plans for India," *Rediff India*, July 23, 2007, http://www.rediff.com/money/2007/jul/23jaz.htm.

33. September 28, 2009 response to "Al Jazeera English Banned in India," *Reflections: An Indian Muslim's Perspective* blog, August 5, 2007, http:// wishsubmission.wordpress.com/2007/08/05/aje/.

34. Who Decides What We Should/Shouldn't Watch?" *Churumuri*, June 24, 2008, http://churumuri.wordpress.com/2008/06/24/who -decides-what-we-should-shouldn't-watch/.

35. "Q&A: Al Anstey on Al Jazeera in India," December 10, 2010, *Wall Street Journal*, http://blogs.wsj.com/indiarealtime/2010/12/10/qa-al-anstey -on-al-jazeera-in-india/.

36. "Al Jazeera English Comes to India," *Hindu*, December 8, 2010, http:// www.hindu.com/2010/12/08/stories/2010120863632400.htm.

37. M. Obaid Siddiqui, interview (via e-mail) by the author, January 9, 2011.

38. Comment posted on "Q&A: Al Anstey on Al Jazeera in India," *Wall Street Journal*.

39. Shawn Powers and Mohammed el-Nawawy, "New Media and the Politics of Protest: A Case Study of Al Jazeera English in Malaysia," in Michael Kugelman, ed. *Kuala Lumpur Calling: Al Jazeera English in Asia* (Washington, DC: Woodrow Wilson International Center for Scholars, 2008), 65–82.

40. Tony Birtley, interview (via e-mail) by the author, February 4, 2011.

41. Facebook page for Saima Mohsin, http://www.facebook.com /SaimaMohsin. Questions and responses can be found in postings between February 4 and 8, 2011.
42. Kamal Hyder, interview (via e-mail) by the author, January 25, 2011.
43. Robert D. Kaplan, *Monsoon: The Indian Ocean and the Future of American Power* (New York: Random House, 2010), xi.
44. Ibid., 322.

CHAPTER 7

Covering Gaza, 2008–2009: A Palestinian View

Rima Najjar Merriman

In 2009, Al Jazeera English (AJE) was nominated for an International Emmy in the news category for its coverage of both sides during the Israeli assault on the Gaza Strip.[1] During the relentless December 2008–January 2009 Israeli bombardment of the Gaza Strip, Palestinian journalists, including those affiliated with the AJE, were the only witnesses left on the scene. Was their reporting "independent" and "balanced"? What story did they get out? In a sense, these reporters could be said to have been "embedded," by default, with the Palestinians. They continued to work, "braving air raids and ground offensives, overcoming technical difficulties and while having to bear constant anxiety for the safety of their families."[2]

"While other networks are increasingly severed from Gaza as phone lines are cut and 75 percent of the territory is without electricity, Al Jazeera is bringing its approximately 140 million English- and Arabic-speaking viewers live images of bombings, tanks rolling through Gaza's farmland, and interviews with civilians and aid workers inside Gaza city," wrote Shane Bauer in a January 6, 2009 article, "Al Jazeera Breaks the Israeli Media Blockade."

"Like all of the networks, Al Jazeera gives constant hard-hitting interviews with politicians and analysts from Israel, the West Bank, and the rest of the Arab world. But while others can only balance pundits with more pundits, Al Jazeera has been taking the viewer to the scene to weigh the words of politicians against the reality on the ground."[3]

After the Israeli pounding of the Gaza Strip was over, commentators around the world quickly picked winners and losers: "War has a way of lifting or bringing down media outlets," wrote award-winning journalist and TV producer Daoud Kuttab. "CNN made its debut in the first American war on Iraq. Al Jazeera Arabic succeeded with the second Intifada and this war on Gaza, the clear winner was Al Jazeera International." According to Kuttab, Aljazeera International did its job with "professionalism and balance" and "kept its poise and won the respect of many around the round."[4]

The Gaza Strip is essentially a huge refugee camp. It is only 28 miles long and about 5 miles wide, with a population of approximately 1.6 million people, 3 quarters of whom are registered refugees (a total of 1.1 million in 8 separate camps), and whose education and general welfare have been taken over by UNRWA since the 1948 Arab-Israeli war, when these Palestinians fled to the Strip or were forced to flee from Jaffa, towns and villages south of Jaffa, and from the Beersheva area in the Negev (all now part of Israel), and were not allowed to return. The refugee camps have one of the highest population densities in the world, with a growth rate of 3.35 percent. About 65 percent of the population is under the age of 25, 43.5 percent of the employable population is unemployed and unable cross the border to find work, and in 2009, 69 percent were living below the poverty line.[5] In an in-depth feature on English.aljazeera.net, Mark Levine traces Gaza's "misery today" to "the late Ottoman period, decades before the war of 1948 transformed the Gaza Strip from a minor port and agricultural hinterland into one of the most overcrowded places on earth."[6]

On the other hand, Israel's military is ranked among the top in the world: it is currently eleventh, according to GlobalFire.Power.com. In 1967, it occupied the Gaza Strip, which had been under Egyptian rule since the establishment of the state of Israel in 1948. As it has done and continues to do in the occupied West Bank and in Jerusalem, Israel established Jewish colonies in the Gaza Strip and subjugated its inhabitants in a variety of ways. In 2005, recognizing that he could no longer subjugate Gazans in a cost-effective manner, Prime Minister of Israel Ariel Sharon removed 8,500 Israeli colonizers and unilaterally withdrew Israeli troops behind a wall enclosing Gaza. However, in spite of the withdrawal, Israel continued to exercise a terrible grip on the Strip.[7] According to some analysts, Sharon's policy of making sure that "the Palestinians will not be reaping any rewards from Israel's withdrawal" led directly to the January 25 legislative election in Gaza of the militant Islamist Palestinian group Hamas, which is considered to be a terrorist organization by Israel, the United States, and Europe and is considered to be a resistance group by Palestinians.[8] A poll conducted by An Najah University in the occupied West Bank reported that the majority of Palestinians credited strikes by Hamas and Jihad for the withdrawal.[9]

Following Hamas's victory in the elections, Israel used various ploys to paralyze the services the Palestinian Authority (PA) provides to Palestinians in the Gaza Strip, as well as the West Bank. Israel has direct control of the PA tax system and, as a result, indirect control of all functions of the PA. It has used this control, as well as control of all borders and all nonpopulated areas, to keep a tight grip on the Palestinian population, especially in the Gaza Strip.[10] As Aljazeera's senior political analyst Marwan Bishara shows, Israel's occupation is a colonial dictatorship, taking all and giving nothing in return.[11]

The barebones narrative of Israel's assault of December 2008 and January 2009 on Gaza is as follows: On December 19, 2008, the political-military resistance arm of Hamas (Ezzedin al-Qassam) in the besieged Gaza Strip announced that it would no longer continue the cease-fire, which had already been broken by an Israeli infantry unit on November 4, when it entered the blockaded Gaza Strip and killed four Hamas gunmen. At the time, American media, busy with Barack Obama's election in November, largely ignored the Israeli military attack on Hamas.[12] On January 5, CNN's Rick Sanchez finally confirmed that Israel had broken the cease-fire.[13]

In a desperate bid to force Israel to ease its stepped-up blockade on the Gaza Strip, Hamas, as reported by AJE, announced that the six-month cease-fire "will not be renewed as long as there is no real Israeli commitment to all of its conditions....There is nothing that encourages us to continue with a deal that did not achieve the results we hoped for." Ayman Mohyeldin, the then AJE's correspondent in Gaza,[14] explained that Gazans are highly skeptical about the cease-fire. "They say, so far, the existing truce has not brought any gains to the people in Gaza. People say the ongoing siege is a stark example of how Israel has treated Gazans." AJE also reported on violations against the cease-fire by noting: "There have been sporadic violent clashes along the Israeli-Gaza border in the past two months, with both sides accusing each other of violating the truce. Israeli troops have carried out raids within the Strip while Hamas fighters have launched rocket attacks on southern Israel."[15]

Hamas continued to fire rockets on Israel, which then promptly blasted the Gaza Strip with 200 rockets that were fired between December 19 and 27. An Israeli air offensive coded "Cast Lead" commenced on December 27, after an Israeli civilian was killed in Netivot. Israeli ground operations began on January 3, 2009, and continued until Israel adopted a unilateral cease-fire in Gaza on January 17, after refusing to comply with a UN Security Council vote calling for an immediate cease-fire on January 9.

The news coverage of Israel's devastating assault on the Gaza Strip, which reported "reckless and indiscriminate" shelling of residential areas, the use of human shields and massive violations of human rights, especially on the part of the Israeli military, led to worldwide protests "supporting both Israel and the Palestinians."[16] In covering the terrible assault, AJE succeeded in putting a face to the Israeli onslaught in Gaza. As one man from Gaza told AJE, "I can't believe the world is watching and no one is doing anything."[17] During the bombings, AJE coverage showed what was really happening on the ground; it was only later, after the damage had already been done, that this was properly brought to the world's attention. In 2009, AJE reported "The aerial and ground attacks have risen in volume and ferocity and have shifted focus from civil security offices, public service buildings and mosques, to random bombardment of entire neighborhoods, empty fields within the periphery of these neighborhoods and vacated or partially vacated buildings. Now, Israeli forces have taken to directly targeting and destroying residential buildings and homes, civilian cars transporting entire families and schools that provide shelter for the thousands of displaced families in the Gaza Strip." The same report shows how the Gaza bombings fit into the larger picture of Israel's decades-long displacement of Palestinians, and describes personal stories that evoke memories of the Palestinian "nakba" in 1948, when Israel was established by force.[18]

A 575-page UN fact-finding report was issued in September of 2009. This report accused Israel's military as having "deliberately" and "disproportionately" attacked the Gaza Strip with the intent to "punish, humiliate and terrorize a civilian population."[19]

Although the report blurs the distinctions between those resisting a brutal occupation and those perpetrating it, it does include a comprehensive indictment not only of the Israeli assault on the Gaza Strip, but also of Israel's oppression of Palestinians, detailing such practices as the fragmentation of the Palestinian population, the restrictions on movement and access, the unchecked violent attacks on Palestinian civilians by Jewish settlers, discriminatory practices, wholesale political detentions and torture, extrajudicial killings, the "silent transfer" of Palestinians in East Jerusalem, the de facto annexation of 10 percent of the West Bank on the Israeli side of the separation wall, the settlement expansion, land expropriation, and the demolition of Palestinian homes.[20]

In 2011, Richard Goldstone, one of the four authors of the report, retracted some of the conclusions, though not the findings, in a *Washington Post* op-ed.[21] This was followed by a call from the U.S. Senate for the UN to rescind the "lies and libels" against Israel,[22] and accusations against Goldstone from other quarters of "bizarre behavior" and caving in to pressure.[23] On April 14, the coauthors of the UN report rejected Goldstone's retraction, saying, "There is no justification for any demand or expectation for reconsideration of the report as nothing of substance has appeared that would in any way change the context."[24]

Regardless of the politics surrounding the report, especially in the U.S. Senate, the fact remains that the death toll, as is usual with any military engagement between Israel and the Palestinians, given the vast imbalance in power between the two sides, was disproportionate. On the Palestinian side, according to B'Tselem, an Israeli organization, "1,385 Palestinians were killed, 762 of whom did not take part in the hostilities. Of these, 318 were minors under age 18. More than 5,300 Palestinians were wounded, of them over 350 seriously so." On the Israeli side, "During the operation, Palestinians fired rockets and mortar shells at Israel, with the declared purpose of striking Israeli civilians. These attacks killed three Israeli civilians and one member of the Israeli security forces, and wounded dozens. Nine soldiers were killed within the Gaza Strip, four by friendly fire. More than 100 soldiers were wounded, one critically and 20 moderately to seriously."[25]

Yet, American mainstream television media were carefully reporting; for example, "Youngsters on both sides of the border are being killed, injured and traumatized by the fighting in Gaza," as ABC anchor Charles Gibson put it in a lead-in to a piece on "children of war" for the January 8 edition, 2009, of *World News Tonight*.[26]

One especially gruesome characteristic of any military engagement between the Israelis and Palestinians is its foregone conclusion. In a chapter called "Child's Play" in *The Punishment of Gaza*, veteran Israeli journalist Gideon Levy describes how the sitting-duck nature of the Gaza Strip and its inhabitants provided the Israelis with a "war deluxe": "it is child's play—pilots bombing unimpeded as if on practice runs, tank and artillery soldiers shelling houses and civilians from their armored vehicles, combat engineering troops destroying entire streets in their ominous protected vehicles without facing serious opposition."[27] Israel used missiles launched from unmanned combat aerial vehicles called drones and dropped white phosphorous bombs. "Phosphorus ignites in oxygen at temperatures of more than 30C. It is almost impossible to put out and, if it comes into contact with human flesh, can burn to the bone."[28]

The Palestinians' tragic and decades-long struggle for self-determination, their "weak ragged organization,"[29] their rudimentary and improvised weapons, and the urban guerilla nature of their fighting (meaning, by definition, irregular sabotage and harassment of a stronger force) set the stage for the Israeli assault, which many in the news media have come to see as "the punishment of Gaza," rather than a "war," thanks largely to the reporting of AJE, whose coverage, along with footage made available to foreign media by Ramattan, a Palestinian news agency based in

Gaza City, is credited with turning world opinion against Israel. The coverage was an antidote to the Israeli military's "new media war," which had heavily invested in and continues to invest in social media in order to disseminate Israeli military propaganda as well as Israeli-centric reporting, especially in the United States.

The news itself became a casualty of the assault, with six journalists killed by Israeli forces, two while on the job, between December 27, 2008, and January 17, 2009, and "at least" three buildings housing media outlets hit directly, and, some would argue, deliberately, by the Israeli air fire. Moreover, Israel closed the Gaza Strip to foreign journalists, disallowing even the practice of "embedding" of such journalists with Israeli troops.[30]

A general belief that has surfaced in recent years is that "Reporting independently from the front lines of war is an increasingly rare engagement for journalists working for major international media outlets. From Iraq to Afghanistan, reporters are increasingly embedded with Western military forces, operating without independence."[31] Nevertheless, in the case of Israel, international reporters embedded with the Israeli military during the Israeli attack on Lebanon in July–August 2006 managed to negatively expose the Israeli army. As a consequence of such lessons, not only was access into the Gaza strip denied to foreign journalists, but a two-kilometer wide area around the strip was also designated off-limits.

The reasons behind this closure as given by the Israeli military were to help safeguard journalists' lives during air strikes and to ensure that journalists would not obstruct military operations during the ground offensive. However, Israeli army spokesman Avital Leibovich told Journalists Without Borders "that the Israeli authorities viewed the media as a propaganda tool, a weapon being used by Hamas, and it should therefore be destroyed on the same basis as any other military target."[32] On the other hand, early in the attack, the Israeli military uploaded a significant amount of footage to a YouTube account,[33] including images of Israeli shipments of humanitarian aid for the besieged Gazans and of "precision strikes" at weapons that were supposedly hidden in a mosque. That this kind of footage was made available to reporters was meant primarily to justify the air attacks and secondarily to show that there is no humanitarian calamity in Gaza. According to BBC world affairs correspondent Paul Reynolds, "Both these aims are intended to place Israel in a strong position internationally and to enable its diplomacy to act as an umbrella to fend off calls for a cease-fire while the military operation unfolds."[34] In Israel, in the largest circulation newspaper, Yediot Aharonot hailed the surprise air strikes with a front-page headline saying "Better Late Than Never." Its rival Maariv blared the headline "Fighting Back."[35]

AJE has also provided coverage of some of the less popular Israeli views. Just a year prior to the commencement of the Israeli bombing of Gaza, AJE reported that an Israeli rights group had released a report criticizing the Israeli government and saying that the occupation of Gaza continued through Israel's "invisible hand": "Despite the removal of illegal settlements and permanent army bases from Gaza in August 2005, Israel continues a form of occupation . . . This includes control over Gaza's air space and territorial waters, its borders, the movement of goods and people, the taxation system, fiscal policy and the population registry."[36] It is worth mentioning here that the PA views Al Jazeera as "pro-Hamas, a biased impediment to the 'peace process.'"[37]

The press in the West Bank does not traditionally have a positive record of allowing the exercise of freedom of the press, a repressive situation exacerbated by the Israeli occupation and the ongoing hostilities between the two major Palestinian political factions, Hamas and Fateh. An April 2011 Human Rights Watch report[38] documented abuses against journalists by the haphazard and very lightly armed collection of units called the "Palestinian Security Forces" in the West Bank[39] and by Hamas "Internal Security Services" in the Gaza Strip, many of whose members do double duty by also acting as "operatives" of the Izz al-Din al Qassam Brigades, according to a March 24, 2009, report by the Israel Intelligence Heritage & Commemoration Center.[40]

Khalid Amayrah, a Palestinian journalist and Hamas supporter who has written for a number of media outlets, including AJE, and who covered the assault on Gaza from the West Bank responded to questions about his experiences with censorship or obstruction:

I have never been mistreated or persecuted by Hamas; I write anything I want without facing any problem from Hamas. Most of the problems I have faced came from the PA in the West Bank; they detained me several times for saying things they said were not supposed to be said. The PA is sensitive to all questions that would expose or embarrass it, including questions pertaining to human rights violations, torture in PA jails, collaboration with Israel, including security coordination, accusations of PA willingness to concede on fundamental issues such as Jerusalem and the refugees and also other issues related to corruption, nepotism, and cronyism . . . As to the Israelis, they deny me access to information, they bar me from entering Jerusalem, they bar me from traveling abroad. They also deny me a press card. I am subjected to all these restrictions. The Israelis are quite virulent with regard to press freedoms for Palestinians, but they are much smarter in applying their policy in comparisons to PA.[41]

Amira Hass, an Israeli journalist working for Haaretz who had been kicked out of the Gaza Strip by Hamas just one month before Israel had attacked the Strip, and who subsequently stayed there four months, gathering testimonies from scores of people, said of AJE:

> As a journalist, I expect the media to pose difficult questions which are not pleasant to Power, and to relate to troubling internal social issues. Of course, during the onslaught on Gaza, the first priority was to show the reality of Gazans under fire, especially that—deliberately or not—Israel had made sure beforehand that hardly any journalists be there. In that sense, Al Jazeera English professionally challenged Israel's attempts at portraying the attack as something it was not: a war of defense. It exposed the propaganda nature of Israeli electronic reporting.[42]

In the Egyptian state-controlled media as covered by AJE, there was also "hardly any fact-checking that Israel broke the cease-fire first" or questioning of Israeli policies and statements. In one of its programs,[43] AJE reported very presciently on the "fault lines" in the Egyptian media that reached a pitch during the Israeli assault on Gaza, causing a ripple effect. The report describes how the media disconnect between the tightly controlled anti-Hamas state TV and the intensive campaign of criticism by the liberal and Islamist oppositional print media "could have real consequences for the country and the region." A country like Egypt, the broadcaster says, "risks becoming collateral damage." "With more than 1000 Palestinians dead, this is a global story that most of the global media still cannot get." In the Global Village part of the program, a viewer says that independent blogging that takes the Egyptian government to task on its stand on the Gaza assault hopes "to bring about a popular uprising of some sort."[44]

Of the U.S. coverage of the assault on Gaza, AJE makes a point through a piece by Habib Battah that focuses on the U.S. media's almost grotesque compulsion to give equal space to images of Israeli suffering next to images portraying the carnage visited on Palestinians: "If an Israeli woman had lost five daughters in a Palestinian attack, would *The Washington Post* run an equally sized photograph of a relatively unharmed Palestinian woman, who was merely distraught over Israeli missile fire?" In fact, this is what the *Post* did in reverse. Battah explains: "To understand the frustration often felt in the Arab world over U.S. media coverage, one only needs to imagine the same front page had the situation been reversed." He adds, "Like many major news organisations in the US, *The Washington Post* has chosen to cover the conflict from a perspective that reflects the US government's relationship with Israel." He goes on to address the following categories of reporting of the assault to which AJE is sensitive and how these are missing or distorted in the U.S. media: Arab frustrations, stripped context, missing Palestinian perspective, missing the victim's perspective when the victim is Palestinian and missing Palestinian voices.[45]

Palestinian journalists have often complained about not being considered credible by foreign media such as the BBC, the CNN, and France 24. As a manager of Ramattan complained to Reporters without Borders, "We are not credible because we are Palestinian. Anyone is considered to be better than us and this even if we have long years of media experience. Today we need to feel that we are no less worthy than others and that we provide work of quality."[46] AJE covered a story on January 26, 2009, about a Palestinian videographer (Ashraf Mashrawi) who was accused on an Internet site of faking footage he had shot of the futile attempt of a Norwegian medical team to resuscitate his brother, a victim of an Israeli rocket attack. The site falsely claimed that his brother had been dead before arriving at the hospital.[47]

Ali Abunimah, author of *One Country: A Bold Proposal to End the Palestinian Impasse*,[48] cofounder of the Electronic Intifada and a tireless critic of National Public Radio's (NPR) coverage of Palestinian and Israeli news, suggests that this attitude toward Palestinian journalists, and by extension, to the bashing of Arab media outlets like Al Jazeera, is "a thinly disguised racist element."[49] This racism manifests itself in a general attitude both in the press and when it comes to the granting of public offices, especially in the United States. A reporter on the Middle East, an officer in the American diplomatic corps, government, or a Middle East scholar or pundit who has Jewish ethnic ties to the Middle East is deemed credible on the subject of Israel until proven otherwise. However, the opposite is true for persons of Arab descent, whether they are American or any other nationality. The assumption is that anything Arab is also somehow anti-American.

A study by researchers William Youmans and Katie Brown at the University of Michigan, Ann Arbor, found that Americans who watched AJE news coverage found it to be fair when branded with a CNN International logo. People watching the same clip who were told it was Al Jazeera were more likely to conclude that the story was biased. They warned, "If those who remain prejudiced against AJE mobilize around this view and oppose cable carriage of AJE, it could offset gains in AJE's reputation.... to the detriment of international relations."[50]

At the same time as the media are dismissive of Palestinian reporting associated with an Arab media organization like Al Jazeera and wary of it as "biased," the mainstream media in the Western world and especially in the United States easily embrace Israeli-centric coverage of the conflict between Israel and the Palestinians. The Associated Press, for example, is "usually the only global wire service taken by U.S. newspapers." It operates without oversight: "Editors around the country simply accept its reporting at face value." And, most importantly, "Even when an AP report carries a Palestinian dateline and even a Palestinian byline, in the large majority of cases the article was actually written in Israel, frequently by an Israeli editor."[51] A blog cosponsored by two nonprofit, nonpartisan American think tanks "without ethnic ties to the region," specializing in media analysis, the Council for the National Interest and If Americans Knew, records a clear pattern of alleged "distortions and omissions" in the reporting on the Israeli occupation by the Associated Press. The case studies published on the blog have titles such as "Letting AP in on the Secret: Israeli Strip Searches," "AP Erases Video of Israeli Soldier Shooting Palestinian Boy," "Just Another Mother Murdered," "Anatomy of a Cover-Up: When a Mother Gets Killed Does She Make a Sound?"[52]

Although the coverage of the Gaza "punishment" remained no more than "background noise" in the mainstream TV news outlets in the United States, dominated by the "carefully-scripted talking points of the Israeli spokespeople,"[53] video clips of AJE reporting show that it did manage to rectify some of the "omissions and distortions" that have long been transmitted by journalists such as AP's Matti Friedman, who was recently exposed ("deconstructed") on israelpalestinenews.wordpress.com,[54] and to explain and analyze more fully, something that British television news, for example, has consistently failed to do in covering the conflict between the Palestinians and Israelis.[55]

As catalogued, these "omissions and distortions" have to do with the underreporting of Palestinian children's deaths, word choices (e.g., the use of "incursion" for what is, in reality, a massive invasion), editorial decisions, the wording of headlines, and choice of context. More insidious than the framing and semantics of the reporting is the "engendering a false parity by stretching the notion of journalistic balance to encompass power, culpability, and legitimacy as well."[56] Here, for example, is how AJE describes the launch of Israel's ground offensive on the Gaza Strip on January 4, 2009. What is most striking about this passage is its stark simplicity and clarity:

> Ayman Mohyeldin, Al Jazeera's correspondent in Gaza City, said that the scene in Gaza was one of "fear and terror."
>
> He said that there were reports of heavy fighting between Israeli forces and Palestinian fighters in areas such as Zaytoun, near Gaza City, as several loud explosions rocked the territory.

Palestinian medical sources say at least 464 Palestinians have died and more than 2,000 had been injured since Israel began aerial bombardment of Gaza more than a week ago.

Four Israelis have also been killed by Palestinian rockets fired into southern Israel during the past week.

Israel, meanwhile, extended its naval blockade of Gaza early on Sunday, from six nautical miles to 20 nautical miles, preventing humanitarian aid and protest vessels from trying to break the siege.[57]

In his exposé of how the U.S. domestic media covered the news of the assault on Gaza,[58] Lawrence Pintak concludes that "the humanity, the scale and the context of the conflict" was "AWOL," particularly on television. These dimensions, however, are all present and accounted for in the coverage of AJE. American alternative media, especially on the Internet, made use of such coverage to get the word out for those who cared to know.

For example, of the 18 news stories posted on the webpage of If Americans Knew, called "What Everyone Needs to Know about Israel/ Palestine," which lists "Videos on December 2008– January 2009 Attack on Gaza,"[59] 12 items are from AJE and the other 6 are from *Democracy Now!*, the Guardian of London, Alternet, C-Span, CNN, and one is a YouTube clip showing UK Jewish MP Gerald Kaufman speaking out against the invasion of Gaza, concluding with "They're not simply war criminals, they're fools,".

The 12 AJE video reports (the longest of which lasts less than five minutes) manage to convey and contextualize the horror visited on the caged Gazans without resorting to showing "a steady stream of vivid images of bloodshed accompanied by commentary thick with moral outrage,"[60] a strategy that Al Jazeera Arabic had chosen for its reporting, or exercising the "restraint" of Al Arabia, which was supposedly motivated by fear of "inciting terrorism." At the same time, AJE reporting avoids the Israeli-centric framing, semantics, and implication that Hamas has the same ability to cause damage as the Israeli military.

One of the video clips listed on the site, which is titled "Delicate EU-Gaza Diplomacy,"[61] is a snapshot of how European diplomats are uncomfortably and carefully reacting to anti-Israeli sentiments with words such as "unnecessary," "provocation," and "disproportionate." Fateh and Hamas are recognized by Czech foreign minister Karel Schwarzenberg as being participants in negotiations. In the video, protesters against Israel, including the Jewish, speak out, one of whom says, "This is an unnecessary war that won't bring peace." The Israeli government's view was publicized by reporter Jonah Hull: "The Israeli government believes war is now the only way to guarantee security," and we hear French foreign minister Bernard Kouchner buying into Israel's justification of its assault by describing it as a "response" to Hamas's "provocation," albeit "certainly disproportionate." All this occurs in less than three minutes.

Images and words devoid of "newspeak" are transmitted by a clip posted on the site that aired January 5, a day after the report on EU "diplomacy." This clip is titled "More Children Killed as War on Gaza Continues"[62] and shows us the aftermath of "an indiscriminate strike" on a refugee camp on the outskirts of Gaza City. Hospitals are "bursting at the seams" with casualties: "An entire family, five children and their parents perished in the attack." We watch the image of a Palestinian man tenderly holding a tiny dead body and placing it gently next to the bodies of three other children. We see a father ushering his three wounded children into hospital, including one dazed child with a head wound waiting to be cared for. Context is provided: "Gaza has been under siege for years, and shortage of medicines and humanitarian supplies has only worsened." "The people of Gaza have nowhere to flee" is noted in the Israeli defense minister's warning that the ground offensive may go deeper into Gaza to find and eliminate Hamas and its rockets. Mohammad Vall (the reporter) concludes: "It's not clear what strategy Israel is going to pursue to achieve that without causing carnage among Palestinian civilians in the most densely-populated spot on Earth."

To those in the news media who may have felt pressured to pause defensively over the wording of "indiscriminate shelling," that is, to stop to consider whether the shelling was truly indiscriminate or merely a lapse in the vaunted precision skills of the Israeli air force, AJE provides a subsequent report in June to vouch for its accuracy relying on Human Rights Watch as a source.[63] In addition, its reporters and cameramen show direct evidence as they go along. In one of the clips listed on If Americans Knew, dated January 19, Sherine Tadros visits an apartment block in Tar El Hawa, where "doctors and nurses from the nearby hospital, the Al-Quds Hospital, were staying." The building shows "clear evidence...of heavy artillery shelling...you can see that it's not just the areas that were targeted specifically that have been destroyed, but also nearby residential flats and areas that have also been subjected to heavy bombardment and heavy artillery shelling." And, again, the motif of being trapped with no possible exit appears like a mantra as Tadros says: "it's this feeling of being trapped inside this war zone as the fighting goes on around you that is so difficult for the Palestinian civilian population here to cope with."[64]

In another video clip, Tadros reports on the Sammouni family in Gaza City, whose house was demolished by Israeli forces after the family had been ordered to stay in it for safety. Twenty-seven members of the family died and another ninety Gazans remained trapped under the rubble, with rescue efforts hampered by Israeli forces.[65]

There are two more video clips on the If Americans Knew site from AJE, dated January 5 (the assault on Gaza was by then into its tenth day). One clip shows an account from a Palestinian father whose seven-month-old child has just been killed in the conflict, and the other is a four-minute report called "Gazans Flee Homes and Seek Refuge in UN Schools." The latter clip opens with reference to the "humanitarian crisis in Gaza," noting that about 13,000 have fled their homes because of Israel's continued "onslaught" on Gaza. The source for the number cited is identified as the UN. Images of men, women, and children taking refuge in a school are shown.

Choosing her words carefully and accurately, Sherine Tadros (the reporter) says, "In Gaza, nowhere is safe and nobody is immune from the onslaught." A mother with young children speaks on camera through a translator. "What have the children done to deserve this?...We want to go home and eat and sleep like everyone else.... Where is the great Arab world?...They've left us. Shame on them." An elderly man, Sobhi Rizk, speaks through a translator. Tadros explains that 61 members of his family are in the shelter. The man's granddaughter, Amal, still a child, speaks at length through a translator, "overwhelmed," and crying as she speaks. "I'm crying for the children of Gaza who have been thrown in the street.... We don't know what this war is about." Tadros concludes by emphasizing a crucial point: Gazans are besieged: "Refugees are a casualty of every war, but in Gaza there is nowhere safe to flee. Israel says its enemy is Hamas, but while it fights its battle, it keeps a million and half people trapped inside the war zone it's created."

If Americans Knew also lists the AJE video report of the Israeli shelling that landed only meters away from a UN refugee camp school, "killing 40 people and injuring 45." In less than three minutes, it gives us a "thin slice" of the situation, showing the panic, grief, and fear sown among the Gazan population in Jabaliya refugee camp, mentioning that only a few hours earlier, Israeli shelling had hit another UN school, killing three members of the same family. We hear a Hamas representative saying, "I think it's a new massacre and this holocaust in Gaza [*sic*]," and an Israeli spokesperson describing Hamas as "an indespicable [*sic*]...terror organization that chooses to booby trap his own people." But as usual, AJE gets quickly to the bottom line: all of the crossings out of Gaza remain closed. "Israel insists it's not targeting civilians and its strikes are accurate, but as the death toll rises and schools get hit, Israel may find it that much harder to explain its actions and defend its offensive to the outside world."

On January 9, AJE aired an interview with Taghreed al Khodary, a journalist trapped in the center of Gaza "trying to move from family to another family, just to feel what it is like for families, for kids for parents." She describes the Catch-22 she and the other inhabitants are experiencing:

> Everybody thinks Israel will bomb a mosque which is nearby less than 100 meters away from where I live; some in the neighborhood escaped...into another neighborhood, which is also dangerous...Israelis dropped many leaflets in every inch of Gaza, saying evacuate and they announced telling people evacuate to the city but also in the city they are dropping leaflets warning the population to leave...you don't know what's a target any-more; you don't know who is living in your neighborhood anymore; there are no Hamas leaders in my neighborhood, but you don't know who is supporting Hamas; you don't know who is in the military wing anymore; you are feeling in a trap everywhere in Gaza.[66]

Speaking on *Democracy Now!* in February 2011, Marwan Bishara, senior political analyst at AJE, said, "we listen to the people, and we report the story as is....The fact that Washington sees people as terrorists, as jihad-ists, as radicals, as extremists, and the most autocratic and the worst of kleptocracies in the world as moderate, as allies, as friends of the United States, is an insult to the American people."[67]

The achievement of AJE is that it succeeded, through its reporting, in counteracting the propaganda the Israeli military had spread before and during the assault on Gaza, with the American mainstream media's willing help. So, for example, by allowing viewers to see and hear Gazans quietly assembling over the rubble of mosques to pray, it showed that terrorism is not inextricably linked to their schools or mosques.

An AJE video report by journalist Ayman Mohyeldin titled "Praying in Defiance of Israel's War in Gaza—09 Jan 09"[68] shows footage of a crowd of Palestinian men and boys gathering to pray amidst the rubble of a destroyed mosque (Mohammad Mosque). The report includes the voiceover translation of an interview with an Imam (Dr. Mohammad Bakheet), who calmly voices the sentiments of those around him: "To the people around the world and in Moslem countries, I say your silence allows for this aggression to continue, and to those praying here, I say this is our mosque, and I will pray here till judgment day and we will rebuild this mosque even bigger." It also includes the story of Abu Mohammad, who had fled his neighborhood to stay with his daughter close to the destruction. Abu Mohammad tells us that he "was moved by a sense of purpose to pray on the site of the destroyed mosque." He adds, "Our faith cannot be destroyed by missiles."

AJE has been gradually dispelling the myth that Israel is a free and democratic nation that is under attack by terrorists. AJE's senior political analyst Marwan Bishara points out that "No other dictatorship in the region has been as indifferent and destructive for so long over those it ruled, as the Zionist regime has been in Palestine." He goes on to note that "In reality, Israel has directly or indirectly driven Palestinians out of their homeland, confiscated their properties, rejected their right to return to their homeland despite UN resolutions, and occupied and colonised the rest of their homeland for the last four decades." Bishara puts into context Israel's 2008/2009 bombing of Gaza by saying that Israel "didn't hesitate to use lethal, excessive force time and again against those under its occupation. The most recent war crimes have been documented and detailed in various UN reports, including that of Judge Goldstone regarding the 2008/2009 war on Gaza, which added or changed little in regards to the reality on the ground."[69]

AJE has also fairly shown the other side of the Palestinian struggle as being one of resistance, rather than terrorism. In Gaza, Palestinians continue to "struggle with poverty amid an ongoing blockade, while also recovering from Israel's war on the territory earlier," AJE reports. There, where Hamas has ruled in recent years, AJE portrays the organization's "resistance and struggle against Israel" rather than the acts of terrorism that are depicted in Western media. One year after the start of the 2008 Israeli bombing of Gaza, AJE provided coverage of a mass rally against Israeli occupation, including Ismail Haniya's speech in which he told the crowds that "Hamas will not go back on its line of resistance and struggle until it achieves for our people their freedom and independence, God willing." Such coverage has provided a more balanced view of Hamas's rule in Gaza.[70]

And from Hamas's headquarters in Damascus, Musa Abu Marzouq—the deputy head of Hamas' political bureau—told AJE's Shane Bauer in an interview:

> We are defending ourselves.
>
> When you talk about any occupation, people should resist the soldiers and the army who occupy their country.
>
> We don't have weapons sophisticated enough to launch at exact targets.
>
> We are sending a message: "You can't provide security to your side until you bring security to the Palestinian side."
>
> We are looking for freedom and for security for the Palestinian people. This is our message to Israel.
>
> They need to understand that we are working for an independent state.[71]

AJE has also allowed a wide variety of activists, academics, and scholars to express views that are nearly taboo in Western media. Ali Abunimah, for example, describes the 2008 Israeli bombing of Gaza as posted on AJE's website as follows: "Operation Cast Lead, as Israel dubbed it, was an attempt to destroy once and for all Palestinian resistance in general, and Hamas in particular, which had won the 2006 election and survived the blockade and numerous US-sponsored attempts to undermine and overthrow it in cooperation with US-backed Palestinian militias."[72]

Moreover, AJE also shares the less popular views of Western leaders about Israel that are often ignored by Western media. As AJE states in one report: "David Cameron, the British prime minister, has urged Israel to lift the blockade of the Gaza Strip, describing the current state of the Palestinian enclave as a 'prison camp.' "[73]

"Demand Al Jazeera" is an AJE marketing site that has links to a very long list of articles published by American media, such as the *New York Times* to the *New Yorker*, about its coverage.[74] The general consensus is that AJE's reporting on the 2011 revolution in Egypt is a triumph. "Its sudden visibility and importance became a big story.... There was a plainspoken clarity and a depth to A.J.E.'s coverage, and a refreshing lack of strong personalities gumming up the transmissions."[75] But in the eyes of this researcher, AJE had already proven itself long before in the thorny thickets of reporting on Israel.

LIST OF IN-DEPTH REPORTS POSTED ON THE AJE SITE

"War on Gaza: All the latest reports and analysis from Gaza, Israel and around the world."

> Last Modified: 01 Jan 2009 15:37 GMT War on Gaza
> Palestinian men bear trauma of war"
> Al Jazeera reports on the growing mental health problems among Palestinian men.
> Zeinah Awad in Gaza Last Modified: 01 Feb 2009 12:34 GMT
> Gazans pledge to rebuild
> Emerging from the rubble, they hope to restore their lives."
> Safa Joudeh in Gaza Last Modified: 27 Dec 2009 13:04 GMT
> War crimes convictions after Gaza?
> If war crimes have been committed in Gaza, prosecuting suspects will not be simple."
> Anita Rice Last Modified: 22 Jan 2009 19:07 GMT
> Gaza conflict 'remains unsettled'
> Alastair Crooke tells Al Jazeera Israel fell short and Hamas came out stronger from the war."

Last Modified: 22 Jan 2009 23:59 GMT
Palestinian factions united by war
But will the veneer of a unified front against Israel hold up to the ceasefires?"
Shane Bauer in Damascus Last Modified: 20 Jan 2009 09:33 GMT
Waging the web wars
A new media expert examines how Hamas and Israel defended their positions online."
Riyaad Minty, Al Jazeera's new media analyst Last Modified: 27 Dec 2009 13:02 GMT
Who will save the Palestinians?
Middle East historian says Palestinians must change the rules of resistance."
Mark LeVine Last Modified: 27 Dec 2009 13:03 GMT
Arab-Israelis lament war on Gaza
Arabs in Israel say the war has increased divisions between Israeli-Arabs and Jews."
Rachel Shabi in Israel Last Modified: 27 Dec 2009 12:59 GMT
Gaza: The endless cycle of trauma
Middle East analyst Sandy Tolan explains how history is repeating itself."
Sandy Tolan, Middle East analyst Last Modified: 27 Dec 2009 12:57 GMT
Gaza diary: To die with hope
One Gazan's diary of life under Israeli bombardment."
Mohammed Ali in Gaza City Last Modified: 27 Dec 2009 13:01 GMT
War amongst the people'
Defence analyst assesses Israel's preparedness for a new type of conflict."
Paul Beaver Last Modified: 03 Jan 2009 12:14 GMT War on Gaza

Notes

1. "88.1 FM WESU to Broadcast 'Al Jazeera English,'" April 29, 2011, http://www.middletownpress.com/articles/2011/02/12/news/doc4d56099e298bf127201259.txt

2. Reporters without Borders, "Israel/Gaza Operation 'Cast Lead': News Control as Military Objective," February, 2009, p. 6.

3. Shane Bauer, "Al Jazeera Breaks the News Media Blockade," *New American Media*, January 6, 2009, http://news.newamericamedia.org/news/view_article.html?article_id=db5f72890b1f8e4fad37c77329277907, April 29, 2011.

4. Daoud Kuttab. "Winners and Losers in Gaza," *Daoud Kuttab*, January 23, 2009, http://www.daoudkuttab.com/?p=524.

5. The United Nations Agency for Palestine Refugees.

6. Mark Levine, "Tracing Gaza's Chaos to 1948," *Al Jazeera English*, July 13, 2009, http://english.aljazeera.net/focus/arabunity/2008/02/2008525185737842919.html, April 29, 2011.

7. See B'Tselem, http://www.btselem.org.

8. "Aimless in Gaza," *New York Times*, July 15, 2005, http://www.nytimes.com/2005/07/15/opinion/15fri2.html?8br, April 29, 2011.

9. "Poll: Most Palestinians Credit Terror for Israeli Withdrawal," *World Tribune*, July 27, 2005, http://www.worldtribune.com/worldtribune/05/front2453578.936111111.html, April 29, 2011.

10. See B'Tselem, http://www.btselem.org. Israel must prevent a humanitarian crisis in the oPt.

11. Marwan Bishara, "The Middle East's Oldest Dictatorship," *Al Jazeera English*, April 21, 2011, http://english.aljazeera.net/indepth/opinion/2011/04/201142114189933416.html

12. Jim Lobe and Ali Gharib, "US Media Didn't Report Israeli Ceasefire Violation," *Electronic Intifada*, January 8, 2009, http://electronicintifada.net/content/us-media-didnt-report-israeli-ceasefire-violation/7941, April 29, 2011.

13. "CNN Confirms Israel Broke Ceasefire First," April 29, 2011, http://www.youtube.com/watch?v=KntmpoRXFX4.

14. As of 2011, he is the chief of AJE's Cairo bureau.

15. "Gaza-Israel Truce in Jeopardy," *Al Jazeera English*, December 15, 2008, http://english.aljazeera.net/news/middleeast/2008/12/20081214144 33365449.html, April 29, 2011.

16. "Attack on Gaza: Worldwide Protests," *Guardian*, January 8, 2009, http://www.guardian.co.uk/world/gallery/2009/jan/08/gaza -humanrights?INTCMP=ILCNETTXT3487, April 29, 2011.

17. "Gazans Tell of Ordeal as War Rages," *Al Jazeera English*, January 15, 2009, http://english.aljazeera.net/focus/2009/01/20091155194386203.html, April 29, 2011.

18. Safa Joudeh, "Displaced and Desperate in Gaza," *Al Jazeera English*, December 27, 2009, http://english.aljazeera.net/focus/war_on_gaza /2009/01/200911264110961218.html, April 29, 2011.

19. Richard Goldstone, "Statement by Justice Richard Goldstone on Behalf of the UN Fact Finding Mission on the Gaza Conflict" (statement delivered to the Human Rights Council, Geneva, Switzerland), September 29, 2009, http://www2.ohchr.org/english/bodies/hrcouncil/specialsession /9/docs/OpeningStatement_GazaFFM_290909.doc, April 29, 2011.

20. Norman G. Finkelstein, "*'This Time We Went Too Far': Truth and Consequences of the Gaza Invasion* (New York: OR Books, 2010), 131.

21. Richard Goldstone, "Reconsidering the Goldstone Report on Israel and War Crimes," *Washington Post*, April 1, 2011, http://www .washingtonpost.com/opinions/reconsidering-the-goldstone-report -on-israel-and-war-crimes/2011/04/01/AFg111JC_story.html, April 29, 2011.

22. "Senate Calls on UN to Revoke Report on Israel," *Seattle Times*, April 15, 2011, http://seattletimes.nwsource.com/html/nationworld /2014783807_apussenateisraelunreport.html, April 29, 2011.

23. Roger Cohen, "The Goldstone Chronicles," *New York Times*, April 7, 2011, http://www.nytimes.com/2011/04/08/opinion/08iht -edcohen08.html?ref=opinion#, April 29, 2011.

24. "Gaza War Report Co-authors Reject Goldstone's Retraction," *Haaretz Daily Newspaper*, April 14, 2011, http://www.haaretz.com/news /diplomacy-defense/gaza-war-report-co-authors-reject-goldstone-s -retraction-1.355951?localLinksEnabled=false, April 29, 2011.

25. B'Tselem, "One Year since Operation Cast Lead, Still No Accountability," December 27, 2009, http://www.btselem.org/English/Gaza_Strip /20091227_A_year_to_Castlead_Operation.asp, April 29, 2011.

26. Lawrence Pintak, "Gaza: Of Media Wars and Borderless Journalism," *Arab Media Community* (Middle East Center of St. Antony's College, University of Oxford, January 2009), 4.

27. Gideon Levy, *The Punishment of Gaza* (London/New York: Verso, 2010), 102. See also Rima Merriman, "A Cruel Cat and Mouse Game," *Electronic Intifada*, May 20, 2006: "The Israelis call it a war, but it is really a contemptible and cruel cat and mouse game, with the mouse firmly held under the cat's paw or locked up in a cage to which the cat has free and easy access," http://electronicintifada.net/content/cruel-cat -and-mouse-game/5967, April 29, 2011.

28. "Gazan Mother Tells of White Phosphorous Pain," *Al Jazeera English*, March 26, 2009, http://english.aljazeera.net/news/middleeast/2009/0 3/200932618435772724.html, April 29, 2011.

29. Levy, *The Punishment of Gaza*, 102.

30. Reporters without Borders, "Operation 'Cast Lead': News Control as a Military Objective," February 15, 2009, http://en.rsf.org/palestinian -territories-operation-cast-lead-news-control-15-02-2009,30310.html, 3, April 29, 2011.

31. Stephan Christoff, "Robert Fisk on Gaza and the Media," *Rabble.ca*, February 23, 2009, http://www.rabble.ca/news/robert-fisk-gaza-and -media, April 29, 2011.

32. Reporters without Borders, "Operation 'Cast Lead': News Control as a Military Objective," 6.

33. "Youtube—Idfnadesk's Channel," April 29, 2011, http://www.youtube .com/user/idfnadesk.

34. Paul Reynolds, "Propaganda War: Trusting What We See?" *British Broadcasting Corporation*, January 5, 2009, http://news.bbc.co.uk/2 /hi/7809371.stm, April 29, 2011.

35. Israel Media on Defensive over Gaza War Coverage (AFP), January 14, 2009.

36. Laila El-Haddad, " 'Invisible Hand' of Israel in Gaza," *Al Jazeera English*, October 27, 2007, http://english.aljazeera.net/news/middleeast/2007 /01/2008525134238230569.html, April 29, 2011.

37. Gregg Carlstrom, "The PA vs. Al Jazeera: The Palestine Papers," *Al Jazeera English*, January 26, 2011, http://english.aljazeera.net/palestine papers/2011/01/201112612212385624.html, April 29, 2011.

38. International Freedom of Expression Exchange, "Human Rights Watch Report Documents Rise in Attacks, Detentions of Journalists in West Bank and Gaza," April 7, 2011, http://www.ifex.org/palestine/2011/04/07 /security_report/, April 29, 2011.

39. Esther Pan/Council on Foreign Relations, "Reorganizing the Palestinian Security Forces," October 4, 2005, http://www.cfr.org/israel/middle-east-reorganizing-palestinian-security-forces/p8081, April 29, 2011.

40. Intelligence and Terrorism Information Center at the Israel Intelligence Heritage & Commemoration Center (IICC), "Mounting Evidence indicates that during Operation Cast Lead (and in ordinary times) members of Hamas's internal security forces served as commanders and operatives in Hamas's military wing (Izz al-Din al-Qassam Brigades)," April 29, 2011, http://www.terrorism-info.org.il/malam_multimedia/English /eng_n/pdf/hamas_e067.pdf

41. Khalid Amayrah, e-mail message to the author, April 23, 2011.

42. Amira Hass, e-mail message to the author, April 22, 2011.

43. Al Jazeera English, *Inside Story*, January 26, 2009.

44. Al Jazeera English, "Egyptian Media Coverage of Gaza," January 26, 2009, http://english.aljazeera.net/programmes/listeningpost/2009/2 009/01/200911684521632980.html, April 29, 2011.

45. Habbib Battah, "In the US, Gaza Is a Different War," *Al Jazeera English*, January 7, 2009, http://english.aljazeera.net/focus/war_on _gaza/2009/01/2009185448204690.html, April 29, 2011.

46. Reporters without Borders, see also http://israelpalestinenews.wordpress .com/

47. Al Jazeera English, "Inside Story, Egyptian Media Coverage of Gaza," January 26, 2009, http://english.aljazeera.net/programmes/listeningpo st/2009/2009/01/200911684521632980.html, April 29, 2011.

48. Ali Abunimah, *One Country: A Bold Proposal to End the Palestinian Impasse* (New York: Metropolitan Books, 2006).

49. Ali Abunimah, "Letter to NPR for Al-Jazeerah Bashing," Abunimah. org, October 14, 2001, http://www.themodernreligion.com/terror/wtc -npr-radio.html, April 29, 2011.

50. William Youmans and Katie Brown, "Can Al Jazeera English Leverage its 'Egypt Moment' into an American Audience?" *Arab Media and Society* 12 (Spring 2011), http://arabmediasociety.com /index.php?article=768&printarticle, April 29, 2011.

51. http://israelpalestinenews.wordpress.com/

52. Ibid.

53. Pintak, "Gaza: Of Media Wars and Borderless Journalism," http://www .arabmediasociety.com/topics/index.php?t_article=237, April 29, 2011.

54. "AP's Matti Friedman: An Israeli Citizen and Former Israeli Soldier," *Associated Press Deconstructed*, April 13, 2011, http://israelpalestinenews

.wordpress.com/2011/04/13/aps-matti-friedman-israeli-citizen-and-former-israeli-soldier/, April 29, 2011.

55. Greg Philo and Mike Berry, *Bad News from Israel* (London: Pluto Press, 2004).

56. Muhammad Idrees Ahmad, "The BBC: Eyeless in Gaza," *Electronic Intifada*, January 6, 2009, http://electronicintifada.net/content/bbc-eyeless-gaza/7926, April 29, 2011.

57. Al Jazeera English, "Israeli Ground Troops Enter Gaza," January4, 2009, http://english.aljazeera.net/news/middleeast/2009/01/20091322357629723.html, April 29, 2011.

58. Pintak, "Gaza: Of Media Wars and Borderless Journalism," http://www.arabmediasociety.com/topics/index.php?t_article=237, April 29, 2011.

59. If Americans Knew, "December 2008—January 2009 Attack on Gaza: Videos," April 29, 2011, http://www.ifamericansknew.com/cur_sit/dec08videos.html

60. Pintak, "Gaza: Of Media Wars and Borderless Journalism," 2.

61. Al Jazeera English, "Video: Delicate EU-Gaza Diplomacy," January 4, 2009, http://www.ifamericansknew.com/cur_sit/diplo.html, April 29, 2011.

62. Al Jazeera English, "Video: More Children Killed as War on Gaza Continues," January 5, 2009, http://www.ifamericansknew.com/cur_sit/children.html, April 29, 2011.

63. Al Jazeera English/YouTube, "Inside Story—Collateral Damage? 30 June 09," June 30, 2009, http://www.youtube.com/watch?v=TWYkGFuDpOk, April 29, 2011.

64. Sherine Tadros, Al Jazeera English, "Video: Aftermath of Attacks on Tar El Hawa District," January 16, 2009, http://www.ifamericansknew.com/cur_sit/tarelhawa.html, April 29, 2011.

65. Sherine Tadros, Al Jazeera English, "Family Members Die in Israeli House Demolition," January 18, 2009, http://www.ifamericansknew.com/cur_sit/house.html, April 29, 2011.

66. Al Jazeera English/YouTube, "Trapped Gaza Journalist Talks to Al Jazeera—09 Jan 09," January 8, 2009, http://www.youtube.com/watch?v=NBWQJ1BxMrI, April 29, 2011.

67. Al Jazeera English, "'The Genie Is Out of the Bottle': Assessing a Changing Arab World with Noam Chomsky and Al Jazeera's Marwan Bishara," February 21, 2011, http://english.aljazeera.net/programmes/empire/2011/02/20112211027266463.html, April 29, 2011.

68. "Ayman Mohyeldin," World News Network, April 29, 2011, http://wn.com/Ayman_Mohyeldin

69. Marwan Bishara, "The Middle East's Oldest Dictatorship," *Al Jazeera English*, April 21, 2011, http://english.aljazeera.net/indepth/opinion/2011/04/201142114189933416.html, April 29, 2011.

70. Al Jazeera English, "Hamas Vows to Continue Resistance," December 14, 2009, http://english.aljazeera.net/news/middleeast/2009/12/20091214152114620921.html, April 29, 2011.

71. Shane Bauer, "Hamas: We Will Win War in Gaza," *Al Jazeera English*, January 13, 2009, http://english.aljazeera.net/news/middleeast/2009/01/200918155333111890.htm, April 29, 2011.

72. Ali Abunimah, "GAZA: ONE YEAR ON 'Israel Resembles a Failed State,'" *Al Jazeera English*, December 28, 2009, http://english.aljazeera.net/focus/gazaoneyearon/2009/12/200912269262432432.html, April 29, 2011.

73. Al Jazeera English, "Cameron Urges Lifting of Gaza Siege," July 28, 2010, http://english.aljazeera.net/news/middleeast/2010/07/2010727131527583794.html, April 29, 2011.

74. Al Jazeera English, "Demand Al Jazeera: US Media Coverage of Al Jazeera," February 24, 2011, http://english.aljazeera.net/demandaljazeera/2011/02/20112883136279551.html, April 29, 2011.

75. Nancy Franklin, "Falling for A.J.E.," *New Yorker News Desk*, February 16, 2011, http://www.newyorker.com/online/blogs/newsdesk/2011/02/al-jazeera-english.html, April 29, 2011.

CHAPTER 8

Covering Gaza, 2008–2009: An Israeli View

Eytan Gilboa

INTRODUCTION

On December 27, 2008, Israel launched a limited military operation, code-named Operation Cast Lead (OCL), against Hamas in Gaza.[1] On January 3, 2009, it began a ground operation designed to secure areas within the Gaza strip from which Hamas launched rockets against Israeli cities and towns. A cease-fire was announced on January 17 and Israel withdrew its forces on January 21.

Hamas and Israel have been involved in violence since Hamas was established. Hamas conducted numerous terrorist acts inside Israel, even after Israel and the PLO signed the Oslo peace accords. Since 2001, Hamas has also been firing rockets and mortar shells into Israeli cities and towns, and has sent suicide bombers to blow up buses, coffee shops, supermarkets, universities, and cinema houses.

Undoubtedly, as any other country in a similar war situation, Israel had the right to self-defense, and, therefore, had the right to respond by force to Hamas terrorism and attack its strongholds inside Gaza. The only question was of proportionality. The battle against Hamas was between a state and a nonstate actor; and was fought between soldiers in uniform and combatants dressed in civilian clothing operating inside civilian population, often using women and children as human shields.[2] OCL raised serious questions about just war, rules, and laws of war, and the roles of international organizations such as the UN. It also challenged the media, especially the global all-news networks.

Media coverage of warfare has always been problematic. Philip Knightley observed that during wars, the war correspondent or the truth has always been the first casualty.[3] In the past decade, coverage of war has become even more complicated. Scholars and journalists have argued that war correspondents moved from detachment to involvement, from verification to assertion and from objectivity to subjectivity.[4] They criticized primarily American and British correspondents who covered the wars in Afghanistan and Iraq. The founders of Al Jazeera Arabic and later Al Jazeera English (AJE) shared these reservations and promised to follow different practices and to present the true facts and the real picture of what was happening in the battlefields.

Scholars working on the media roles in conflict resolution and reconciliation also suggested that AJE may be performing reconciliation roles in contemporary global confrontations, particularly those that developed in the Middle East and the Muslim world following the terror attacks of 9/11.[5] OCL provides an excellent opportunity to test all these hypotheses. This chapter attempts to answer three questions:

1. Was AJE coverage of OCL different from the Western media coverage of recent wars, and to what extent did the relatively new and promising network cover OCL accurately and fairly?
2. Did the OCL coverage follow the principles of peace journalism and conciliatory media?
3. In covering OCL, did AJE live up to its Code of Ethics?

Most research on AJE in general and coverage of OCL in particular presented data and arguments from an Arab or Muslim perspective. The basic thesis has been that the Western media coverage was distorted and biased in favor of Israel and that only AJE presented and described the true facts on the ground.[6] This work presents the topic from an Israeli perspective. It demonstrates many problems in the AJE coverage of OCL and raises questions about the claims made about the network's contributions to accurate, unbiased, and conciliatory coverage of conflicts and wars.

This chapter begins with a summary of relevant theories and principles of peace journalism and conciliatory media. It continues with the context of OCL as seen from an Israeli perspective. This section is important because professional coverage and the conciliatorily function require a presentation of context from the perspectives of both sides. The next section deals with the most critical issue of any contemporary war coverage: casualties and proportionality. A central part of the chapter explores issues of AJE framing of OCL via both content and comparative analysis. The concluding section uses the data and the theoretical approaches to assess AJE's performance in OCL.

Theoretical Approaches

Two theoretical models could serve to analyze AJE role in OCL: "war journalism" and the "conciliatory medium model." The first contrasts war journalism with peace journalism while the second is an application or extension of peace journalism to AJE. Both models provide effective criteria to assess AJE coverage of OCL.

Peace journalism argues that the media emphasize violence and refrain from legitimizing nonviolence and conflict resolution.[7] Journalists, scholars, and practitioners have criticized coverage of violence and offered alternative approaches. Several criticized just coverage of warfare, while others offered broader criticism and suggested more comprehensive approaches needed to confront coverage of the conflicts' wider dimensions. John Galtung argued that the media generally follow the "low road" of war journalism in reporting conflict: chasing wars, the elites that run them, and a "win-lose" outcome.[8] His alternative approach, the "high road" of peace journalism, focuses on conflict formation, the people from all sides who suffer from violence, and a "win-win" solution. According to Galtung, war journalism focuses on who advances and who capitulates at what cost to human lives and material. This coverage polarizes and escalates because it calls for hatred and more violence to avenge or stop "them." It sees "them" as the problem and dehumanizes "them."

War journalism is driven by propaganda and manipulation and is, therefore. biased and distorted. In contrast, Galtung wrote, peace journalism explores the reasons behind the violence and provides a voice to all parties, as well as empathy and understanding. It focuses on suffering on the whole and humanizes all sides. Peace journalism is more truthful and attempts to deescalate violence by highlighting peace and conflict resolution as much as violence.

Similarly, Ross Howard distinguished between "traditional journalism" and "conflict-sensitive journalism."[9] The first covers only "the bare facts," while the second also explores solutions, new ideas, and new voices. Traditional journalism presents only bad news, does not seek other sides or points of view, assigns blame, uses emotional language such as terrorism or massacre, and takes sides. On the other hand, conflict-sensitive journalism presents balanced reports and only what is known; it uses words carefully and refrains from emotional terms, seeks explanation and comment from all sides, and looks for solutions.

Simon Cottle suggested that under certain conditions, the media can perform a conciliatory role in conflicts, both domestic and international.[10] His model includes seven components: (1) Exposing events or actions that the mainstream media ignores; (2) Inspiring public debates among ruling and opposition leaders of parties and groups; (3) Conducting interviews without fear or censorship; (4) Using personal accounts and testimonies; (5) Reconciling the past with the present; (6) Willingness and ability to criticize itself and other media; (7) Ability to interact in a globalized world with the aim of dismantling historically and anachronistic images of the "other."

Building on the principles of peace journalism and reconciliatory media, Mohammed el-Nawawy and Shawn Powers defined "conciliatory media" as media that "deviates from the 'war journalism' style...and instead contributes to creating an environment that is more conducive to cooperation, negotiation and reconciliation."[11] They further suggested that this type of media "can help alleviate tensions grounded in stereotype and myth and enhance a global understanding of events in ways that encourage open-mindedness among audiences." A medium may become conciliatory if it follows the following 11 principles:

1. Providing a public place for politically underrepresented groups;
2. Providing multiple viewpoints on a diversity of controversial issues;
3. Representing the interests of the international public in general, rather than a specific group of people;
4. Providing firsthand observations from eyewitnesses of international events;
5. Covering stories of injustice in the world;
6. Acknowledging mistakes in journalistic coverage when appropriate;
7. Demonstrating a desire toward solving rather than escalating conflicts;
8. Avoiding the use of victimizing terms, such as martyr or pathetic, unless they are attributed to a reliable source;
9. Avoiding the use of demonizing labels, such as terrorist or extremist, unless they are attributed to a reliable source;
10. Abstaining from presenting opinions that are not substantiated by credible evidence;
11. Providing background, contextualizing information that helps viewers fully understand the story.

It is easy to discern, however, that several of these principles, such as 2, 4, or 10 belong to principles of any reliable professional journalism, while several others, ostensibly the more unique characteristics, such as 8 or 9, clearly negate the principles of peace journalism. Principle 3 is also problematic; who determines the "interests of the international public"?

El-Nawawy and Powers used interviews with AJE journalists and viewers in several countries and have determined that AJE has adopted many of their 11 characteristics, "and thus it may prove to provide a conciliatory function when it comes to covering politically and culturally divisive issues". Obviously, general interviews and surveys are insufficient to support this argument. Only analysis of several specific cases and events that must include content analysis can help to determine whether AJE is a conciliatory medium. OCL provides an excellent opportunity to test the el-Nawawy and Powers thesis.

CONTEXT AND BACKGROUND

One of the main principles of both peace journalism and conciliatory medium is the responsibility of the media to provide adequate context and background for events and processes. Israel argued that before, during, and after OCL, AJE failed to provide the necessary context for any understanding of the operation, and that omitted and ignored significant issues including the Hamas charter and approach to Jews and Israel, the Hamas deliberate missile attacks on Israel cities and towns since 2001, the Israeli withdrawal from Gaza in 2005, the smuggling of weapons, rockets, and missiles to Gaza via tunnels dug beneath the border between Gaza and Egypt, the military alliance with Iran and the capturing and holding of an Israeli soldier—Gilad Shalit.

The Hamas charter adopted in 1988 is one of the most extreme anti-Semitic and anti-Israeli documents ever written and distributed. Select articles dealing with Jews and Israel appear in Appendix 1. Hamas denies any right to the Jews in any part of the land of Israel. It wrote that the conflict with Israel is religious and political, between Muslims and the Jewish "infidels." All of Palestine is Muslim and no one has the right to give it up. Jihad (holy war) is the only way to "liberate" Palestine. The charter is filled with overt anti-Semitism. The Jewish people have only negative traits, are controlling the world including the international media, and are responsible for all the wars and disasters of the twentieth century.

In accord with its charter, Hamas rejects the Oslo peace process and all the agreements Israel signed with the PLO and the Palestinian authority. It opposes peace, any compromise with Israel, and any Israeli-Palestinian negotiations. Hamas's stated goal is to destroy Israel and replace it with a theocratic Islamic Palestinian state. It preaches hatred and violence on all its media outlets, in mosques and schools, and carries out numerous terrorist attacks on Israeli civilians. It has also turned Gaza into a frontal Iranian base.[12] Hamas fighters are trained in Iran and the organization receives substantial annual sums of money from Iran. In violation of all rules and laws of warfare and international law, Hamas has deliberately fired missiles against Israeli civilians from within densely populated areas in Gaza, and is holding an Israeli soldier, Gilad Shalit, denying him the privileges granted to prisoners of war by the Geneva Convention, such as visits by representatives of the International Red Cross and correspondence with relatives. Due to its extremist ideology and violence, Hamas has been placed on a list of terrorist organizations by the United States and many countries in Europe.

AJE frequently uses the term "Israeli occupation" even in reference to Gaza. This is misleading because Israel withdrew its citizens and soldiers from Gaza in August 2005. At the time, there were 8,000 Israeli settlers living in 21 villages. All the villages were destroyed. The Israeli disengagement, as the withdrawal was called, was controversial in Israel because the right opposed it, and the left thought that any Israeli territorial withdrawal should be pursued in return for reciprocal Palestinian steps toward peace. In January 2006, there was a dramatic change in Palestinian politics. Hamas won the Palestinian Parliamentary elections and established with Fatah a Government of National Unity. Between June 7 and 15, 2007, however, Hamas used brutal force to assume sole control over Gaza. It was estimated that Hamas killed over 100 Fatah members and wounded over 500. Hamas cruelty and brutality surfaced when they threw Fatah members from buildings to the ground or shot them in the knees.[13] For Israel, after the takeover, Gaza became an enemy entity.

Despite the withdrawal and the Hamas takeover of Gaza, Israel continued to supply basic commodities to the residents of Gaza including electricity, fuel, food, medicine, and water. This supply is probably unprecedented in the history of warfare. A country was supplying the basic commodities to an enemy during a state of war. Despite the withdrawal and the aid, Hamas and other radical Palestinian organizations such as the Islamic Jihad continued and even escalated the firing of rockets and mortar shells into Israeli cities and towns. Figure 8.1 shows the number of rockets and shells fired by year from 2001 to 2010. In 2008 alone, prior to OCL, almost 2,500 rockets and shells were fired. The weapons weren't accurate; Israel invested considerable resources to protect its citizens, and, therefore, the number of civilians killed and the damage were limited. Yet, no government can tolerate this continuing type of terrorism deliberately directed against 1 million citizens.

It is crucial then to establish the correct causation between provocation and response. Israel imposed a partial blockade over Gaza only because of the missile attacks. If there were no attacks, there wouldn't have been a blockade. Egypt shared the Israeli concern about Hamas conduct and violence, and for its own reasons imposed a similar blockade on its border with Gaza. Obviously, ordinary life became difficult due to Hamas's autocratic regime and the indiscriminate attacks on Israel. The

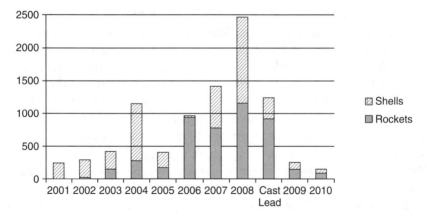

Total: 9,070 (4728 Rockets and 4342 Mortar Shells)

Figure 8.1 Rockets and Mortar Shells Per Year

Source: Jerusalem: Israel Ministry of Foreign Affairs, 2010. http://www.mfa.gov.il/MFA/Terrorism-+Obstacle+to+Peace/Hamas+war+against+Israel/Missile+fire+from+Gaza+on+Israeli+civilian+targets+Aug+2007.htm

isolation of Hamas and the sanctions failed, however, and the attacks on Israeli cities and towns continued. The people in the targeted areas exerted enormous pressure on the government to stop Hamas terrorism.

Unfortunately, none or very little of this important context appeared in the AJE coverage. Since context is a crucial element in peace journalism and conciliatory media, AJE failed this test. It focused only on the tragic consequences and human suffering of the Palestinians during OCL. It failed to question Hamas ideology and practice, and its responsibility for the death and destruction. Given this context, at least in Israeli eyes, the people of Gaza also have to share responsibility for the suffering. They voted for Hamas knowing well where its political platform and use of force will lead them.

CASUALTIES AND PROPORTIONALITY

One of the major claims repeatedly made by AJE and other networks was that Israel employed disproportionate force in Gaza. Proportionality has always been a significant factor in the evaluation of warfare. Even if an actor has the right to self-defense, it must be executed in full compliance with the laws of wars and international law. Proportionality and the status of citizens in combat zones are covered in various laws and conventions. Terrorist organizations, like Hamas, however, are playing a double game with the laws of war; they demand adherence from states but exempt themselves.

Proportionality is based primarily on cost in human life and destruction. A comparison between the Palestinian and the Israeli casualties was often used to support the claim that Israel was using disproportional force in OCL. The number and the identity of the Palestinian casualties has been a subject of much debate and controversy. At the end of OCL, Hamas first announced that 1,330 Gazans were killed. At the end of February 2009, this number increased to 1,414 and then again to 1,452.[14] The two increases weren't supported by any evidence of new discoveries of bodies or death of wounded people. Hamas didn't provide information on its own casualties and explained that it wouldn't do so "until victory."

A thorough Israeli investigation of names, affiliation, and employment of every casualty yielded the following results: a total of 1,166 Palestinian were killed; 709, the great majority, were Hamas combatants and officials of the security services, and members of other terrorist organizations such as Islamic Jihad; 295 noncombatants were killed, 89 of them under the age of 16, 49 women, and 157 men whose involvement in the battle is unclear.[15] In November 2010, Hamas interior minister Fathi Hamad confirmed the results of the Israeli investigation. He said in an interview with the London-based Arabic language daily *Al-Hayat* that 250 of its police officers were killed in addition to the 200–300 members of the Al-Qassam Brigade and 150 security personnel.[16] Thus, about 70 percent of the Palestinian casualties were combatants or members of the security services and only 30 percent were civilians.

The proportionality debate also failed to note the reasons for the ratio between Palestinian and Israeli casualties. They can be easily found in diametrically opposed approaches of Hamas and Israel toward military strategies, life, and death. While Israel made every possible effort to protect its people, both soldiers and civilians, from Hamas fire, the latter did everything it could to increase the number of casualties in Gaza by firing and fighting from schools, mosques, private homes, and even from hospitals. In yet additional flagrant violation of the laws and rules of war, Hamas fighters didn't wear uniforms, thus making every Gazan civilian a suspect. Under these difficult and challenging circumstances, contrary to Hamas' disregard for human life, the Israeli military made endless efforts to refrain from hurting noncombatants. Ahead of numerous military actions that had be taken in heavily populated areas, the IDF warned Palestinians to leave war zones via phone calls to their homes, dropping leaflets and broadcasting messages. In view of all these facts, during OCL, Israel employed measured and proportional force.[17]

It should be noted that several human rights organizations, Palestinian, Israeli, and global, including, for example, Human Rights

Watch and Amnesty International, accepted the Hamas figures without performing serious investigations of their own.[18] The Goldstone Committee, established by the UN Council on Human Rights to investigate alleged Israeli war crimes in OCL, cited the false figures of Hamas and the human rights organizations, also without performing a serious investigation of their own.[19] The Goldstone Committee included members such as Christine Chinkin from the UK and Hina Jilani from Pakistan who already made up their mind even before the investigation started. For these reasons Israel decided not to cooperate with the committee. The committee report accused Israel of deliberately targeting civilians in OCL and enormously damaged Israel's image and reputation in the world. The report, however, is filled with fabricated facts, questionable testimonies, false accusations, and baseless conclusions, and consequently was severely criticized and discredited.[20] On April 1, 2011, Richard Goldstone, the committee chair himself, retracted the report's conclusions, including the accusation of deliberate targeting of civilians.[21]

FRAMING ANALYSIS

Framing has become one of the dominant theories of media effects. Entman defined framing in the following way: "Selecting and highlighting some facets or events or issues, and making connections among them so as to promote a particular interpretation, evaluation, and or solution."[22] Unlike the earlier theory of "agenda setting," which suggests that the media only tells audiences what issues to think about, framing suggests that the media takes a position on controversial issues, and it tells audiences what to think about the issues. Framing demonstrates the power of contemporary media to shape and influence public opinion. Application of framing analysis reveals how the media present and package messages with the aim of affecting public opinion and ultimately the attitudes of politicians and policymakers.

Blondheim and Shifman suggested that both Hamas and Israel attempted to influence the framing of OCL via three main scripts: power, vulnerability, and disaster.[23] Power refers to courage, persistence, performance, and determination to win the battle. Vulnerability refers to actual and perceived threats and capabilities to cope with them. Disaster means severe breakdown in basic necessities of life, supplies, and services including shelter, food, medicine. Hamas employed all the three types of scripts but focused on the humanitarian one. Israel attempted to project vulnerability due to the years of Hamas missile attacks on cities and towns, and denying the scope of disaster claimed by Hamas. All of these attempts have failed. During and after OCL, Hamas deliberately concealed the identity of its casualties. The purpose was to blur the lines between combatants and noncombatants and thus to support the false claim that Israel was targeting the whole people of Gaza, not just Hamas fighters. AJE fully adopted the Hamas humanitarian disaster framing and casualties' strategy. It accepted without any questioning the Hamas causality figures and didn't make any effort to investigate who were killed and wounded and under what circumstances.

Framing analysis of the AJE coverage was conducted via two methods: content analysis and comparative analysis. Content analysis focused on a purposive sample of articles from AJE website. Articles that contain the word "Gaza" published during and after OCL, from December 27, 2008, to January 31, 2009. This procedure yielded a total of 21 articles. All the pieces presented one-sided, highly biased, and inflammatory accounts of what was happening on the ground. Typical Headlines include the following: "Where is Humanity? Who Will Save Israel from Itself?," "Israel's Other Voices Go Unheard," "Palestinian Men Bare the Trauma of War," "In the United States, Gaza Is a Different War," "Palestinian Factions United by War," "War Crimes Conviction after Gaza, in Lebanon We Are All Gaza."

Before and during OCL, the Israeli public fully supported the need to stop once and for all the constant missile attacks by Hamas on Israeli cities and towns and alleviate the daily fear of about 1 million people living within the effective range of the missiles. Public opinion polls reveal that about 80 percent of the public supported the operation. A few activists, mostly from the Israeli left and the radical left, opposed OCL demonstrated in Tel Aviv against the Israeli government. AJE amplified the opposition yet cited complaints as if the dissenters didn't get a fair hearing on the Israeli media. On January 7, AJE asserted: "Israel's 'other voices' go unheard, in a climate of widespread support; Israeli opposition to the war struggles to be heard." In another AJE report, titled: "Who Will Save Israel from Itself," the network cited several Israeli or former Israeli radicals, scholars, such as Neve Gordon from Ben Gurion University and Avi Shlaim from Oxford, or journalists Gideon Levi and Amira Haas from *Ha'aretz*, considered in Israel as extreme, hostile persons.

There were no similar reports on any opposition to Hamas policy, strategy, and responsibility for the violence, either because there weren't or because AJE was unwilling to find or broadcast them. On the contrary, in many reports, AJE cited Gazans who expressed support and admiration for Hamas "resistance." For example, on January 10, Tel el Hawa Hamoudi was quoted as saying: "I don't support Hamas. I hate politics. I've hated it all my life. But Hamas has no other option but to resist. Dying for the Palestinian cause is something noble. They are fighting back fiercely because it is the only option they have. They're an Islamic movement and feel they have nothing to lose, because they'll go to heaven." These statements without any comment glorified death and sacrifice so dominant in Hamas theological and political preaching.

AJE widely disseminated without any criticism one of the most ridiculous and outrageous descriptions of the operation: comparing the Israeli incursion to the Nazi atrocities in Poland and Hamas fighting to the January 1943 Jewish uprising in the Warsaw Ghetto. This comparison surfaced in Gaza and the Arab world shortly after the beginning of OCL. One of Hamas prominent leaders, Mahmoud al-Zahar, was the first Arab leader to make the comparison. On January 16, 2009, at the Doha summit, Syrian leader Bashar Al-Assad also stated that the Gaza war was part of a conspiracy to turn Israel into a purely Jewish state, and described this as "the most dangerous brand of Nazism in the modern era."

The comparison between Gaza and the Warsaw Ghetto was absurd on its face. No Jewish organization had ever sworn to destroy Germany and turn it into a Jewish state. No Jewish organization had ever fired thousands of rockets at Germany towns and cities. No Jewish organization had sent suicide bombers into Germany and slaughtered hundreds of Germans while they went about their lawful business. No Gazans were systematically exterminated as were most of the Jews living in the Warsaw Ghetto. Only on February 2, AJE published an article by Mark Levine who still criticized Israel but refuted the Gaza-Warsaw Ghetto analogy. This was too little and too late.

Several AJE reports presented false information as if it were verified and correct. For example, On January 20, Shane Bauer reported from Damascus: "Israel says it has dealt Hamas a crippling blow, but its 22-day onslaught that *killed around 1,300 civilians* and injured at least 6.000 more has brought together a slew of Palestinian factions" (emphasis added). For this AJE reporter, not even a single Hamas fighter participated in the battle, and all the casualties were innocent Palestinian civilians.

The second method employed to analyze AJE framing was to compare its coverage of OCL with coverage of another major global network. The BBC coverage was selected for this comparison. The BBC is considered one of the most professional and reliable global networks. It is by no means a pro-Israeli network. On the contrary, various reports showed that occasionally it exhibited a pro-Palestinian and anti-Israeli bias.[24] A comparison of the AJE and the BBC Timelines of OCL reveals interesting differences. Here are a few typical examples. AJE reported on the first day of the violence, December 27: "Israel begins assault on Gaza, code-named 'Operation Cast Lead,' by launching air raids that kill more than 225 Palestinians." BBC reported in the following way: "Gaza City: Israel launched a wave of air and missile attacks on targets across Gaza. Some 225 people were killed according to local medics. Most are policemen within the Hamas militant movement." Netivot (an Israeli town): "One man killed, several injured in Palestinian rocket attack." Note that AJE failed to identify the Palestinians killed, while the BBC correctly identified them as members of the Hamas security forces. Unlike the BBC, AJE also failed to name the source of the information about the attack, and also the casualties in Israel. AJE mislead its viewers and readers who could have thought that those killed were civilians and that there was no killing and suffering on the other side.

On the second day of OCL, AJE reported the following: "Israeli aircraft bomb the Islamic University in Gaza City and the length of the Gaza-Egypt border, taking out more than 40 tunnels used to smuggle vital goods to the strip." BBC mentioned the strike against "tunnels running between Egypt and Gaza." The AJE reporting was distorted and misleading because the tunnels were primarily used to smuggle weapons and not "vital goods." Also, AJE failed to provide information about the Islamic University in Gaza, which was a Hamas semimilitary base.

On January 1, 2009, AJE reported: "Hamas official Nizar Rayyan is killed along with 14 members of his family in an Israeli raid." Rayyan was one of the top Hamas leaders and an enthusiastic advocate of suicide bombing in Israel. BBC said: "A senior Hamas leader, Nizar Rayyan, was killed in an air strike with at least nine people, including several members of his family. More than 30 rockets fired, including at least one landing in Ashdod and two in Beersheba." Unlike BBC, AJE demoted Rayyan, provided inflated causality figures, and omitted the Palestinian deliberate attacks on Israeli cities and towns.

Another typical example of inaccurate reporting could be found in the January 6 coverage. AJE reported: "An Israeli strike on a UN school in the northern town of Jabaliya kills 43 Palestinians and injures at least 100 who had taken refuge inside the school. Israel strikes hit two other schools, killing two in the Southern town of Khan Younis and three in the Shati refugee camp in Gaza city." Here is how the BBC reported the incident: "At least 40 people were killed—including children—and 55 injured when Israel artillery shells landed outside an UN-run al-Fakhura school in the Jabaliya refugee camp. UN Officials said the school was being used as a refuge for hundreds of people. Israel said its soldiers had come under fire from militants inside the school. A spokesman for Hamas denied there had been any hostile fire coming from the school." Note that AJE said the attack was *on the school* while BBC said an Israeli shell *landed outside the school*. The facts in this incident were as follows: three Israeli shells directed at Hamas combatants firing rockets into Israel from a corner near the UN school landed near them, killed 9, and regrettably also 3 (not 40) nearby civilians.[25]

One month later, the BBC timeline added the following corrective update: "In February 2009, the UN said that a clerical error had led it to report that Israeli mortars had struck a UN run school in Jabaliya, Gaza on January 6, killing about 40 people. Maxwell Gaylord, the UN humanitarian coordinator in Jerusalem, said that the IDF mortars fell in the street near the compound, and not on the compound itself. He said that the UN 'would like to clarify that the shelling and all the fatalities took place outside and not inside the school.'" AJE's message couldn't be clearer. Israel deliberately targeted schools where innocent civilians took refuge, and never bothered to correct the false reporting. The BBC reported on a shell falling outside the school, cited various sources, including Israeli sources, and corrected the false reporting of AJE and other networks after the UN issued a correcting statement.

On several occasions, AJE criticized coverage by other media outlets, primarily the Western ones. For example, Eric Margolis stated on January 5 that Israel succeeded in selling OCL to the Western media as an "antiterrorist operation." He also criticized the Western media for omitting facts about the suffering of the people in Gaza. Similarly, two days later, in a piece titled "In the US, Gaza Is a Different War," Habib Battah accused the mainstream U.S. media of prioritizing Israel's version of the conflict. He also argued that the U.S. media failed to provide an appropriate context, ignored the Palestinian perspective and didn't sufficiently cover the Palestinian suffering. He even added to television news production a new criterion: allocating reporting minutes by the number of casualties. He complained: "Major television channels also adopted the equal time approach, despite the reality that Palestinian casualties exceeded Israeli ones by a hundred fold." Contrary to principle nine in the el-Nawawy and Powers model of conciliatory medium, AJE criticized the other networks but never acknowledged its own mistakes in the coverage of OCL.

CONCLUSIONS

First Al Jazeera, and then AJE promised to bring a new and fresh voice into the international arena. The founders and directors of AJE declared that the network would challenge the Western global networks such as BBC World and CNN International blamed for being biased against

Arabs and Muslims. They said AJE would provide a more accurate and less distorted picture of what is happening in the Middle East and in Muslim countries. They said they would adhere to high standards of professional journalism, free of manipulation, pressure, and censorship so prevalent in the Arab media (see Appendix 2). At the same time, the founders and directors of AJE promised to genuinely represent the interests and public voices of Arabs and Muslims.

All these statements and promises inspired considerable enthusiasm about the network among scholars and commentators.[26] Several even described AJE as practicing peace journalism, and serving as a conciliatory medium in contemporary regional and international conflicts. This study shows, however, that at least in OCL, AJE failed to meet the criteria of peace journalism and reconciliatory media, and perhaps even violated several of the articles listed in its Code of Ethics (Appendix 2). In this particular warfare, AJE's coverage followed the typical symptoms of war journalism. The network failed to provide adequate context of the events leading to OCL, broadcast only bad news, didn't present other points of view, assigned blame, employed emotional language, used terms such as massacres and war crimes, refrained from recommending peaceful solutions, glorified martyrdom and death, took sides and primarily conducted a campaign on behalf of Hamas and the Palestinians. During OCL the imperative of representing the Palestinian cause overtook the code of ethics.

AJE prided itself on being an independent channel ready to challenge any Arab leader and any Arab policy. In practice, it never questioned Hamas's hateful and anti-Semitic charter, never criticized Hamas's strategy of deliberately attacking Israeli cities and towns and terrorizing the population of Gaza. AJE never criticized Hamas for its opposition to negotiations and peace with Israel, its repeated calls for death and sacrifice and use of Gazans as human shields. AJE uncritically used Hamas official sources, while systematically ignoring the Israeli side. AJE glorified the culture of violence, sacrifice, and death preached by Hamas and systematically delegitimized and dehumanized Israel. Finally, AJE didn't preset scenarios of peace and didn't support peace initiatives.

All of these characteristics are exactly opposite the practices of peace journalism and conciliatory medium.[27] Given all these failures, and the results of the framing comparative analysis, viewers and readers of BBC World and CNN International and other global networks received a much more accurate and balanced picture of OCL than did those of AJE. AJE may have positively contributed to certain areas of broadcasting about the Arab world. Unfortunately, so far this hasn't been the case for the Arab-Israeli conflict.

APPENDIX 1: HAMAS CHARTER, 1988, ARTICLES ON JEWS AND ISRAEL

Article 13

[Diplomatic] initiatives, the so-called peaceful solutions and international conferences to find a solution to the Palestinian problem, contradict the Islamic Resistance Movement's ideological position. Giving up any part whatsoever of [the land of] Palestine is like ignoring a part of [the Muslim] faith...Thus such conferences are but one of the means used by the infidels to prevail over Muslim land, and when have the infidels treated the faithful justly? There is no solution to the Palestinian problem except jihad. Regarding the international initiatives, suggestions and conferences, they are an empty waste of time and complete nonsense".

Article 20

That is the Islamic spirit that must prevail in Muslim society. A society facing a cruel enemy who behaves like a Nazi that does not distinguish between man and woman, young and old, must wrap itself in such an Islamic spirit. For our enemy relies on collective punishment. It deprives people [i.e., the Palestinians] of their homes and possessions. It hunts them down in exile and wherever they gather. [The Zionist enemy] relies on breaking bones, shooting women, children and old people, with or without a reason. He opened detention camps to throw into them many thousands of people [i.e., Palestinians], [who live there] in sub-human conditions. In addition, he destroys homes, turns children into orphans and unjustly convicts thousands of young people so that they may spend the best years of their lives in the dark pits of their jails...The Jews' Nazism includes [brutal behavior toward Palestinian] women and children and terrifies the entire [population]. They battle against [the Palestinians'] making a living, extort their money and trample their honor. In their behavior [toward these people] they are as bad as the worst war criminals.

Article 22

Thus [the Jews], by means of their money, have taken over the international communications media: the news agencies, newspapers, publishing houses, broadcasting stations, etc. [Not only that,] they used their money to incite revolutions in various places all over the world for their own interests and to reap the fruits thereof. They were behind the French Revolution, the Communist Revolution and most of the revolutions we have heard about [that happened here and there]. They used their money to found secret organizations and scattered them all over the globe to destroy other societies and realize the interests of Zionism. [Such organizations] include the Freemasons, the Rotary clubs [sic], the Lions [Club], The Sons of the Covenant [i.e., B'nai Brith] and others. They are all destructive espionage organizations which, by means of money, succeeded in taking over the imperialist countries and encouraged them to take over many other countries to be able to completely exploit their resources and spread corruption…they were behind the First World War, through which achieved the abolishment of the Islamic Caliphate, made a profit and took over many of the sources of wealth. They [also] got the Balfour Declaration and established the League of the United [sic] Nations to be able rule the world. They were also behind the Second World War, in which they made immense profits by buying and selling military equipment, and also prepared the ground for the founding of their [own] state. They ordered the establishment of the United Nations and the Security Council [sic] which replaced the League of the United [sic] Nations, to be able to use it to rule the world. No war takes place anywhere in the world without [the Jews] behind the scenes having a hand in it [as it is written in the Qur'an:] "Whenever they fan the flames of war, Allah will extinguish them. They strive [to fill] the land with corruption and Allah does not like the corrupt".

Article 31

Those who believe in the three [monotheistic] religions, Islam, Christianity and Judaism, can live side by side under the aegis of Islam in security and safety, for only under the aegis of Islam can there be complete security.

Article 32

World Zionism and the forces of imperialism are trying in a subtle way and with carefully studied planning, to remove the Arab states, one by one, from the sphere of the conflict with Zionism, eventually of isolating the Palestinian people. The aforementioned forces have already removed Egypt to a large extent, through the treacherous Camp David accords [September 1978]. They are now trying to draw other [Arab] states into [signing] similar agreements, so that they may also be outside the conflict…

The Zionist plan has no limit; after Palestine [the Zionists] aspire to expand to the Nile and the Euphrates. Once they have devoured the region they arrive at, they will aspire to spread further and [then] on and on. Their plan [or plot appears] in The Protocols of the Elders of Zion and their present [behavior] is [the best] proof of what we are saying. Therefore, leaving the conflict with the Zionists is [an act of] high treason and a curse which rests upon whoever [does so].

Source: http://www.terrorism-info.org.il/malam_multimedia /English/eng_n/pdf/hamas_charter.pdf

APPENDIX 2: AJE CODE OF ETHICS

Being a globally oriented media service, Al Jazeera shall adopt the following code of ethics in pursuance of the vision and mission it has set for itself:

1. Adhere to the journalistic values of honesty, courage, fairness, balance, independence, credibility and diversity, giving no priority to commercial or political over professional consideration.
2. Endeavour to get to the truth and declare it in our dispatches programmes and news bulletins unequivocally in a manner which leaves no doubt about its validity and accuracy.
3. Treat our audiences with due respect and address every issue or story with due attention to present a clear, factual and accurate picture while giving full consideration to the feelings of victims of crime, war, persecution and disaster, their relatives and our viewers, and to individual privacies and public decorum.
4. Welcome fair and honest media competition without allowing it to affect adversely our standards of performance and thereby having a "scoop" would not become an end in itself.
5. Present the diverse points of view and opinions without bias and partiality.
6. Recognise diversity in human societies with all their races, cultures and beliefs and their values and intrinsic individualities so as to present unbiased and faithful reflection of them.
7. Acknowledge a mistake when it occurs, promptly correct it and ensure it does not recur.
8. Observe transparency in dealing with the news and its sources while adhering to the internationally established practices concerning the rights of these sources.
9. Distinguish between news material, opinion and analysis to avoid the snares of speculation and propaganda.
10. Stand by colleagues in the profession and give them support when required, particularly in the light of the acts of aggression and harassment to which journalists are subjected at times. Cooperate with Arab and international journalistic unions and associations to defend freedom of the press.

Source: Al Jazeera: http://english.aljazeera.net/aboutus/2006/11 /200852518573369277l.html. Reprinted by permission of AJE.

Notes

1. Research for this study was supported by the Center for International Communication at Bar-Ilan University. The author thanks Chen Pikholz-Ran and Roi Duani for their research assistance.

2. See, for example, A Speech by Hamas leader Fathi Hamad on February 29, 2008, Broadcast by Hamas Al-Aqsa Television: http://www.youtube .com/watch?v=g0wJXf2nt4Y For additional videotapes see http://www .youtube.com/watch?v=J08GqXMr3YE&NR=1 http://www.youtube .com/watch?v=kBYtij4Q7sE&feature=related, Children of Hams, http://www.youtube.com/watch?v=eTGbP55HGi8&feature=related

3. Philip Knightley, *The First Casualty* (New York: Brace Jovanovich, 1975).

4. Howard Tumber and Marina Prentoulis, *Journalism and the End of Objectivity* (London: Bloomsbury Academic, 2012).

5. Mohammed el-Nawawy and Shawn Powers, *Mediating Conflict: Al-Jazeera English and the Possibility of a Conciliatory Media* (Los Angeles: Figueroa Press, 2008); Mohammed el-Nawawy and Shawn Powers, "Al-Jazeera English and Global News Networks: Clash of Civilizations or Cross-cultural Dialogue?" *Media, War & Conflict* 2 (2009): 263–284.

6. Catherine Cassara and Laura Lengel, "Move over CNN: Al Jazeera's View of the World Takes on the West," *Transnational Broadcasting Studies* 12 (2004), http://www.tbsjournal.com/Archives/Spring04 /cassara_lengel.htm; Philip Seib, "Hegemonic No More: Western Media, the Rise of Al-Jazeera, and the Influence of Diverse Voices," *International Studies Review* 7 (2005): 601–615; Leon Barkho, "Unpacking the Discursive and Social Links in BBC, CNN and Al-Jazeera's Middle East Reporting," *Journal of Arab & Muslim Media Research* 1 (1) (2007): 11–29; Magdalena E. Wojcieszak, "Al Jazeera: A Challenge to Traditional Framing Research," *International Communication Gazette* 69 (2) (2007): 115–128.

7. Jake Lynch and Annabel McGoldrick, *Peace Journalism* (Stroud, UK: Hawthorn Press 2005).

8. John Galtung, "Peace Journalism—A Challenge," in *Journalism and the New World Order: Studying War and the Media*, ed. William Kempf and Heikki Luostarinen (Goteborg, Sweden: Nordicom, 2002), 259–272.

9. Ross Howard, *Conflict Sensitive Journalism* (Vancouver, BC: Institute for Media, Policy, and Civil Society, 2003).

10. Simon Cottle, *Mediatized Conflict* (Berkshire, UK: Open University Press, 2006).

11. Mohammed el-Nawawy and Shawn Powers, "Al-Jazeera English: A Conciliatory Medium in a Conflict-Driven Environment?" *Global Media and Communication* 6 (2010): 69.

12. Marie Colvin, "Hamas Wages Iran's Proxy War on Israel," *Sunday Times*, March 9, 2008, http://www.timesonline.co.uk/tol/news/world /middle_east/article3512014.ece

13. Bill Van Esveld, Fred Abrahams, and Darryl Li, *UnderCover of War: Hamas Political Violence in Gaza* (New York: Human RightsWatch, 2009), http://www.google.com/books?id=9ByHZHOmmWQC&print sec=frontcover&hl=iw#v=onepage&q&f=false.

14. *Palestinian Casualties, Operation Cast Lead.* Intelligence and Terrorism Information Center (Tel Aviv: Israel Intelligence Heritage and Commemoration Center, 2009), http://www.terrorism-info.org.il /malam_multimedia/English/eng_n/html/ipc_e021.htm

15. Israel Defense Forces, *Majority of Palestinians Killed in Operation Cast Lead: Terror Operatives,* March 26, 2009, http://dover.idf.il/IDF /English/News/today/09/03/2602.htm

16. "Report: Hamas Admits for First Time Losing More Than 600 Men in Gaza War," *Ha'aretz,* November 1, 2010, http://www.haaretz.com /news/diplomacy-defense/reporthamas-admits-for-first-time-losing -more-than-600-men-in-gaza-war 1.322249.

17. Alan M. Dershowitz, "Israel's Policy Is Perfectly 'Proportionate,'" *Wall Street Journal,* January 2, 2009, Opinion Section,http://online.wsj. com/article/SB123085925621747981.html; Michael J. Totten, "Gaza and the Law of Armed Conflict," *Commentary,* March 1, 2009, http:// www.commentarymagazine.com/2009/01/03/gaza-and-the-law-of -armed-conflict/; Justus Reid Weiner and Avi Bell, "The Gaza War of 2009: Applying International Humanitarian Law to Israel and Hamas," *San Diego International Law Journal* 11 (2009): 5–42.

18. Human rights organizations have issued questionable reports about Israel's conduct in the conflict with the Palestinians including reports on OCL. *NGO Gaza War Myths Revisited* (Jerusalem: NGO Monitor, 2010), http://www.ngo-monitor.org/article/ngo_gaza_war_myths_revisited

19. The UN Human Rights Council (UNHRC), which appointed the Committee, has been for a long time the most ridicules and irresponsible UN organization. It has been lead by "champions" of human rights such as Iran, Libya, Cuba, Saudi Arabia, China, and Russia and has focused disproportionally on Israel and the Palestinian-Israeli conflict. In March 2006, UNHRC replaced the ineffective and corrupt UN Commission for Human Rights, but sine then hasn't done much better. From 2006 to 2010, Israel had been condemned in 32 resolutions comprising 48 per-rcent of all resolutions passed. See reports by UN Watch: http://www .unwatch.org/site/c.bdKKISNqEmG/b.1289203/k.BDAE/Search /apps/s/search.asp

20. Peter Berkowitz, "The Goldstone Mess," *Policy Review* 166 (2011), http://www.hoover.org/publications/policy-review/article/73356; Dore Gold, *The UN Gaza Report: A Substantive Critique* (Jerusalem: Jerusalem Center for Public Affairs, 2009), http://www.jcpa.org /text/GoldGoldstone-5nov09.pdf; see also http://www.youtube .com/watch?v=NJhkWGZ5oB8 Richard Landes, "Goldstone's Gaza Report—Part One: A Failure of Intelligence," *Middle East Review*

of International Affairs 13 (2009), http://www.gloria-center.org /files/20100125102300.pdf; Richard Landes, Goldstone's Gaza Report—Part Two: A Miscarriage of Human Rights," *Middle East Review of International Affairs* 13 (2009), http://www.gloria-center .org/meria/2009/12/landes2.html; *The Main Findings of the Goldstone Report versus the Factual Findings* (Tel Aviv: Meir Amit Intelligence and Terrorism Information Service, 2010), http://www.terrorism-info.org.il /site/content/t1.asp?Sid=13&Pid=334

21. Richard Goldstone, "Reconsidering the Goldstone Report on Israel and War Crimes," *Washington Post*, April 1, 2011, http://www .washingtonpost.com/opinions/reconsidering-the-goldstone-report-on -israel-and-war-crimes/2011/04/01/AFg111JC_story.html

22. Robert Entman, "Framing: Toward Clarification of a Fractured Paradigm," *Journal of Communication* 43 (1993): 51–58.

23. Menahem Blondheim and Limor Shifman, "What Officials Say, What Media Show, and What Publics Get: Gaza, January 2009," *Communication Review* 12 (2009): 205–214.

24. *BBC Watch Reports,* http://www.bbcwatch.com/

25. See report in *Ha'aretz*, February 3, 2009, www.haaretz.com/hasen /spages/1061189/html

26. See, for example, Nalia Hamdy, "Arab Media Adopt Citizen Journalism to Change the Dynamics of Conflict Coverage," *Global Media Journal* 1 (2010): 3–15.

27. For several positive contributions of the media to Arab-Israeli peacemaking, see Eytan Gilboa, "Media Diplomacy in the Arab-Israeli Conflict," in *Media and Conflict: Framing Issues, Making Policy, Shaping Opinions*, ed. Eytan Gilboa (Ardsley, NY: Transnational, 2002), 193–211; Eytan Gilboa, "Media-Broker Diplomacy: When Journalists Become Mediators," *Critical Studies in Media Communication* 22 (2005): 99–120.

CHAPTER 9

AJE's Conciliatory Role: Covering the "Ground Zero Mosque" Controversy

Mohammed el-Nawawy

The proliferation of satellite news and the explosion of mediums of news consumption have created an environment where most viewers can tune into a broadcaster that describes news in ways they find to be culturally, politically, and ideologically agreeable. As a result, news broadcasters today are more likely to harden existing opinions and attitudes, encourage stereotypical thinking of cultural "others," create ideological disharmony among their audiences, and lead to increasingly isolated public spheres.[1]

This disharmony has often been exemplified in the media coverage of religiously driven conflicts. In this context, Bagir argued that "Unfortunately, more often than not, the media have played a negative role [in covering these conflicts] by aggravating [them] through...partial, biased and provocative news reporting as well as slanted opinions."[2]

Among this hardening media environment, one news organization stands out: Al Jazeera English (AJE), which is considered by many an anomaly when it comes to its journalistic mission and identity. It stands out from its competitors in that it presents a challenge to the existing paradigms guiding international news broadcasters. It is neither dominated by geopolitical nor commercial interests, and is the first of its kind to have the resources, mandate and journalistic capacity to reach out to typically isolated and ignored audiences throughout the world. It represents a challenge to "the myth of the mediated center," while providing a test case for examining the conciliatory potential of a global satellite channel.[3] AJE's model of journalism offers an alternative to today's mode of news journalism that continues to encourage stereotypical and counterproductive attitudes toward cultural "Others." AJE's programing represents a fresh break from the traditional news agenda of other global news giants.[4]

This chapter provides an assessment of the AJE website coverage of the controversy that surrounded the building of an Islamic center on Park 51 in New York City. Because of the center's proximity to Ground Zero, it has been referred to by most American media as the "Ground Zero Mosque." The chapter utilizes an 11-point scale outlining the characteristics of a media that can play a conciliatory role in society. The chapter tests this scale by using a qualitative textual analysis of the channel's website to investigate whether its coverage of the controversy provided a conciliatory function by creating a general culture of tolerance and encouraging reconciliation among the cultural antagonists involved in this controversy.

BACKGROUND OF THE "PARK 51 MOSQUE" CONTROVERSY

A proposal to build a US$100 million Islamic center, known as Cordoba House, on Park 51, in New York City's Lower Manhattan stirred a national controversy in the American media about whether a "Ground Zero Mosque" would be offensive to the families of the September 11 victims. "Some Sept. 11 victims' families and others view the proposed mosque site—in a building damaged by debris from the attacks—as very much part of the terrain of death and sorrow surrounding the trade center."[5] The proposed 100,000 square foot site is located "in a neighborhood that includes bars, strip clubs, and an off-track betting facility. Still, it is 'hallowed ground' to many who oppose the Islamic Center—including politicians using it to batter [U.S.] President [Barack] Obama."[6] Moreover, the proposed mosque "drew hundreds of fever-pitch demonstrators, with opponents carrying signs associating Islam with blood, supporters shouting, 'Say no to racist fear!' and American flags waving on both sides. Opponents demanded that the mosque be moved farther from the site where more than 2,700 people were killed on September 11, 2001... The dispute has sparked a national debate on religious freedom and American values."[7]

"The location of the proposed 13-story community center and mosque, at 51 Park Place (known as Park 51), is not part of Ground Zero, and isn't even visible from the former site of the World Trade Center."[8] In fact, the mosque is two blocks from Ground Zero and 300 yards from the World Trade Center memorial. The proposal's mastermind, Imam Feisal Abdul Rauf, is an American Muslim whose work is focused on interfaith dialogue and spiritual connections between the Muslim world and the West. "Cordoba House is a project of Rauf's organization, the Cordoba Initiative, whose name honors the tolerance among Muslims, Christians and Jews that flourished [under a Muslim caliphate] in the Spanish city of Cordoba a thousand years ago."[9] However, "critics seized on the name as a signal that Rauf... had Islamic hegemony in mind."[10]

This initiative captured the headlines of mainstream American media, which were divided between support and opposition to the project. According to Rauf, "A project meant to foster understanding has become unduly mired in conflict and what he described as misconceptions of a clash between Islamic and American values."[11] Generally, the American media coverage of Park 51 center was skewed. "While challenging some of the 'facts' that opponents put forward and refraining from calling for a ban on the community center, the more centrist [American] corporate media entertained the lies and bigotry of anti-Muslim forces to an alarming degree."[12] Some observers argued that the opposition to the Islamic center "can be attributed to Islamophobia and a media culture that is often receptive to it."[13]

A lead editorial in the *New York Daily News* exemplified the divisions surrounding the mosque controversy by citing a poll conducted by Quinnipiac University "showing that 54 percent of New Yorkers do believe...[Rauf, the key figure of the center proposal] has a constitutional free exercise-of-religion right to build the mosque...near Ground Zero. But [according to the poll] 53 percent, including many Muslims and supporters of the right to build believe 9/11 sensitivities (in those areas) should carry the day."[14] Another editorial published in the *New York Times* described the discourse surrounding the Islamic center's controversy as vitriolic commentary, pitting Muslims against Christians, Tea Partiers against staunch liberals, and September 11 families against one another.[15] A *Philadelphia Inquirer* editorial placed the Islamic center story "in the context of elevated anti-Muslim sentiment in the country since September 11, and the coinciding Islamophobic activism, which includes anti-mosque movements in...[various states] as well as in New York. The editorial described the opposition to building the center as "part of a larger movement to ban Islam in the U.S."[16]

In this context, Esposito noted that "Globalization and an increasingly multicultural and multireligious America (and Europe), with their significant Muslim populations, tests the mettle of Western democratic principles of free speech and freedom of worship."[17] According to Esposito, it is unfortunate that "American attitudes toward Islam and Muslims often blur the line between the peaceful and rational mainstream majority of Muslims on the one hand and the acts of a small but dangerous minority on the other...Why should Muslims who are building a center be any more suspect than Jews who build a synagogue or center or Christians who build a church or conference center?"[18]

Esposito, as cited in Salim, argued that "Publishing houses, journals, consulting firms, and the media seek out that which captures headlines and all too often confirms stereotypes and fears of extremism and terrorism. Think how often any reference to an Islamic organization inevitably includes adjectives like "fundamentalism," "conservativeness," and "extremist."[19] Along the same lines, Murphy argued that "for a significant minority, Islam itself—not the choices of some of its adherents—appears to be the foe. In essence,...[the proposal to build an Islamic center near Ground Zero] is a message of rejection to America's small but growing Muslim minority."[20] Alatas noted that the Western media very rarely focus on "inter-religious encounters of peace" despite the fact that such encounters have been common among Muslims, Christians and Jews. Media coverage of these encounters "would help all to restore their faith in the goodness of humanity."[21]

It is worth noting that President Barack Obama defended the proposal to build the Islamic center near Ground Zero and argued that "as a citizen, and as president, I believe that Muslims have the same right to practice their religion as anyone else in this country."[22] New York City mayor Michael Bloomberg also defended plans to build the center, which in addition to the prayer area would include a swimming pool, gymnasium, restaurant, and culinary school.[23] "Being American, [Bloomberg said], means holding tight to constitutional freedoms and the rule of law, especially under pressure to capitulate."[24]

COVERING CONFLICT IN A MASS-MEDIATED ENVIRONMENT

Today, rather than having a single network dominating the international news scape, satellite news broadcasters have popped up around the world, each with a slightly different take on international events. Narratives guiding the public's understanding of events are increasingly and more easily contested, and thus the "battle" to control the flow of information has become intense, particularly during times of conflict. As competition over the airwaves has increased, it has become especially difficult to discern under what circumstances particular broadcasters have influence, and among what audiences. With a plethora of news organizations broadcasting information around the world, it has become much easier for audiences to tune into the organization that is oftentimes aligned with their opinions and worldviews, a change in the news scape that calls into question whether news organizations are actually educating audiences or rather providing people with information that is simply used to further their preexisting opinions and attitudes.

Moreover, this expanded role for media in society presents newly formed challenges, especially in the context of international conflict. While media technologies have always played a role in international conflict, today's network society has dramatically increased the ways in which media technologies are utilized in conflicts, the number of media organizations producing and disseminating information during conflict, as well as the means to better monitor and understand mediated communications from afar.[25]

It is along these lines that Seib argues that "the connectivity of new media is superseding the traditional connections that have brought identity and structure to global politics."[26] Tumber and Webster describe the changes in terms of a move from the traditional forms of "industrial war" toward mass-mediated conflicts, or "information wars," placing the varied media outlets and technologies at the center of discussions of how to best navigate and understand contemporary international conflict. In short, they argue that the military assets alone no longer govern the outcome of international conflict, and success and failure are increasingly dependent on controlling the flow of information and the associated "hearts and minds" of the global citizenry.[27] Accordingly, media organizations are often being treated as actors within international conflicts, able to shape and refine opinions of people and even governments.

Between War and Peace Journalism

The news media "often give priority to conflict and war at the expense of playing a positive role in attempts to bring about peace."[28] The bureaucratic structure and professional constraints of news organizations make them prone to covering conflict. "News organizations recognize conflict and revolution more easily than they do slower, more subtle forms of social change...As story tellers, journalists constantly seek and exploit narrative tension. The time constraints of newsgathering make reliance on opposing sources a quick and simple way to tell stories across many content areas...Conflict, then, is not merely one of the types of stories that journalists cover; in many respects, it is the very mode through which journalists normally understand and interpret the world."[29] According to Pauly, "News work places journalists at the very nexus of political and social conflict...News offers condensed and powerful moral fables, in which violence figures as a narrative shorthand for the roles, motives, and ethics of the participants."[30] The quandary facing the news media, according to Simon Cottle, as cited in Pauly, "is that almost all forms of significant social conflict now have come to be 'mediatized'—that is, media 'are capable of enacting and performing conflicts as well as reporting and representing them.'"[31]

In this context, Gilboa argued that the media role in intensifying and worsening conflict can be reversed: "This reversal, however, is difficult to achieve. It is always easier to foment conflict than resolve it, and the media's role in conflict resolution is more complicated than the roles of those dominating the violence phase."[32]

Despite these challenges, scholars have argued for a new form of journalism—peace journalism—as a means of "de-escalation-oriented conflict coverage." This type of coverage "would have to include a self-critical and realistic view of own goals, and it must take into account that the opponent might also feel threatened and in acting in a defensive role."[33] Lynch and McGoldrick define peace journalism as that which takes place "when editors and reporters make choices—of what stories to report and about how to report them—that create opportunities for society at large to consider and value non-violent responses to conflict."[34] Galtung, a pioneer in the field of peace journalism studies, argues that media in times of conflict should focus on conflict transformation, a move the requires journalists who are empathetic and understanding; able to provide a platform for all parties and voices to express themselves; and focuses on the negative impact of violence, such as damage and trauma.[35] Similarly, Wolfsfeld notes that it is the responsibility of reporters in the war zones "to provide as much information as possible about the roots of the problem and to encourage a rational public debate concerning the various options for ending it."[36] Wolfsfeld explains that, at times, encouraging rational deliberation among alienated groups can encourage all parties to refrain from escalating violence and engage in thoughtful consideration of ways to end the conflict.[37]

It is also important to note that peace journalism authors are not calling for journalists to sanitize their coverage of conflicts, nor focus solely on calls for peace and cooperation. Rather, advocates argue that journalists describe violence in terms of its political, economic, and social motivations, rather than a natural or inevitable consequence of otherwise uncontrollable events. By exposing violence as either a dire or irresponsible choice for dealing with an existing conflict, peace journalists can encourage nonviolent responses to conflicts that are otherwise viewed through a highly politicized lens.[38]

A major weakness in the peace journalism literature is a failure among peace journalism scholars to consider the roles that collective identity—religious, ethnic, national, and transnational—can have on the propensity for groups to either take to violence or consider nonviolent solutions to conflicts. This oversight is especially problematic given the growing area of scholarship examining the role that media—especially electronic and new media—can have on the constitution and wherewithal of collective identities.[39] This oversight is particularly important given that the current war on terror, similar to the cold war before it, exemplifies the importance of examining the role of media not only in its coverage and investigation of the material aspects of war, but also in the construction and propagation of the underlying ideologies that are so influential in shaping the sociopolitical environments that can result in conflict.[40]

According to Bagir, peace journalism can be achieved in the media coverage of multicultural, multireligious, and multisectarian issues. To do so, journalists "have to penetrate deep into the hitherto terra incognita of the religious communities they report on. Indeed, there is no better way to understand a community than to mingle directly with the people ... [Moreover], exchange programs between journalists across religions have to be designed and carried out as much as possible ... [And] libraries of resources related to inter-religious issues as well as to media coverage of such issues have to be built and made easily accessible for journalists and editors."[41]

CONCILIATORY MEDIA SCALE

"Conciliatory media" is a term that was coined by el-Nawawy and Powers, and is defined as any news media that can contribute to creating an environment that is more conducive to cooperation, negotiation, and reconciliation. To further illustrate the criteria of a conciliatory medium, el-Nawawy and Powers developed an 11-point typology, outlining the precise characteristics of a media that can serve a conciliatory function, as follows:[42]

- Providing a public place for politically underrepresented groups;
- Providing multiple viewpoints on a diversity of controversial issues;
- Representing the interests of the international public in general rather than a specific group of people;
- Providing firsthand observations from eyewitnesses of international events;
- Covering stories of injustice in the world;
- Acknowledging mistakes in journalistic coverage when appropriate;
- Demonstrating a desire toward solving rather than escalating conflicts;
- Avoiding the use of victimizing terms, such as martyr or pathetic, unless they are attributed to a reliable source;
- Avoiding the use of demonizing labels, such as terrorist or extremist, unless they are attributed to a reliable source;
- Abstaining from giving opinions that are not substantiated by credible evidence;
- Providing background, contextualizing information that helps viewers fully understand the story;

While this is an idealized media form that can be hard to find in today's mostly commercially driven media, it can be argued that AJE satellite channel has adopted many of the characteristics included in the conciliatory media typology and thus may prove to provide a conciliatory function when it comes to covering politically and culturally divisive issues.

Ibrahim Helal, AJE's former deputy manager for news and programs, suggests: "The 'South' here is not meant to be geographical. It is symbolic. It is a lifestyle because in the West, you have a lot of South as well. In Britain, you have South. In Europe, you have South. The South denotes to the voiceless in general."[43] The network promises that it contains the technological capacity and the ideological wherewithal to provide new and productive fora for cross-cultural communications.

Addressing AJE's mission, Nigel Parsons, the former AJE managing director, said, "This was a chance, a blank piece of paper to do things differently. And I do think that we have shaken up a very tired old industry. I do think we have raised the bar. Everyone said that there was nothing different to do or be done. I think to a large measure that we have achieved what we have set out to do. We do provide more analysis. We do provide more depth. We do cover untold stories."[44]

Serving as a "voice to the voiceless" is a concept that is unfamiliar among many Western news media networks. Helal argues: "The AJE way of journalism is a bit different from the West because we tend to go faster to the story and to go deeper into communities to understand the stories, rather than getting the [news] services to give us the information...We try to do our best to set the agenda by searching for stories others cannot reach or don't think of." Moreover, Helal suggests that the nature of AJE's stories and the angles they focus on contribute to their standing out as a network compared to Western news media.

Early research on the content, ideological underpinnings, and operation of AJE all indicate that its approach to and production of news differ significantly from that of other major transnational media organizations like CNN International and BBC World. Content analysis points to a repeated and thorough effort at producing programing that has more depth than most contemporary televised news, as well as an agenda that emphasizes issues of particular importance to those living outside the postindustrialized Western world.[45]

In this context, Waddah Khanfar, Al Jazeera's director general, explains: "Our philosophy of reporting is a human sentiment paradigm rather than the power center. We shift away from the power. Our relationship with power is always to question power, rather than to give power more domain to control. We have to empower the voiceless, rather than to empower the pulpit...or the powerful only."[46]

AJE has a news agenda that aims at "redressing global imbalances in the flow of information."[47] According to Parsons, AJE is "the first news channel based in the Mideast to bring news back to the West." Moreover, AJE focuses less on "breaking news," oftentimes of little significance to a majority of the world's citizens, and the "soundbite culture"' that characterizes many of its Western counterparts. News items on AJE "are generally longer and snappier [than its Western counterparts] while documentary-style shows abound…its stories seem to introduce more angles than would be the case with 'conventional' all-news networks."[48]

With an initial budget of over US$1 billion, mostly coming from the emir of Qatar, AJE has opened up four broadcasting centers (in Qatar, the UK, Malaysia, and the United States) and 21 supporting bureaus in Africa, Latin America, and Asia, parts of the world that have often been marginalized or altogether neglected by the mainstream Western media. Thanks to its sizable and remarkably market-independent resources, AJE is not subject to the economic pressures that have caused a decline in the quality of the many Western media.[49] Even the BBC World Service, although publicly funded via a grant-in-aid by the UK's Foreign and Commonwealth Office, relies on some commercially viable programing to sustain its budget. According to Kieran Baker, AJE's regional news editor for the Americas, cited in Hanley, "This station [AJE] may be the last bastion of public broadcasting."[50] Along the same lines, Naheda Zayed, AJE's news editor in Washington, DC, observes: "We are not driven by the dollar or constrained by commercialization pressures as many other news networks. And this gives us great liberty in the way we approach our stories."[51]

According to AJE's Code of Ethics, AJE presents "diverse points of view and opinions without bias or partiality." Moreover, it "recognizes diversity in human societies with all their races, cultures and beliefs and their values and intrinsic individualities in order to present unbiased and faithful reflection of them." And it "acknowledges a mistake when it occurs, promptly corrects it and ensures it does not recur." AJE's corporate profile further expresses its unique mission: "The channel gives voice to untold stories, promotes debate, and challenges established perceptions…The channel [sets] the news agenda, bridging cultures and providing a unique grassroots perspective from underreported regions around the world to a potential global audience of over one billion English speakers."[52]

Given its aims, resources, structure, and size, AJE provides a breath of fresh air and an interesting case study for examining the role of mass media in the cross-cultural conflict in the twenty-first century.

Textual Analysis of AJE Website Coverage of the Proposed Islamic Center

Textual analysis entails "seeing texts in terms of the different discourses, genres and styles they draw upon and articulate together."[53] Conducting textual analysis requires studying the actual text and interpreting the meaning(s) constructed through that text. In this study, the textual analysis of the AJE website stories on the controversy surrounding the Islamic center on Park 51 stretched over a four-month period: from the beginning of June to the end of September 2010. This time frame captured the height of the controversy surrounding this proposed center. In the textual analysis, the 11-point conciliatory media scale mentioned above was put to the test to see if the stories surrounding this controversy on the AJE website were conducive to a conciliatory environment by meeting some or all of the points included in the scale.

The researcher used the search terms: "Ground Zero Mosque," "Park 51," "Muslim Center," "Islamic Center," "Cordoba House," "Cordoba Mosque Initiative," "Prayer Hall," and "New York Islamic Center" to find stories. These search terms identified only 20 articles on the AJE website during the abovementioned time frame.

The few number of stories on AJE website dealing with the proposed Islamic center controversy was a stark contrast to the large number of stories on the Islamic center that had been presented by the American media. In this context, Al Anstey, AJE managing director, noted in an e-mail correspondence with the author that

> It certainly wasn't an editorial decision not to cover the story heavily. The reality is as a global channel there were a number of strong stories running at the time. In addition to the Mosque, we were covering the floods in Pakistan; the Chilean miners; the Israeli abuse photos; the strikes in South Africa; and of course the continuing clean up of the BP oil spill [in the Gulf of Mexico]. So the global news agenda was busy at the time. I fully understand that the US networks will have been covering the story at a different position in their bulletins as their focus is different to ours, but in the context of the stories happening at the time on the world stage I think this was one very important story among many. I...[believe] the stories we did [regarding the Islamic center] were balanced and provided important context as well.[54]

Of the 20 AJE stories, 9 stories (45 percent) were produced by AJE staff, 8 (40 percent) were produced by news agencies, and 3 stories (15 percent) were coproduced by AJE and news agencies. So, the reliance on foreign news agencies in this context was obvious in many of

AJE stories. It can be argued here that AJE could have used more of its own resources and staff writers to produce its own stories on the issue at hand. In this context, Loomis conducted a study of how the websites of AJE, BBC, CBS, and CNN covered world news, and he found that the AJE website "used fewer of its own reporters to gather information than any of the other agencies...[AJE website] did quote a greater number of sources in its articles, but those used were from the same traditional institutional sources used by others." According to Loomis, if AJE is concerned about providing its Western audience with a different point of view, "perhaps...[it] should place a greater effort on presenting stories from the unique Middle Eastern vantage point that has made Al Jazeera so widely known. Those stories...need to be created from a Middle Eastern understanding of which few in the West seem to have access."[55]

However, looking at the structure of AJE stories from a different angle, one could also argue that AJE website, by relying on a mix of sources and news agencies in addition to its own reporters and writers, is keen on "providing multiple viewpoints" on the controversial issue of the proposed Islamic center. This meets one of the criteria listed in the 11-point conciliatory media scale. Moreover, using this mix of stories from Western perspectives (represented mostly in stories coming from news agencies) as well as non-Western views (represented in using AJE website's own staff) is an indication that AJE "represents the interests of the international public in general, rather than a specific group of people." Again, this meets a second criterion in the conciliatory media scale as reflected in the selection of the AJE website stories.

The multiplicity of viewpoints was evident in an article about one episode of the AJE program *Inside Story*. This article titled "Obama and US Muslims" had a video of the episode, and it probed the question of treatment of Muslims in the United States in light of the proposed Islamic center. The video showed a discussion, including a Republican strategist, an advocate of the separation between church and state, and a spokesperson for the Council on American-Islamic Relations (CAIR). The Republican strategist strongly opposed the center, while the CAIR spokesperson supported it. The church and state separation advocate mediated the two abovementioned opposing sides with opinions that were factual and evidence-based. It was very strategic to invite all three members. The views of the supporting and opposing groups were expressed, along with mediating facts and evidence providing clarity for the statements. This allowed for the news report to be balanced. Moreover, the news anchor served as a mediator, stepping in when needed, but in no way providing his own opinion on the issue at hand. There were also news feeds at the bottom of the screen while the guests were debating the issue. This served to further explain what was not being said about the Islamic center.

Even some of the photos used in the stories helped provide multiple viewpoints on the issue. For example, in a story that was posted on September 12, 2010, under the title "US Mosque Row Feeds Radicals," a big photo was included that showed the building that would house the proposed Islamic center in the background with "Islamophobic signs" reading "Islam is a false religion," and "Stop the insanity" in the foreground. In the photo, there was also a Cross with the term "Repent" engraved in it.

In the analysis, it was noticed that the proposed Islamic center was referred to in the body of most AJE stories as "Islamic culture center," "Park 51," or so-called Ground Zero Mosque. This may be an indication that the AJE website coverage was more conciliatory than other broadcasters. In a way, "Ground Zero Mosque" is inaccurate, opinionated, and may lead to further tension since it has negative connotations. In this context, Michael Calderone, media reporter for Yahoo, said in an interview with the show "On the Media" on National Public Radio that "It is incumbent upon the media to look critically at who benefits the most from dubbing this project the Ground Zero Mosque. I think clearly it's those who want to tie it to 9/11 in some sort of way. And if that's clear, then I would think that editors would be a bit more wary."[56]

In its attempts to refrain from using the term Ground Zero Mosque in the body of its stories, the AJE website coverage, it can be argued, followed a third criterion on the conciliatory media scale by "abstaining from opinions that are not substantiated by credible evidence." However, in this context it is worth mentioning that the term Ground Zero Mosque was still mentioned in some of the stories' headlines in the AJE website despite the fact that it was referred to in the body of the articles by different terminology. The possible explanation for this usage is that since most networks had been using the term Ground Zero Mosque, this term had become more familiar to audience members who are more likely to use it in their Internet searches. If an online news outlet decides to use different terminology, it may not reach an audience. Therefore, AJE website might have conformed to the terminology used in the Western mainstream media in its stories' titles so that readers can find its stories. But once they find them, they would realize that the body of the story used different, more accurate terminology. Some AJE stories even alluded to the fact that Ground Zero Mosque was used inaccurately by some popular discourses and media outlets and explained why it was inaccurate. This is a very tactful and effective way to stand out in an inconspicuous way and without losing the audience. It is also an indirect way of "acknowledging mistakes in journalistic coverage," which is a fourth criterion on the conciliatory media scale that is reflected in the AJE website stories. In fact, in one of the AJE website stories posted on August 14, 2010, it was mentioned that "The project is popularly called the 'Ground Zero Mosque,' perhaps a slight misnomer on two counts: It will not be located at Ground Zero, but rather at...Park Place...Nor is it a mosque: Planners will...build an Islamic community center called Cordoba House, which will house a mosque, an auditorium, a swimming pool and a bookstore."[57]

Another story that acknowledged mistakes in the journalistic coverage of the proposed center in the American media was posted on September 4, 2010, under the title "Debating the 'Ground Zero Mosque.'" This story shed light on an episode of AJE's the *Listening Post*, a show that assesses the international media coverage of various global issues. This story was accompanied by a video that talked about the "false narrative in American news media when it comes to Islam."[58] One paragraph in the story reads: "If you [come] across the American media, then we doubt you missed this story. Plans to build an Islamic community center near the site where the World Trade Center used to stand...has triggered a heated, often irrational and frequently inaccurate debate...Our News Divide this week looks at a community center that initially slipped through the news agenda, was dragged back into it by new media and was then blown out of all proportion when the mainstream [media] had another go at it." So, in a way this story highlighted and explained how the proposed Islamic center controversy was exaggerated by the U.S. media outlets.

Most stories analyzed used a variety of webpage features, such as individual photos of the Park 51 mosque, officials press conferences, or demonstrations; videos of rallies and protests for and against the proposed center; links to other relevant stories, and feedback links allowing the readers to comment on the reported stories. A majority of stories also provided a balanced, noninflammatory coverage of the issue. For example, in a story that was reported by AJE staff and posted on June 20, 2010, the lead reads: "A proposal to build an Islamic Center near Ground Zero, where the twin towers of the World Trade Center once stood in the US city of New York, [was] met with loud opposition from some Americans."[59] Using the term "some Americans" in this context is an indication that not most or all Americans oppose it. The story included a video showing opponents chanting anti-Islam slogans. The video also included quotes from people at the scene of the protests. For example, one of the center supporters was quoted as saying: "Building [this] center can serve as a monument to peace." The story alluded to the fact that local authorities and neighborhood residents welcomed the center, but "a small, vocal group led by the Stop Islamization of American movement says the center has no business being near Ground Zero." This story, like most others on AJE website, provided a fifth criterion on the conciliatory media scale, as reflected in the AJE stories, by "providing firsthand observation from eyewitnesses of the event."

Another story posted on August 4, 2010, included a quote from NYC Mayor Bloomberg supporting the proposed center. This was followed by a sentence reading: "[This] was a setback for opponents of the mosque, who say it disrespects the memory of those killed on September 11."[60] This sentence gave credit to the opponents' stance and opinion. Another story, posted on August 14, 2010, tried to present an understanding of the proposed center by explaining the history behind it and why it was criticized. One paragraph in the story reads: "The project has been attacked on three grounds: One of them is simply anti-Muslim bigotry based on smears...A second criticism is the location, which some Americans say is insensitive to the victims of the [9/11] attacks...Critics say it would be inappropriate to build a mosque on the 'hallowed ground' of Ground Zero...As several commentators have pointed out, there is also a strip club...just one block north of the mosque site."[61] This paragraph was accompanied by a detailed map showing the readers where the proposed center will be located. The story also sheds light on the proposed center's imam (Abdul Rauf), by discussing his background and his public diplomacy and interfaith dialogue efforts under the previous and current U.S. administrations. This reflects a sixth criterion on the conciliatory media scale as reflected in the AJE stories, which is "providing background, contextualizing information that helps audience fully understand the story." This story was successful in providing a multifaceted context in which to debate the issue by including a background of the proposed center and its leader.

Another story that provided context to the issue was posted on September 13, 2010, and it included an interview with Imam Rauf, the executive director of the Cordoba Initiative, who shed some light on the background of the proposed center and noted that he was looking into "all options...to resolve debate over center's location." According to Rauf, the center's proposed location was important despite its controversial nature. "We need a platform where the voice of moderate Muslims can be amplified...This is an opportunity that we must capitalize on so the voice of moderate Muslims will have a megaphone," he said.[62] This story helped humanize the leaders behind the center, particularly Imam Rauf, who was not well-known to most Americans before this controversy started surfacing on the American media.

It is worth mentioning in this context that most AJE website stories alluded to the fact that the proposed center is not on Ground Zero. For example, one story posted on August 14, 2010, stated that the center lies "two blocks from what has become known as Ground Zero."[63] This article provided a highly insightful balance between the Democrats' and Republicans' views and the supporters and opponents of the proposed center. Under the title "Respecting Differences," one paragraph in this story reads: "New York City Mayor Michael Bloomberg, an independent who has been a strong supporter of the mosque project, welcomed Obama's . . . [support of the center] as a 'clarion defense of the freedom of religion' . . . But top Republicans . . . have already announced their opposition . . . Opponents including some relatives of the victims of September 11 attacks see the prospect of a mosque so near the destroyed trade center as an insult to the memory of those killed. Some of the victims' relatives, however, are in favor."

Along the same lines, another story posted on August 23, 2010, included the perspectives of both supporters and opponents to the center. In this story, which included a photo of a slogan reading "No Mosque here," the lead paragraph reads: "Hundreds of supporters and opponents of the proposed Islamic cultural center near the World Trade Center site in New York have staged rallies." So, the opening paragraph, or the lead, set the stage for a balanced coverage of the two sides. Then, the story went on to reflect both sides' opinions by including the content of the anticenter slogans, such as "No Mosque, no way" and "Not all Muslims are terrorists, but all the terrorists were Muslim." Then the story quoted a retired school teacher who supported the center as saying: "This has become a political tool to preach hatred. The peace-loving Muslims did not attack us."[64] The story, however, did not include direct quotes or interviews with the opponents of the center. This might have helped humanize the center's supporters more than its opponents.

But the Islamic center opponents were quoted and interviewed in another story titled: "Don't Panic, It's Only Islamic." This story started out with a balanced lead that reads: "Approximately, 400 people gathered in lower Manhattan this weekend to protest about the building of an Islamic cultural center . . . The demonstration was countered by a much smaller group of people who turned up nearby to shout slogans in favor of the complex." The story then proceeded to quote some of the demonstrators who opposed the center. One such opponent said: "I don't want the mosque here . . . I know what Constitution says but they are spitting in our face, the mosque people." Another opponent said: "They're putting a flag on their victory. This is not about peaceful Islamic people. This is about extremist groups that are going to be here. A third opponent was quoted as saying: "The issue here is not religious freedom; the issue is it's holy sacred ground and what is most interesting is how they can't understand that." The paragraph following these quotes reads: "In the same street as the proposed mosque there is an off-track betting shop and a nightclub where cars can regularly be found semi-naked." This latest sentence makes the readers think about the issue at hand and combats the view of the "holy sacred ground."

Another story that helped show how AJE website did provide background, contextualizing information had to do with the U.S. pastor, Terry Jones, who threatened to burn the Quran (Muslims' holy book) in the state of Florida. In this story, Jones was quoted as saying that if the location of the proposed Islamic center in NYC were to be moved, "it would be a sign from God to call off the Quran burning."[65] This was an interesting perspective that not all news stories had covered. It also helped the audience members make connections between various stories that revolved around the same theme, which is the negative perception of Islam and Muslims in America.

It was noticed in the analysis that AJE website stories generally avoided using "victimizing" and "demonizing" labels, unless they are attributed to a reliable source, thus meeting a seventh and eighth criterion in the conciliatory media scale as reflected in the AJE website stories regarding the proposed Islamic center. For example, the anti-Muslim and racist slogans were only referred to in the context of showing the flyers that some opponents to the center carried.

It was also noticed in the analysis that AJE website interviewed U.S. public figures, who were supportive of the plans to build the Islamic center, and they provided optimistic messages of tolerance, acceptance, and open-mindedness. One such figure was the Reverend Jesse Jackson, who was quoted in a video saying: "American is a work in progress, and will pass the test of tolerance. You have the right to fight for what is right...And ultimately you will prevail."[66]

Of the 20 stories analyzed on the AJE website, only 2 were opinion pieces written by guest writers. Diversity of opinion was evident in the AJE selection of these two pieces as one was written by a Muslim and the other was written by an atheist. One of them was posted on August 31, 2010, under the title "Unveiling Fear & Prejudice." Written by a Muslim scholar (as obvious from his name), this piece had an acerbic tone. It opened with an idealistic and ultimately euphoric view of how the proposed center can change U.S.-Muslims relations, yet almost instantly adopted a pessimistic and bitter tone that lamented the fear that exists in the Muslim-Western relations. The concluding paragraph reads: "Today, there seems to be reciprocal Muslim and Western fear. The anti-Muslim prejudice that tempts the benighted mind inside Western individuals...must be resisted by all. This is vital lest Euro-American Muslims become the victimized masses at the margins of the new millennium."[67]

In the second opinion piece, whose writer admitted to be "of the atheist tradition," it was titled "In the Face of Islamophobia." Overall, the piece called for conciliation and tolerance. The writer, Sean Bonner, reminded "those who in recent times having voiced their right to speak out against the building of the Cordoba House (for its close proximity to the [9/11] site), that the United States was founded on the principles of self-representation and a spectrum of personal freedoms." Bonner argued that "religious freedom and tolerance are core American values."[68]

CONCLUDING REMARKS

The textual analysis of the few stories dealing with the proposed Islamic center or "Park 51 Mosque" that were presented on the AJE website showed that it satisfied 8 points of the 11-point typology that was described above. In other words, this strongly indicates that AJE network has a great potential to play a conciliatory media function, especially when it comes to highly charged and controversial issues such as the one being addressed in this chapter.

One of the remaining three criteria on the conciliatory media scale that could not be applied to the coverage of the proposed Islamic center by AJE website called for "providing a public place for politically under-represented groups." The author is not in a position to firmly and assert-ively make a decision about which side is more represented than the other in the controversy surrounding the proposed center. Obviously, AJE website did present highly balanced coverage of the two sides (support-ing and opposing the center) in a way and a manner that had not been reflected in the coverage by many other networks in the West. In a way, one can argue that the opinions and the voices of those supporting the proposed Islamic center were generally suppressed in the Western media. But whether these voices are politically underrepresented is hard to affirm. For example, Imam Abdul Rauf, the mastermind of the proposed center, has been given an opportunity to play a key role in the interfaith dialogue through efforts adopted by the U.S. State Department over the past few years. One of the AJE website stories mentioned that Imam Abdel Rauf had participated in exchange programs organized by the U.S. Department of State and he also served as an advisor to the U.S. Federal Bureau of Investigation.[69]

The second of the three conciliatory media scale criteria that could not be applied to the AJE website coverage of the proposed Islamic center has to do with "covering stories of injustice in the world." It can be argued that the Obama administration has treated this story with justice and fairness since it wholeheartedly supported the proposal to build a mosque and an Islamic center near Ground Zero, citing the clause of freedom of religion under the U.S. First Amendment. The bigger issue remains, however, which is the Islamophobia that still lingers in many circles in the United States, and the question of whether a Muslim can be a "true American." It is this Islamophobia that has led to the fierce opposition among some public circles in the United States to building the proposed Islamic community center and mosque. It is the "otherness" of Muslims or anything Islamic that has led to the controversy and the fierce debate around whether or not to build an Islamic center in New York, at a time when this should not have been an issue to start with. If the issue had to do with building a church or a synagogue near Ground Zero, maybe it would not have caused this uproar or stirred this public controversy. Islamophobia "is a problematic neologism, and the one that is currently the most common term used to refer to bigotry, discrimination, policies and practices directed towards Islam and...Muslims."[70] "The current Islamophobia...,a destructive force for a globalizing world, may not be countered by an embrace of 'cultural difference' without engaging the political dimensions of the emerging world order, global communication and culture."[71] It can be argued that some media outlets in the West have contributed to this Islamophobic spirit by using demonizing terms to describe Islam and Muslims and by framing Islam as a religion of terror and hatred. That is why it is encouraging to have a network like AJE, which adopts most of the functions under the conciliatory media typology. Rather than spending too much time and resources on covering the issue of Park 51 center, which wasn't really about justice, AJE did focus on covering other stories of injustice in the world. This was partly exemplified in the quote from Al Anstey, AJE managing director, which was mentioned earlier in the chapter.

The third and last of the three criteria that could not be applied to the AJE website coverage of the Islamic center has to do with "demonstrating a desire towards solving rather than escalating conflicts." It can be argued that while the AJE website stories dealing the proposed Islamic center reflected a genuine attempt to avoid escalating conflict by avoiding the use of demonizing labels; providing multiple perspectives on the issue; and including background contextualizing information, still one cannot firmly conclude that AJE can contribute to solving conflict. This argument goes to the heart of "peace journalism," which, as discussed above, has to create opportunities for a peaceful environment. However, this role and mission can be doubtful in some cases, including the one at hand in this study. In fact, a media outlet's ability to solve conflict is particularly questionable when there is a hostile environment that is not conducive to reconciliation to start with. This is the kind of environment that has been surrounding the proposed mosque and community center. It is a hatemongering environment, where voices of reason and reconciliation are being overshadowed by extremism, racism, and radicalism.

In this context, Hanitzsch argued that "A peaceful culture is a precondition of peace journalism, rather than its outcome. In a culture in which a life has virtually no meaning and violence seems an appropriate measure of conflict resolution, peace journalism is not likely to evolve." According to Hanitzsch, "The inherent logic of news production is...[a major] limitation of peace journalism...It is difficult, if not impossible, to implement the values of peace journalism in traditional news formats where space and time constraints do not allow a detailed elaboration of backgrounds and causes of violence as well as its consequences."[72]

In the context of the issue at hand in this study, one can argue that a network like AJE can play a role in reducing the tension between supporters and opponents of the "Park 51 Mosque." But the issue is much bigger and more complicated than having an Islamic community center in lower Manhattan; it is the growing suspicion and fear of Islam that lingers in the American psyche. There was little that AJE could do to cut through the hateful discourse that surrounded the media coverage of Park 51 center. No broadcast network has the ability, in and by itself, to solve this problem.

NOTES

1. Kai Hafez, *The Myth of Media Globalization* (Cambridge: Polity, 2007).
2. Haidar Bagir, "Harnessing Inter-religious Harmony through Media Agencies," in *Covering Islam: Challenges & Opportunities for Media in the Global Village*, ed. Syed F. Alatas (Singapore: Center for Research on Islamic and Malay Affairs, 2005), 133–148.
3. Nick Couldry, "Transvaluing Media Studies," in *Media and Cultural Theory*, ed. James Curran and David Morley (London and New York: Routledge, 2006, 186), 177–194.
4. Mohammed el-Nawawy and Shawn Powers, "Al-Jazeera English: A Conciliatory Medium in a Conflict-Driven Environment?" *Global Media and Communication* 6 (1) (2010): 61–84.
5. Jennifer Peltz, "Imam Exploring Mosque Options," *Charlotte Observer*, September 14, 2010, 3A.
6. Brad Knickerbocker, "Ground Zero Mosque Debate Hits the Streets of New York," *Christian Science Monitor*, August 22, 2010, 1p.
7. Verena Dobnik, "Heated Rallies over Project Near Ground Zero: 'No Mosque, No Way!' vs. 'Say No to Racist Fear!'" August 23, 2010, http://

www.news889.com/news/world/article/92097--heated-rallies-over-project-near-ground-zero-no-mosque-no-way-vs-say-no-to-racist-fear.

8. Steve Rendall and Alex Kane, "The Media's Construction of the 'Ground Zero' Mosque," *Extra,* October, 2010, 8, 8–9.

9. Ibid.

10. Lisa Miller, Nayeli-Rodriguez and Will Oremus, "War over Ground Zero," *Newsweek* 156 (7) (August 16, 2010): 26–33.

11. Jennifer Peltz, "Imam Exploring Mosque Options," *Charlotte Observer,* September 14, 2010, 3A.

12. Rendall and Kane, "The Media's Construction of the 'Ground Zero' Mosque," 8–9.

13. Ibid., 9.

14. Nat Hentoff, "Unifying Muslim Community after Ground Zero Mosque Uproar," September 13, 2010, http://www.cato.org/pub_display.php?pub_id=12129.

15. Javier Hernandez, "Planned Sign of Tolerance Bringing Division Instead," *New York Times,* July 13, 2010, http://www.nytimes.com/2010/07/14/nyregion/14center.html.

16. Rendall and Kane, "The Media's Construction of the 'Ground Zero' Mosque," 9.

17. John Esposito, "Islamophobia and the Muslim Center at Ground Zero," *CNN Opinion,* July 19, 2010, http://articles.cnn.com/2010-07 19/opinion/esposito.muslim.center_1_muslim-center-muslim-community-mosque-construction?_s=PM:OPINION.

18. Ibid.

19. Farrukh Salim, "Exploring U.S. Media Reporting about 'Islam' and 'Muslims': Measuring Biased or Unbalanced Coverage," *Graduate Major Research Papers and Multimedia Projects* (2010) Department of Communication Studies and Multimedia, McMaster University.

20. Dan Murphy, "Is Ground Zero Mosque Part of Culture War or Symbol of Tolerance?" *Christian Science Monitor* (2010): 1.

21. Syed Alatas, "Is Objective Reporting on Islam Possible? Contextualizing the 'Demon," in *Covering Islam: Challenges & Opportunities for Media in the Global Village,* ed. Syed F. Alatas (Singapore: Center for Research on Islamic and Malay Affairs, 2005, 48), 41–51.

22. Sheryl Stolberg, "Obama Strongly Backs Islam Center Near 9/11 Site," *New York Times,* August 13, 2010, http://www.nytimes.com/2010/08/14/us/politics/14obama.html.

23. Sara Frazier, "Half of Poll Respondents Oppose Mosque Near WTC; Majority Say People Have Right to Build It," *Los Angeles Times,* September 3, 2010, http://www.latimes.com/news/nationworld/nation/wire/sns-ap-us-nyc.mosque-poll,0,6110330.story.

24. Lisa Miller, Nayeli-Rodriguez, and Will Oremus, "War over Ground Zero," *Newsweek* 156 (7) (August 16, 2010): 26–33.

25. Manuel Castells, *The Rise of the Network Society*, 2nd ed. (Oxford: Blackwell, 1999).

26. Phillip Seib, *"The Al-Jazeera Effect: How the New Global Media Are Reshaping World Politics* (Washington, DC: Potomac Books, 2008), 175.

27. Howard Tumber and Frank Webster, *Journalists under Fire: Information War and Journalistic Practices* (London: Sage, 2006).

28. Thomas Hanitzsch, "Situating Peace Journalism in Journalism Studies: A Critical Appraisal," *Conflict & Communication Online* 6 (2) (2007): 1–9 [1].

29. John Pauly, "Is Journalism Interested in Resolution, or Only in Conflict?" *Marquette Law Review* 93 (1) (2009): 7–23 [7].

30. Ibid., 12.

31. Ibid., 22.

32. Eytan Gilboa, "Media and Conflict Resolution: A Framework for Analysis," *Marquette Law Review* 93 (1) (2009): 87–111 [88].

33. Wilhelm Kempf, "Conflict Coverage and Conflict Escalation," in *Journalism and the New World Order: Studying War and the Media*, ed. Wilhelm Kempf and Heikki Luostarinen (Goteberg, Sweden: Nordicom, 2002), 227–255.

34. Jake Lynch and Annabel McGoldrick, *Peace Journalism* (Stroud, UK: Hawthorn Press, 2005), 5.

35. Johan Galtung, "Peace Journalism—A Challenge," in *Journalism and the New World Order: Studying War and the Media*, ed. Wilhelm Kempf and Heikki Luostarinen (Goteberg, Sweden: Nordicom, 2002), 259–272.

36. Gadi Wolfsfeld, *Media and the Path to Peace* (Cambridge: Cambridge University Press, 2004).

37. Ibid.

38. Jake Lynch and Annabel McGoldrick, *Peace Journalism* (Stroud, UK: Hawthorn Press, 2005).

39. Jeffrey Alexander and Ronald Jacobs, "Mass Communication, Ritual, and Civil Society," in *Media, Ritual and Identity*, ed. Tamar Liebes and James Curran (London: Routledge, 2998), 23–41.

40. Jeff Lewis, *Language Wars: The Role of Media and Culture in Global Terror and Political Violence* (London: Pluto Press, 2005).

41. Bagir, "Harnessing Inter-religious Harmony through Media Agencies," 133–148.

42. El-Nawawy and Powers, "Al-Jazeera English: A Conciliatory Medium in a Conflict-Driven Environment?" 61–84.

43. Ibrahim Helal, Personal interview, April, 2008, Doha, Qatar.

44. Nigel Parsons, Personal interview, April, 2008, Doha, Qatar.

45. Roland Schatz, "Widening the Perspective: Al Jazeera International Enriches Media Landscape," March 8, 2007, *Arab Media Center*.

46. Waddah Khanfar, Personal interview, November, 2007, London, UK.

47. Naomi Sakr, "Challenger or Lackey? The Politics of News on Al-Jazeera," in *Media on the Move: Global Flow and Contra-Flow*, ed. Daya K. Thussu (London: Routledge, 2007, 120), 116–132.

48. Habib Battah, "Al-Jazeera's New Frontier," *Middle East Broadcasting Journal*, July/August (2007), http://www.mebjournal.com/component /option,com_magazine/func,show_article/id,309/.

49. Robert McChesney, *Rich Media, Poor Democracy: Communication Politics in Dubious Times* (Champaign: University of Illinois Press, 2000).

50. Delinda Hanley, "Al-Jazeera English: The Brave New Channel They Don't Want You to See," *Washington Report on Middle East Affairs*, September/October (2007): 24–25.

51. Naheda Zayed, Personal interview, April, 2008, Washington, DC.

52. "Al-Jazeera English Code of Ethics," http://english.aljazeera.net /aboutus/2006/11/ 2008525185733692771.html, January 15, 2011.

53. Norman Fairclough, *Analyzing Discourse: Textual Analysis for Social Research* (London: Routledge, 2003).

54. Al Anstey, e-mail correspondence with the author, 2011.

55. Kenneth Loomis, "A Comparison of Broadcast World News Web Pages: Al Jazeera English, BBC, CBS, and CNN," *Electronic News* 3 (3) (2009): 143–160.

56. "The Semantics of the 'Ground Zero Mosque,'" On the Media, National Public Radio, http://www.onthemedia.org/transcripts/2010 /08/20/01, August 20, 2010,

57. "Prayer Hall or Provocation," English.aljazeera.net, August 14, 2010.

58. "Debating the 'Ground Zero Mosque,'" English.aljazeera.net, September 4, 2010.

59. "Protests against 9/11 Muslim Center," English.aljazeera.net, June 20, 2010.

60. "Ground Zero Mosque Approved, 2010," English.aljazeera.net, August 4, 2010.

61. "Prayer Hall or Provocation," English.aljazeera.net, August 14, 2010.

62. "US Imam Weighs Mosque Solution," English.aljazeera.net, September 13, 2010.

63. Obama Backs "Ground Zero Mosque," English.aljazeera.net, August 14, 2010.

64. "New Yorkers Rally over Mosque Plan," English.aljazeera.net, August 23, 2010.

65. "US Pastor 'Suspends' Quran Burning," English.aljazeera.net, September 10, 2010.

66. "Jesse Jackson Backs Mosque Plan," English.aljazeera.net, September 11, 2010.

67. Larbi Sadiki, "Unveiling Fear & Prejudice," English.aljazeera.net, August 31, 2010

68. Sean Bonner, "In the Face of Islamophobia," English.aljazeera.net, August 29, 2010.

69. "Prayer Hall or Provocation," English.aljazeera.net, August 14, 2010.
70. Erik Love, "Confronting Islamophobia in the United States: Framing Civil Rights Activism among Middle Eastern Americans," *Patterns of Prejudice* 43 (3–4) (2009): 401–425.
71. Mehdi Semati, "Culture, Difference, and Islamaphobia in the Age of the Global" (Paper presented at the International Communication Association, San Francisco, CA, 2007).
72. Hanitzsch, "Situating Peace Journalism in Journalism Studies: A Critical Appraisal," 1–9 [1].

CHAPTER 10

Conclusion: AJE in the World

Philip Seib

In the vastly expanded contemporary universe of journalism, Al Jazeera English (AJE) has developed with less fanfare than attended the first years of its parent, Al Jazeera Arabic. The news cacophony is louder and more distracting today than it was in 1996, when the Arabic channel was born. Having a lower profile worked to AJE's advantage, as the channel's leadership sorted out issues of format, logistics, and management.

All this changed with the Arab revolutions of 2011. AJE became a high-profile news provider, the go-to source for English-language coverage of events in Egypt and elsewhere. Even in the United States, with the channel's limited cable and satellite access to viewers, people went in droves to the AJE website and watched streaming coverage from Cairo's Tahrir Square and other sites at the heart of the uprisings. AJE executive Tony Burman reported that as of February 3, traffic to AJE's live online stream had increased 2,500 percent, with 60 percent of that coming from the United States, where an estimated 7 million Americans watched 50 million minutes of AJE coverage.[1] YouTube, a simulcast on Link TV, and excerpts on some PBS stations also attracted viewers who wanted to see AJE's extensive and intensive coverage.

AJE's performance as a leading purveyor of information during an event of global significance underscores the importance of devoting serious attention to AJE's current and prospective role in journalism and politics. As the preceding chapters have illustrated, the channel's ambitions are significant, its achievements to date merit recognition, and its prospects are such that the channel could well become one of the world's most authoritative sources of news.

This chapter concerns itself with the future—particularly how AJE may affect the bridges yet to be built between news and international relations during an era in which communication technologies and information flows change constantly, and the definition of "media" remains in flux. Similarly, we have entered an era of reconfigured geopolitics, when the "nation-state" may be more virtual than physical and when diplomacy may be taking an unprecedented turn toward becoming an enterprise among people rather than between governments.

In all these matters, AJE will be a noteworthy factor.

AL JAZEERA AS POLITICAL PLAYER

To understand the future political significance of AJE, it is important to appreciate the past—to recognize the historical importance and regional influence of its Arabic-language parent. AJE is very much a child of the Arabic channel, and despite its level of editorial independence this relationship remains crucial.

When Al Jazeera Arabic first went on the air in 1996, few observers expected the channel to amount to more than a quickly forgettable publicity stunt by a country that most people could not locate on a map. After all, viewers in the region seemed content with the steady, albeit drab, government-run news media, and if they wanted a broader perspective, they could access the BBC, CNN, and other such sources.

But that dismissive attitude, which was found mostly in the West, was built on a false assumption: that the Arab television news audience did not care where its information came from. In reality, there was a hunger among Arab viewers for news about their lives that they could trust and in which they could claim ownership. For too long they had had to rely on staid outsiders such as the BBC, the CNN, and other non-Arab information sources to tell them what was happening in their own lives. This was an improvement, but in only a limited way, on the news programing that was tightly controlled by Arab governments and featuring dreary-looking broadcasts and "news" that only the most credulous would accept.

Al Jazeera changed all that. First, it looked different. Its original staff, many of whom came from the short-lived BBC Arabic television channel (a new version now exists), knew the importance of appealing to viewers whose visual tastes were increasingly shaped by international cinema and by the new channels they were beginning to watch as satellite dishes sprouted throughout the region. With generous financial support from the Qatari government, Al Jazeera was able to feature eye-catching state-of-the-art production values that held viewers' attention.

More important was the content—an unprecedented expansion of pan-Arab journalism into topics that almost all other television channels in the region (with the exception of some in Lebanon) dared not address. Other Arab states soon felt Al Jazeera's sting, as stories were aired about corrupt governments that neglected their own people's needs (and the needs of neighboring Palestinians) while officials enriched themselves. By the time of the 2000 intifada, Al Jazeera had become the principal television source for news about Arabs reported by Arabs. Its coverage featured an Arab perspective, which some critics denounced as bias, but it was a slant that attracted and retained viewers. And because of its willingness to take on previously sacrosanct individuals and institutions, the channel engaged its audience's interest and enjoyed its trust.

Beyond the journalistic approach Al Jazeera brought to its newscasts was the relative intellectual transparency that infused its talk shows. Free-wheeling commentary about politics, women's issues, and the archaic nature of much of Arab life changed public discourse, bringing into communal conversation topics that had previously been discussed only in whispers or in media venues outside the popular mainstream. Religion also featured prominently, with the well-known cleric Yusuf Al Qaradawi presiding over his own program, and with Islam's dominant role in the region clearly recognized. The channel appeared undaunted by the intrinsic volatility of the politics-religion mixture.

Al Jazeera's talk shows are often loud, the journalists often insistent, and the coverage sometimes sensational. Pull all these pieces together and you have an entertaining news product not unlike commercially successful counterparts in other parts of the world. It quickly won a huge audience in the region and forced governments to take note. At first, those in power in states that were covered critically by the channel regarded Al Jazeera as a minor irritation, but soon it was more than that, as coverage fueled restiveness within countries whose governments could no longer count on their own, well-behaved news media to keep a lid on public opinion. As is noted in chapters 7 and 8, in January 2009 it was Al Jazeera that fueled public anger throughout the region about Arab governments' failure to respond to the war in Gaza. People took to the streets in places like Dubai, where political demonstrations—other than those sanctioned by government—were rare. The target of the protests was not Israel but rather the leaders of Egypt and other Arab states.

As a result of the channel's sometimes incendiary coverage, the emir of Qatar began hearing regularly from aggrieved neighbors, but Al Jazeera was rarely reined in (except in cases in which Qatar's own interests were involved). So, some Arab governments shut down Al Jazeera's operations in their countries, a practice that has continued, although in the aftermath of the 2011 revolutions this might change in some countries.

Here are some examples: in October 2010, the Moroccan Ministry of Communications withdrew accreditation from the channel's staff in the country, citing a failure to follow "the rules of responsible and serious journalistic work." The Moroccan authorities said that Al Jazeera's coverage "seriously distorted Morocco's image and manifestly damaged its interests, most notably its territorial integrity" in reports about Western Sahara, territory that is the subject of a continuing dispute between Morocco and the Algerian-backed Polisario Front.[2] A few weeks later, the Kuwaiti government closed Al Jazeera's bureau in that country, accusing the channel of interfering in Kuwait's internal affairs by reporting about a violent police response to a public gathering organized by the Kuwaiti opposition.[3] Tunisia had never allowed Al Jazeera to open a bureau there, but when the Tunisian revolution of 2011 began, Al Jazeera nevertheless played a significant role, aggregating social media content and broadcasting it to the many Tunisians who might not have had access to the Internet. The Tunisian coverage, although from afar, was potent, and it gained attention from those in Egypt and elsewhere whose reaction was, "If Tunisia, why not us?"

Outside the region, the most significant government criticism of Al Jazeera has come from the United States, particularly during the George W. Bush administration, which objected to the channel's coverage of the wars in Afghanistan and Iraq, coverage that often emphasized the cost of conflict in terms of civilians' lives. Nervous Western governments used the label "the Osama bin Laden network" to characterize Al Jazeera, a tactic that worked well among those who had never seen the channel's newscasts and were ready to believe that it was part of an Arab terrorist conspiracy.

Al Jazeera may have been a convenient villain in the West, but in terms of audience loyalty in the Arab world, being perceived as an irritant to Arab governments and the United States did no harm to the channel's popular standing. Attacks on the channel enhanced its credibility as an independent voice, and such controversies showed that Al Jazeera *matters.*In terms of its balance sheet, however, some governments' annoyance with the channel led to significant loss of advertising (from Saudi Arabia, in particular), but the Qatari emir's deep pockets ensured the channel's continued operations.

Perhaps most significantly, these varied factors contributed to an altered public sphere in the Arab world, brought about by an "Al Jazeera effect" that extended beyond the Qatari news organization to numerous other regional satellite channels and then to Internet-based media that have empowered individuals and groups in unprecedented ways. "News," which for so long had largely been a product of Arab officialdom, had become something that people were beginning to trust as being on *their* side, and, therefore, as a tool of intellectual liberation in a society that tended to frown on such. When combined with the deluge of information through social media, Al Jazeera and other news providers became key factors in the transformation of Arab politics.

After its first decade, Al Jazeera's journalistic credentials and political influence were well established within the Arab world, which includes—because of the channel's global satellite reach—the Arab diaspora worldwide. Further, the channel was acclaimed by some both within and outside the Middle East as a "voice of the Arabs," attaining a goal of Egyptian president Gamel Abdel Nasser when he created a radio station of that name in 1953. But this notion of Al Jazeera as a pan-Arab focal point is an overstatement—as is the notion that any media outlet could be the "voice" of 350 million Arabs—and should be treated carefully. Al Jazeera itself does not make this claim. The idea emerges from the same mindset that declares there to be an "Arab street." In reality, on almost every issue, there are many Arab streets. There is no more a singular "Arab street" than there is a "European street" or an "Asian street."

There are plenty of Arabs who have little use for Al Jazeera, thinking it too loud and too radical. The Saudi-backed Al Arabiya channel, which is based in Dubai, is Al Jazeera's principal rival. It has a more conservative, establishment-oriented outlook than does Al Jazeera, and maintains equally high production standards. Although sometimes overlooked outside the Middle East (partly because of Al Jazeera's skillful and pervasive self-promotion), Al Arabiya has a large and loyal audience base.

Nevertheless, Al Jazeera's voice has been significant. The channel has audience and influence, but its reach has its limits. To maintain and expand influence requires an audience that can grow. The direction for expansion was clear. Fewer than 400 million people worldwide speak Arabic, but the most widely spoken language in the world is English.

The commercial possibilities of expanding into English are obvious: more audience means more advertising revenue. But given Al Jazeera's emir-ensured financial security, the commercial aspects of expansion should not be overrated. Despite "Al Jazeera" being one of the world's most recognized brands, the organization's expansion agenda was not primarily driven by expectations of profits (although the emir has made clear that his generosity might not last forever). Rather, a principal ambition of the Al Jazeera leadership is to change journalism, and by so doing change international politics.

The two goals are closely related. Journalists who claim to have no political agenda are being disingenuous. Why bother to do journalism if your coverage has no effect? Whether the news story is about the failures of a local housing project or about global warming, the information journalists deliver should provide news consumers with knowledge that they can use to develop and enhance opinions and then act upon them. That is a political outcome. Critiquing governments' performance has similar political ramifications. Wadah Khanfar, Al Jazeera's director general, said: "We have to challenge centers of power. When they are trying to hide facts, people should learn that governments from now on cannot brush away stories and cannot hide the truth."[4] Few journalists would disagree with that.

AL JAZEERA AS VIRTUAL STATE

By early 2011, Al Jazeera was moving forward with plans to further expand its array of channels by creating Al Jazeera Turkish, Al Jazeera Swahili, and Al Jazeera Balkans. None of these would have as large a language-based audience as AJE, but the expansion is evidence of the overall Al Jazeera mission to upgrade international journalism and, not incidentally, extend its own influence.

To understand the true reach of Al Jazeera's channels, and particularly AJE, it is necessary to look at the world with a perspective that is not limited by the territorial delineations of conventional maps. In the era of satellite television and the Internet, borders that once could obstruct communication, as well as block passage of people and goods, are decreasingly relevant. For instance, unless a government is willing to shut down its Internet system for a prolonged time, which would be disastrous for any country that is part of the global economic community, information flows cannot be stopped. In the digital era, no long-term equivalent of radio jamming exists, except for rare countries such as North Korea that do not care about interaction with the rest of the world. Traditional national borders, now more than ever before, also do not define the locus of a national or ethnic population or, for that matter, a television audience.

Consider Pakistan as an example. What is "Pakistan" today? Is it the land mass northwest of India, as is shown on maps and recognized as a legal entity? Or is it, in reality, a virtual state that exists partly in its traditional space, but also with pieces in the United Kingdom, home to nearly a million Pakistanis, and Saudi Arabia, with even more Pakistanis living there, and the United Arab Emirates and more than 20 other locales around the globe with large Pakistani populations? With easily available tools such as mobile phones, Facebook, and various other Internet-based devices, plus satellite television and radio, members of the Pakistani diaspora can maintain unprecedented connectivity. Wherever they may be, these people are, if they choose to be, linked to each other and to their homeland in ways that make them still very much a part of a "Pakistan" that is both virtual and very real.

This virtual state phenomenon applies to other nationalities as well, such as Haitians, Turks, Senegalese, and many others, and to groups that are not, as a matter of international law, nationalities with recognized states, such as Kurds. A more difficult-to-define group, in terms of whether it wants to be or can be connected, is the *ummah,* the global Muslim community, almost 80 percent of which does not speak Arabic and a considerable portion of which speaks English. Might AJE, given its base in a Muslim country and its kinship with a news organization widely perceived as having significant ties to Islam, prove to be a catalyst in pulling together the English-speaking *ummah?*

As the channel's audience grows in Pakistan, India, and other places with substantial Muslim populations, survey research (a particularly imprecise discipline in some of those locales) may eventually determine if this affinity exists. Al Anstey, managing director of AJE, noted that AJE has a "shared heritage" with the parent Arabic channel; "We have the same DNA," he said. He also said that this audience might be attracted by AJE being "comprehensive in our coverage of the Middle East," adding that although plenty of other news organizations also cover the region extensively, audience members with an emotional stake in events there "don't necessarily feel comfortable" with reporting by those without true grounding in the Arab world. In terms of having the credibility to build audience, he observed, the question may be viewers' judgment about "which prism are we looking through?"[5]

The 2008–2009 Gaza war coverage underscored the significance of the AJE prism. As the only English-language television news organization with crews inside Gaza, its reporting—replete with graphic images of Palestinian casualties, many of them children—was certain to find a receptive audience among those whose sympathies were with the residents of Gaza as well as those who were dissatisfied with coverage that relied heavily on sources provided or controlled by Israel.

A case can be made that the Gaza coverage was simply good journalism, and any pro-Palestinian political impact was an unintended (although predictable) ripple effect. Or, an alternative case can be made that AJE's coverage was politically driven, with bias carried to the point of intentional distortion. These arguments are made in chapters 7 and 8. Whatever the merits of these respective arguments, the Gaza story was a breakthrough for AJE in that its monopoly on on-site English-language reporting helped the channel build trust in its news product among an audience that was, because of language, familiar with Al Jazeera (Arabic) news only by reputation.

Such coverage will align AJE in the public's mind with the Arabic channel, but it is unclear how that will affect audience size. By its nature, the AJE audience will be something of a virtual entity, as English-speakers are more thoroughly dispersed around the globe in substantial numbers than are those who speak any other language. Over the long term, will perceptions of journalistic affinity with the Arabic channel help AJE build audience in Pakistan, for instance, but hurt it in the United States? If so, is that a trade-off AJE is willing to accept?

A good guess is, probably not. Although AJE can survive without the advertising dollars that would be produced by having a large American audience, if the channel's goal is influence rather than affluence, then the U.S. market is essential. That means that AJE must be particularly sensitive about how its political outlook and the "prism" that Anstey spoke of are perceived, especially by audiences who are skeptical about the objectivity of the overall Al Jazeera organization.

The 2011 coverage of the Arab revolutions helped alleviate some people's concerns about the channel's being seen as a partisan player. The reporting from the streets where the uprisings were occurring, particularly in Egypt, could be characterized as more "prodemocracy" than "pro-Arab." Although the subject matter was intensely political, audience sympathies were largely one-sided—with the protestors and against the established order—which is not the case with issues related to Israel, a topic that Al Jazeera coverage as other Arab channels do, with a strong anti-Israel viewpoint.

Nevertheless, the political complexities of the region necessitate restraint in any applauding of the collective Al Jazeera enterprise as being a champion of Arab democratization. Critics have noted that Al Jazeera—particularly the Arabic channel—pulled its punches in its coverage of turmoil in Bahrain (Qatar's next-door neighbor), and that the channel's coverage of Syria overstated the scope of the anti-Assad protests there and underestimated the influence of the Muslim Brotherhood in the newly tumultuous politics in Syria and elsewhere.

Qatar's leaders appear to be little bothered by such criticisms. They apparently see the entire Al Jazeera enterprise as a vehicle to help take them, over the long term, to greater international prominence. Beyond broadcasting, they have played this game shrewdly and effectively. Qatar is one of the rare Arab states that talks with controversial neighbors such as Israel and Iran. It has served as a host for peace talks related to Lebanon, Sudan, and other conflict zones, and it regularly organizes debates and major conferences about the world economy and other global issues. It uses its wealth to strengthen friendships, such as by investing heavily in less prosperous Arab neighbors.[6] It displayed its ambition in its successful bid for the 2022 FIFA World Cup, with promises of air-conditioned stadiums, a bridge to Bahrain, and other futuristic innovations.

Qatar is redefining the concept of superpower—with oil and gas wealth superseding armed might, with its media-political powerhouse of Al Jazeera, and with its dynamic imagination overshadowing its tiny size. Qatar has the highest economic growth rate in the world (19.4 percent in 2010), the highest per capita GDP in the world (US$145,300 in 2010), and an unemployment rate under 1 percent.[7] These factors help insulate Qatar's rulers from the turmoil that has boiled over in much of the rest of the region. Unlike Saudi Arabia, Qatar has proved willing to adapt its religious and political standards in ways that make the country a comfortable partner for other nations. It has embraced flexibility over rigidity.

Al Jazeera was created partly to enhance Qatar's public diplomacy, giving the state an identity that would be recognized by publics as well as governments, particularly in the Middle East. In a dispatch among the WikiLeaks documents released in late 2010, U.S. ambassador to Qatar Joseph LeBaron wrote: "Al Jazeera's ability to influence public opinion throughout the region is a substantial source of leverage for Qatar, one which it is unlikely to relinquish. Moreover, the network can also be used as a chip to improve relations. For example, Al Jazeera's more favorable coverage of Saudi Arabia's royal family has facilitated Qatari-Saudi reconciliation over the past year." Al Jazeera denied that it had been used as a political tool in this way, stating, "This is the U.S. embassy's assessment, and it is very far from the truth."[8]

Wielding influence is, however, part of what Al Jazeera does, and it does so overtly. Al Jazeera has created a training center, which works with journalists from underdeveloped countries, and a Centre for Studies, which is a think tank that focuses on geopolitics more than journalism.

Critics of Al Jazeera, who often speak with loudness than exceeds their numbers and their knowledge of the channels' content, may consider Al Jazeera's multilevel expansion to be evidence of malign ambition. But the organization's activities have been undertaken openly, and the argument can be made that it is better for a wealthy state such as Qatar to attain power through a media organization rather than by undertaking a nuclear weapons program or some other menacing enterprise.

*　　*　　*

In the end, the story of AJE comes back to the mission of journalism. As has been illustrated throughout this book, the channel seeks to deliver a journalistic product that is based on a nontraditional world-view. That it is doing so with considerable success is a sign that the channel is maturing in ways that will accrue to its own benefit and that of its viewers. The chapters looking at AJE's efforts in South Asia and Africa underscore this. The channel has made a commitment to being present consistently, rather than relying on transient "parachute journal-ists" whose knowledge about what they must cover is usually minimal. The AJE correspondents are often locals or have extensive experience in their area of coverage. Some are young and unpolished, but many have genuine, enthusiastic interest in the people and events they cover, and this is reflected in their work.

Most important is the nature of stories they present. From Africa comes coverage not always about war or famine, but also about political and economic progress. From South Asia come reports that do not always emphasize poverty or humanitarian emergencies, but rather contribute to viewers' understanding of that region's cultural richness. By setting aside the parochialism that characterizes so much coverage from traditional news organizations, particularly those in the United States, AJE provides its audience with a more truly global perspective.

Although AJE has not as yet achieved all of its goals in traditionally undercovered regions, its efforts distinguish the channel from most other international news providers. Among major news broadcasters or publica-tions, only the *Economist* seems to have a similar commitment to provide consistently broad and sustained global coverage.

Truly rebalancing the news agenda to ensure appropriate coverage for the global South and to "give voice to the voiceless" will take time, as will nurturing audience interest in this widened perspective. As AJE matures, it will face competition not only from traditional news organi-zations, but also—and perhaps more significantly—from online report-ing and aggregating entrepreneurs, and from social media information disseminators. No one can know how the evolution of information will proceed. Will rapid change continue, with Facebook, Twitter, YouTube, and their kin becoming obsolete and replaced by a newer generation of media instruments? What will be the next developments in information technology itself?

Most important, what kind of news will people want? AJE is betting that the technology-driven accessibility of information will in some ways elevate the sophistication of individuals' worldviews, making them more curious about their world. That would be good, and it would benefit not only AJE but also the global intellectual community in which news plays such an important role.

Notes

1. Tony Burman, "The 'Al Jazeera Moment'?" *thestar.com* (Toronto), February 4, 2011, http://www.thestar.com/opinion/editorialopinion /article/933097--the-al-jazeera-moment.
2. "Morocco Suspends Al Jazeera Operations Indefinitely," Committee to Protect Journalists News Release, http://cpj.org/2010/11/morocco -suspends-al-jazeera-operations.
3. "Media Watchdogs Condemn Kuwait for Closing Al Jazeera," *Daily Star* (Beirut), December 15, 2010.
4. "Al Jazeera Now," transcript of *On the Media,* March 26, 2010, www .onthemedia.org/transcripts/2010/03/26.
5. Author interview with Al Anstey, Doha, January 4, 2011.
6. Nicholas Blanford, "Why Qatar Is Emerging as Middle East Peacemaker," *Christian Science Monitor,* May 23, 2008.
7. *CIA World Factbook,* February 20, 2010, https://www.cia.gov/library /publications/the-world-factbook/geos/qa.html.
8. Robert Booth, "WikiLeaks Cables Claim Al Jazeera Changed Coverage to Suit Qatari Foreign Policy," *Guardian,* December 6, 2010.

CONTRIBUTORS

Hussein Amin is a professor in the Department of Journalism and Mass Communication at the American University in Cairo. He holds several key positions in national, regional, and global media. His research interests include global and transnational media with specific reference to the Middle East.

Amelia Arsenault is an Assistant Professor of Communication at Georgia State University and the Media & Democracy Senior Research Fellow at the Center for Global Communication Studies at the University of Pennsylvania's Annenberg School for Communication. She is currently working on a multiyear research project on the activities of international actors in the communications sector in southern Africa.

Mohammed el-Nawawy is Knight-Crane-endowed Chair and Associate Professor in the School of Communication at Queens University of Charlotte. He is the author or coauthor of *Islam dot Com: Contemporary Islamic Discourses in Cyberspace*; *Al-Jazeera: How the Free Arab News Network Scooped the World and Changed the Middle East*; and *The Israeli-Egyptian Peace Process in the Reporting of Western Journalists*. He is the founding editor of the *Journal of Middle East Media* and serves on the editorial boards of *Media, War and Conflict* and *Global Media Journal*.

Tine Ustad Figenschou is a Postdoctoral Fellow in the Department of Media and Communication, University of Oslo. Her PhD thesis, "The South Is Talking Back—Al Jazeera English as a Strategic News Contra-Flow," analyzes to what extent AJE represents a news contraflow. Her work has been published in *Global Media and Communication*, *Media, Culture and Society*, *International Journal of Communication*, and *Journalism*.

EytanGilboa is Professor of Communication and International Relations, Chair of the Communication Department and Director of the Center for International Communication at Bar-Ilan University in Israel. He is also a Visiting Professor of Public Diplomacy at the University of Southern California. His most recent books include *Media and Conflict* and *US-Israeli Relations in a New Era: Issues and Challenges after 9/11*.

Michael Kugelman is Program Associate with the Asia Program at the Woodrow Wilson International Center for Scholars, where he is responsible for research, programming, and publications on South Asia. He is the editor of *Kuala Lumpur Calling: Al Jazeera English in Asia,* and is lead editor for several other publications. He is an op-ed contributor to *Dawn* and the *Express Tribune,* two of Pakistan's major English-language newspapers.

Rima Najjar Merriman is an Assistant Professor of English Literature at Al Quds University. She worked previously as the Coordinator General of Child Rights Planning, a unit in the Palestinian Ministry of Planning, and wrote a chapter on Palestinian children for the *Greenwood Encyclopedia on Children's Issues Worldwide.* She wrote and directed a documentary produced by Al Quds TV titled *The ABCs of Occupation* about the absence of the rule of law in certain areas southeast of Jerusalem.

Shawn Powers is an Assistant Professor at Georgia State University's Department of Communication and is an Associate Director of the Center for International Media Education. He has previously been a Visiting Assistant Professor at the USC Annenberg School London Program and a Visiting Research Fellow at the London School of Economics and Political Science.

Philip Seib is Professor of Journalism and Public Diplomacy and Professor of International Relations at the University of Southern California, and is Director of USC's Center on Public Diplomacy. He is author or editor of numerous books including *Beyond the Front Lines, New Media and the New Middle East, The Al Jazeera Effect, Toward a New Public Diplomacy,* and *Al Jazeera English.*

Will Youmans is a PhD candidate in the Department of Communication Studies at the University of Michigan, Ann Arbor. His writings have been published in the *UCLA Journal of Islamic and Near Eastern Law, Westminster Papers in Communication and Culture,* and the *Middle East Journal of Culture and Communication.*

INDEX